INDIA: A LITERARY COMPANION

INDIA

A Literary Companion

Bruce Palling

JOHN MURRAY

First published in 1992
by John Murray (Publishers) Ltd.,
50 Albemarle Street, London W1X 4BD

A catalogue record for this book is available
from the British Library

ISBN 0-7195-4830-6

Typeset in 12½/12½pt Bembo by Colset Private Ltd, Singapore
Printed and set in Great Britain by
Biddles Limited, Guildford

CONTENTS

ILLUSTRATIONS

(between pages 120 and 121)

The author and publishers would like to thank the following for permission to reproduce illustrations: Plates 1 and 2, Victoria & Albert Museum; Plates 3, 4, 5, 6, 7, 8, 9, 10 and 11, India Office Library (British Library).

AUTHOR'S NOTE

Many people have been exceedingly generous with their time and knowledge in helping me compile and write this book. I would like to offer special thanks to Raghubir Singh, whose suggestions and encyclopaediac knowledge on all aspects of India have been invaluable. Others who have helped me in various ways include John Hatt, Professor Romila Thapar, Aileen and Derek Brown, Sunanda Datta-Ray, R.P. Gupta, Helen Simpson, Mala and Tejbir Singh, John and Bim Bissell, Jaswant Singh MP, W.H. and John Saumarez-Smith, Carol Livingstone, William Hamilton-Dalrymple, Vikram Seth, Baljit Malik, R.V. Pandit, John Lal, Patwant Singh, Ram Mohan Rao, Romesh Sharma, Vishu Singh MP, Alexander Frater, Hugo Kimber, Chris Mullin MP, Nicholas Coleridge, Peter Leggatt, Philippa Scott, Nigel Hankin, Partha Mitta, H.K. Kaul, Professors Lloyd and Susan Rudolph, James Fenton, Punjab Singh, D. Paulus and Ian Buruma.

I am particularly grateful to my agent, Anne McDermid of Curtis Brown, for encouraging me in many ways. Ariane Goodman and Gail Pirkis at John Murray Ltd were also remarkable for their ability to impose order on a somewhat chaotic first draft. I owe a particular debt to numerous booksellers around the world for their kindness and efficiency, notably Fakir Chand in Khan Market, New Delhi, Books of Asia and Heywood Hill in London, plus the staff of the India Office Library, the London Library and the India International Centre in New Delhi.

I would also have been at a loss were it not for those four bedrocks of High Victorian scholarship – the *Imperial Gazetteer of India*, the *Dictionary of National Biography*, the eleventh edition of the *Encyclopaedia Britannica* and the *Oxford English Dictionary*.

In memory of Dhiren Bhagat

INTRODUCTION

A problem – albeit an enjoyable problem – that faces the compiler of a book like this one on India is the extraordinary wealth of material from which one can draw. Certainly the Subcontinent has been exposed to more scrutiny by a greater variety of observers than any other place on earth. Perhaps the breadth of experiences to be had, combined with the relative ease with which foreigners are accepted, explains why so many writers have left such worthwhile accounts. Inevitably my choice has had to be personal and doubtless my prejudices frequently shine through. Nevertheless, I hope that readers will see the point of most, if not all of my selections, and they may get some pleasure from thinking of what they would have included had they been in my place. The writings of William Hickey, Victor Jacquemont, Jawaharlal Nehru, Nirad C. Chaudhuri and V.S. Naipaul on the Subcontinent are wonderfully illuminating and I have quoted from them freely. Their observations charmed or provoked me in ways that changed my whole perspective on the area. However, I was also constantly amazed by the perspicacity of other, strongly contrasting individuals such as Ibn Battuta, Emperor Babur, the Abbé Dubois, Bishop Reginald Heber and Lord William Cavendish-Bentinck. It was a joy reading their work and finding so many points of contact.

I came to the Subcontinent after several years spent in Indochina and south-east Asia but had no idea that it would supplant my interest in those regions so thoroughly. There is no simple explanation for my addiction but it probably has to do with the intensity of existence. There is the excitement of street life, the strength of the cultures, the power of the landscape, and the depth of friendships. I have been permanently altered by my experiences there, which have ranged from being overwhelmed by the glories of nature to seeing a man shot dead in a temple.

The attractions of the Subcontinent are never easy to explain to the squeamish or the faint-hearted. It is also the worst place imaginable for meddlers as there are no end of things that should be rectified. Many of the unadventurous claim they could not bear to travel there because of 'all that ghastly poverty and disease'. This is just an excuse for staying at home garnished with worthless moral superiority. It does nothing to assist a single starving villager. There are other shibboleths that really should be dispelled, but such is their power that even those who know the country still persist in believing them. The biggest is that India is a shining example of the virtues of non-violence. Some even think that Indian foreign policy is somehow based on these principles. The reality is that New Delhi regularly acts like the town bully towards its smaller neighbours. India itself is one of the most heartless and cruel places in the world. But given the circumstances of existence, this is hardly surprising.

Soon after I arrived in New Delhi to work as a foreign correspondent my eye was caught by a touching story of the rescue of a blind teenage girl from a band of callous gypsies. According to the newspaper account, the gypsies had been travelling through a village in southern India with a blinded girl whom they had kidnapped as a baby and used as a beggar. Almost miraculously she recognized the voices of her parents who then managed to rescue her. This had the makings of a heart-rending article but for one reason or another I did not pursue it. Two years later another version of the incident emerged which sounded altogether more plausible. The girl was in fact the natural daughter of one of the gypsies and had been blind from birth. The so-called parents had never set eyes on her before but needed a slave for domestic chores and thought this the easiest way to acquire one. Blood tests were said to have proved that there was no relationship.

Stories as bizarre and brutal as this can be found in the Indian press almost every day, but short of actually visiting the scene of the crime there is no safe way of judging their veracity. India forces you to accept that anything is possible.

Despite its antiquity Indian culture is still subject to strong contradictory strains and influences. The Subcontinent is a giant cauldron whose ingredients are, at one level, merging, while at another they remain wholly separate. Perhaps this explains the supreme tolerance of most people who live there. A recent ingredient, the British, provides some enduring images beyond the obvious ones. On my first trip to India more than a decade ago, I travelled with a friend by train to the foothills of the Himalayas. One of our reserved bunks on the Pathankot Express had been commandeered at a previous station by an Army officer who showed no sign of wanting to comprehend our irritation. Within a few minutes the situation was rectified by a slightly built Sikh ticket inspector. He roused the dozy occupant, lectured him and within a matter of minutes had forced him to vacate the bunk. The idea that rules take precedence over rank is a British import. I cannot think of many countries, especially in the Third World, where such an incident would have had a happy ending.

In India, too, the unexpected is almost commonplace. Recently I was on holiday in western Rajasthan with some Indian friends who had taken over a castle for the New Year. We spent the first few days walking through glorious national parks, visiting temples and trekking to such spectacular ruins as Khumulgar Palace. One day, we asked the *thakkur*, or princeling, of the castle we were staying at whether there were any other interesting places in the vicinity. He vaguely mentioned a smaller fort a few miles away, on the rim of the Aravali Range, but said he hadn't been there for a few years. We set out in a jeep and after negotiating several precipitous slopes and dry river beds we ended up in some of the most memorable landscape I had ever seen. It was obvious that few vehicles had passed this way before because whenever we encountered bullocks or sheep, usually the most blasé of creatures, they almost stampeded in fright. Just before dusk we stopped on the edge of a misty valley which came to an abrupt end at a perpendicular ridge a mile away. There were occasional remnants of Mogul arches and walls around the perimeter of the estate, which was so rundown as to be almost in pure harmony with nature. The stables had long been open to the elements. A series of wells and water pits were bone-dry and in disrepair. The roof of the fort also had large holes where it had simply crumbled away. Curiously, the fort was surrounded by orderly stone huts, which we thought must belong to local tribesmen. However, it turned out that the inhabitants were descendants of a Rajput contingent who had fought on behalf of the ancestors of this fort's *thakkur* and had been rewarded with free accommodation. The villagers gathered outside to see us arrive and told us the *thakkur* himself had left that day on horseback for Jodhpur. His 85-year-old mother was in the house but had never come out of purdah so it was impossible for us to communicate with her in any way. Later, after we had marvelled at the feudal trappings and the extraordinary spectacle of the sun setting on the horizon below us, we chatted to the villagers under an ancient banyan tree just outside the fort's entrance. There were very few adult males among the villagers and none between the ages of 16 and 40 – they had all left in search of work. The villagers recalled once having seen another jeep belonging to somebody in the government but, as for themselves, on the rare occasions they left the place they travelled either by foot or on horseback to the highway, which was only eight miles away. Just before we left I asked them when was the last time a European had been there. I was the first since Independence.

There is much that will change in the Subcontinent in the coming years, often not for the better. Already, Kashmir has been badly affected by the inability of either India or Pakistan to countenance its independence. An even larger problem on the horizon is Hindu revivalism. But I do not think the future is without hope despite my cynicism about Indian politics. Regardless of the manifest failures of the Congress Party over the years, it at least has a structure that allows participation by all castes and faiths. I still have close friendships with politicians of varying hues and I have not yet joined the doom merchants who think that the Subcontinent is on the verge of collapse. India cannot be suppressed for long – it is far too diffuse to respond to singular treatments or simple solutions. I hope that the following pages and extracts give some idea of its complexity as well as its charm and allure.

1

ARRIVAL

> Here are to be seen united in the same individual,
> the greatest contempt for death, the greatest indif-
> ference, the greatest insensibility to physical pain,
> and the most excessive cowardice. Instances are fre-
> quent of the most atrocious cruelty, combined with
> habits of charity; nothing is so contradictory, so
> whimsical, so mad, as these people.
>
> Victor Jacquemont, *Letters from India*

Our first encounter with another culture should stimulate our
sense of curiosity and perhaps lead us to question the basis of
our own seemingly solid and immutable beliefs. If we confine
ourselves to those affluent, orderly countries that owe their
inspiration to Greece and Rome, there is little chance of altering
our perspective on the world. But as travellers over the centuries
have found, the Indian Subcontinent is quite a different matter.

No country offers more in the way of sheer sensory assault
than India. It starts soon after arrival with the smells of incense
and cow-dung and the squabbling, feverish crowds in the cities.
On the streets, there is chaos, or 'functioning anarchy' as one
writer remarked. Providing you are capable of remaining calm
in the face of petty harrassment, you soon learn to cope with
impositions on your time, and occasionally your dignity. After
these minor irritants, the sensory incursions tend to be of more
lasting interest. A hundred years ago, the exotic aspect was
played for all it was worth by many travellers, none less than
Mark Twain:

> This is indeed India! The land of dreams and romance, of
> fabulous wealth and fabulous poverty, of splendour and
> rags, of palaces and hovels, of famine and pestilence, of
> genii and giants and Aladdin lamps, of tigers and ele-
> phants, the cobra and the jungle, the country of a hundred

nations and a hundred tongues, of a thousand religions and two million gods, cradle of the human race, birthplace of human speech, mother of history, grandmother of legend, great-grandmother of Tradition, whose yesterdays bear date with the mouldering antiquities of the rest of the nations – the one sole country under the sun which is endowed with an imperishable interest for alien prince and alien peasant, for lettered and ignorant, wise and fool, rich and poor, bond and free, the one land that *all* men desire to see, and having seen once, by even a glimpse, would not give that glimpse for the shows of all the rest of the globe combined.[2]

The first extant records of Indian life by outsiders were written around 500 BC by Greeks attached to the Persian court. One gives a fanciful description of a tiger, commenting that 'in each jaw it has three rows of teeth and at the tip of its tail is armed with stings by which it defends itself in close fight and which it discharges against distant foes, just like an arrow shot by an archer.' The Greek historian Herodotus provides a brief account of India in his *Histories*, compiled in the middle of the fifth century BC, in which he describes India as being inhabited by a variety of tribes speaking numerous languages, including one group that refused to kill animals and were completely vegetarian.

Nearchus, Alexander the Great's admiral during his campaign to conquer India in the fourth century BC, gives a vivid account of the appearance of the people the invaders encountered in the Punjab.

The dress worn by the Indians is made of cotton produced on trees. But this cotton is either of a brighter white colour than any found anywhere else, or the darkness of the Indian complexion makes their apparel look so much whiter. They wear an undergarment of cotton which reaches below the knee halfway down to the ankles and an upper garment which they throw partly over their shoulders and partly twist in folds round their head. The Indians also wear earrings of ivory, but only the very wealthy do this. They use parasols as a screen for the heat. Their shoes are made of white leather and these are elaborately trimmed, while the soles are variegated, and made of great thickness, to make the wearer seem so much taller.[3]

Other accounts were not quite so measured – another of Alexander's party recounted that elephants 'are so teachable, that they can learn to throw stones at a mark and to use arms, also to sew beautifully'.

There are no records left by travellers during Emperor Ashoka's reign (from *circa* 272BC) but an account of his transition from vanquishing warrior to Buddhist king is preserved in his own rock edicts, though his name and exploits only came to light in a chance discovery earlier this century by a British archaeologist.

The Greek geographer, Strabo, who did most of his research in the great library at Alexandria, composed a fascinating summary of contemporary knowledge of India just before the birth of Christ:

> they speak of people ten feet long and six feet wide, some without nostrils having instead merely two breathing holes above their mouths. There are stories of people who sleep in their ears. There are also certain mouthless people who are gentle by nature and live round the source of the Ganges and they sustain themselves by means of vapours . . . There are places where brass rains from the sky in brazen drops . . .[4]

As the Graeco-Roman world declined, the influence of China grew. The next observer of note to travel to the Subcontinent was Fa Hsien, the first Chinese Buddhist pilgrim to northern India, at the end of the fourth century AD. He spent six years searching for authentic Buddhist scripts to take back to China. Ironically, he referred to India, rather than China, as the 'Middle Kingdom'.

> To the south of this, the country is called the Middle Kingdom (of the Brahmans). It has a temperate climate, without frost or snow; and the people are prosperous and happy, without registration or official restrictions. Only those who till the king's land have to pay so much on the profit they make. Those who want to go away, may go;

those who want to stop, may stop. The king in his administration uses no corporal punishments; criminals are merely fined according to the gravity of their offences. Even for a second attempt at rebellion the punishment is only the loss of the right hand. The men of the king's bodyguard have all fixed salaries. Throughout the country no one kills any living thing, nor drinks wine, nor eats onion or garlic; but chandalas are segregated. Chandala is their name for foul men (lepers). These live away from other people; and when they approach a city or a market, they beat a piece of wood, in order to distinguish themselves . . .

In this country they do not keep pigs or fowls, there are no dealings in cattle, no butchers' shops or distilleries in their market-places. As a medium of exchange they use cowries. Only the chandalas go hunting and deal in flesh.[5]

More than two centuries later, Hsuan Tsang, another Chinese scholar, travelled alone to India to collect more Buddhist texts and relics. He spent thirteen years in the country, visiting most of its regions. His writings give the most detailed account of Indian life in the early seventh century, as in this description of urban life.

As to their inhabited towns and cities the quadrangular walls of the cities are broad and high, while the thoroughfares are narrow tortuous passages. The shops are on the highways and booths line the roads. Butchers, fishermen, public performers, executioners, and scavengers have their habitations marked by a distinguishing sign. They are forced to live outside the city and they sneak along on the left when going about in the hamlets. As to the construction of houses and enclosing walls, the country being low and moist, most of the city-walls are built of bricks, while walls of houses and enclosures are wattled bamboo or wood. Their halls and terraced belvederes have wooden flat-roofed rooms, and are coated with chunam [plaster made of shell-lime and sand] and covered with tiles burnt or unburnt. They are of extraordinary height, and in style like those of China. The houses thatched with coarse or common grass are of bricks or boards; their walls are ornamented with *chunam*; the floor is purified with cow-dung and strewn with flowers of the season; in these matters they differ from us. . . . The inner clothing and outward attire of the people have no tailoring; as to colour a fresh white is esteemed and motley is of no account. The men wind a strip of cloth around the waist and up to the armpits and leave the right shoulder bare. The women wear a long robe which covers both shoulders and falls down loose. The hair on the crown of the head is made into a coil, all the rest of the hair hanging down. Some clip their moustaches or have other fantastic fashions. Garlands are worn on the head and necklaces on the body.[6]

Within a few years of Hsuan Tsang's departure, Islam began to make its presence felt in Sind, on the western edges of the Subcontinent. Early in the eleventh century, Mahmud, a warlord from central Asia, made frequent forays into northern India primarily to pillage temples for loot. One of his companions was Alberuni, a distinguished Persian scholar, who also spoke Greek and quickly mastered Sanskrit the better to study Indian religion and philosophy. His comments about Indian attitudes must be tempered with the knowledge that the local inhabitants were hardly likely to have welcomed these Islamic invaders with open arms.

The Indians believe that there is no country but theirs, no nation like theirs, no king like theirs, no religion like theirs, no science like theirs . . . They are by nature niggardly in communicating what they know, and they take the greatest possible care to withhold it from men of another caste from among their own people, still more of course from any foreigner . . . They are in a state of utter confusion, devoid of any logical order, and in the last instance always mixed up with silly notions of the crowd. I can only compare their mathematical and astronomical knowledge to a mixture of pearls and sour dates, or of pearls and dung . . . Both kinds of things are equal in their eyes since they cannot raise themselves to the methods of a strictly scientific deduction.[7]

In the sixteenth century yet another invader arrived in the Subcontinent. Babur, descendant of Tamerlane and Genghis Khan, and ruler of Kabul, seized Delhi in 1526 and became the first emperor of the Mogul dynasty. His lengthy diary, the *Babur-Nama*, shows the full scope of his genius although he was less than flattering in his description of India.

Hindustan is a country of few charms. Its people have no good looks; of social intercourse, paying and receiving visits there is none; of genius and capacity none; of manners none; in handicraft and work there is no form of symmetry, method or quality; there are no good horses, no good dogs, no grapes, musk-melons or first-rate fruits, no ice or cold water, no good bread or cooked food in the bazaars, no Hot-baths, no Colleges, no candles, torches or candle-sticks. . . .

Except their large rivers and their standing-waters which flow in ravines or hollows, there are no waters. There are no running-waters in their gardens or residences. These residences have no charm, air or symmetry.

Peasants and people of low standing go about naked. They tie on a thing called a *lungata*, a decency-clout which hangs two spans below the navel. From the tie of this pendant decency-clout, another clout is passed between the thighs made fast behind. Women also tie on a cloth one-half of which goes round the waist, the other is thrown over the head . . . Pleasant things of Hindustan are that it is a large country and has masses of gold and silver. Its air in the Rains is very fine . . . The fault is that the air becomes very soft and damp. A bow of those Trans-oxanian countries after going through the Rains in Hindustan, may not be drawn even; it is ruined; not only the bow, everything is affected, armour, books, cloth, and utensils all; a house even does not last long.[8]

The Portuguese had arrived in the Subcontinent a decade earlier than Babur but did not establish themselves in any strength until later in the century. They set up a string of trading outposts along the west coast, notably at Cochin and Goa. It was from there in 1579 that Thomas Stevens, a former scholar at New College, Oxford, who had fled to Rome where he became a Jesuit, wrote a letter to his father in England describing his hazardous voyage to India.

> The first sign of land were certain fowls which they [the Portuguese crew] knew to be of India; the second, boughs of palms and sedges; the third, snakes swimming on the water, and a substance which they call by the name of a coin of money, as broad and as round as a groat, wonderfully printed and stamped of nature; like unto some coin. And these two last signs be só certain that the next day after, if the wind serve, they see land. Which we did, to our great joy, when all our water (for you know they make no beer in those parts) and victuals began to fail us.

After being received in Goa with 'passing great charity', Stevens penned the first account of Indians by an Englishman.

> The people be tawny, but not disfigured in their lips and noses, as the Moors and Cafres of Ethiopia. They that be not of reputation – or, at least, the most part – go naked, saving an apron of a span long and as much in breadth before them, and a lace two fingers broad before them girded about with a string, and no more. And thus they think themselves as well as we with all our trimming.[9]

Though he offered to tell his father more at a later stage about the general lie of the land, no other letters from Stevens are known to have survived. Several years later, however, he was able to assist an early Elizabethan adventurer, Ralph Fitch, who had sailed east on the *Tiger*.

Fitch and his party first stopped at the trading post of Chaul, nine days sailing north of Goa.

> Hither many shippes come from all partes of India, Ormus, and many from Mecca; here be manie Moores and Gentiles. They have a very strange order among them. They worshippe a cowe, and esteeme much of the cows doung to paint the walles of their houses. They will kill nothing, not so much as a louse; for they holde it a sinne to kill any thing. They eate no flesh, but live by rootes and ryce and milke. And when the husbande dieth, his wife is burned with him, if shee be alive; if shee will not, her head is shaven, and then is never any account made of

her after. They say if they should be buried, it were a great
sinne, for of their bodies there would come many wormes
and other vermine, and when their bodies were consumed,
those wormes would lack sustenance, which were a sinne;
therefore they will be burned. In Cambaia they will kill
nothing, nor have any thing killed; in the towne they have
hospitals to keepe lame dogs and cats, and for birds. They
will give meat to the antes.[10]

This last reference is to the Jains, members of a breakaway
religious movement from Hinduism which still survives. Fitch
appears to have been well disposed towards his new environment, stating in one letter that 'It is a brave and pleasant country, and very fruitful. The summer is almost all the year long,
but the chiefest at Christmas; the day and the night are all of
one length.'
   Fitch and his party eventually made the hazardous journey
to the Emperor Akbar's court at Agra, where they stayed for
more than a year before each going their separate ways. Fitch
returned to England after further adventures in Burma and
became closely involved with the Levant Company. He was also
frequently consulted by the East India Company, founded in
1600. His most lasting but anonymous fame is a fleeting
reference by Shakespeare. In *Macbeth*, the first witch remarks
of a sailor's wife that 'Her husband's to Aleppo gone, master
of the Tiger.'
   William Hawkins, second in command of the third expedition of the East India Company, became the first Englishman to show the English flag off the coast of India, on 24
August 1608. Hawkins then hurried off to Agra to present a letter from King James I to the Emperor Jahangir,
who was delighted that this stranger could converse with
him in Turkish. He urged Hawkins to remain as resident
ambassador, which he did. He was promptly made captain of
400 horses, married an Armenian and became one of the court
grandees.
   Rather than rely on such merchant adventurers, the East
India Company sent out Sir Thomas Roe as the first officially
accredited ambassador to Jahangir's court. *En route* to Agra in
1615, he observed that 'The country is plentiful, especially of

cattel, the banians killing none, or selling any to be killed. One day I met 10,000 Bullocks loaded with corn, in one drove, and most days after lesser parcels.'

He was a very different type of character from Hawkins and made a good impression on Jahangir. 'I went to visit the King, and deliver'd him a Present, where I saw abundance of Wealth, but being of all sorts put together without order, it did not look so regular.' Three days later, he went in the evening 'and according to the Mogul's order chose my place of standing, which was on the Right-hand of him on the rising of the Throne, the Prince and young Rama standing on the other side; so I had a full view of what was to be seen, Presents, Elephants, Horses and Whores.'[11]

The Reverend Edward Terry, who became chaplain to Sir Thomas Roe in 1617, was not so sanguine about the country.

> But lest this remote countrey should seem like an earthly Paradise without any discommodities: I must needes take notice there of many Lions, Tygres, Wolves, Jackals (which seeme to be wild Dogs) and many other harmefull beasts. In their rivers are many Crocodiles, and on the Land over-growne Snakes, with other venimouse and pernicious Creatures. In our houses there we often meete with Scorpions, whose sting is most sensible and deadly, if the patient have not presently some Oyle that is made of them, to anoint the part affected, which is a present cure. The aboundance of Flyes in those parts do likewise much annoy us, for in the heate of the day their numberlesse number is such that we can be quiet in no place for them, they are ready to cover our meate as soon as it is placed on the Table, and therefore wee have men that stand on purpose with Napkins to fright them away when as wee are eating: in the night likewise we are much disquieted with Musquatoes like our Gnats, but somewhat lesse: and in their great Cities, there are such aboundance of bigge hungrie Rattes, that they often bite a man as he lyeth on his bed.[12]

After Robert Clive's decisive victory against the French at Plassey in 1757, the British presence and influence in India grew as the East India Company expanded its control. A new

category of immigrant began to arrive – the ne'er-do-well or
remittance man, of whom the most colourful and charming was
William Hickey. Forced by an anxious father to sign up as a
19-year-old cadet officer with the East India Company because
of his amorous and profligate life in London in the 1760s,
Hickey was consigned to 'that common receptacle of all abandoned and undone men, the East Indies!'

In the first of May [1769] we made the coast of
Coromandel, a few miles to the Southward of Pondi-
cherry, running along the land until evening, when falling
calm, we came to an anchor, to wait the land breeze,
which would carry us into Madras roads by daylight of the
following morning. At the usual hour I went to my cot,
but the thoughts of being so near the place of our destination entirely banished sleep, and finding all my efforts in
vain, I put on my clothes and went upon deck. Just
as I got my head above the Companion ladder, I felt an
indescribably unpleasant sensation, suddenly, as it were,
losing the power of breathing, which alarmed me much,
for I supposed it to be the forerunner of one of those horrid
Indian fevers of which I had heard so much during our
voyage. Whilst worried by this idea, my friend Rogers,
whose watch it was, said to me, 'Well, Bill, what do
you think of this? How do you like the delightful breeze
you are doomed to spend your life in?' Enquiring what
he meant, I found that what had so surprised and alarmed
me was nothing more than the common land wind blowing as usual at that hour directly off shore, and so intensely
hot that I could compare it only to standing within the
oppressive influence of the steam of a furnace. At day break
we weighed anchor, standing for Madras, which we had
scarcely reached when we heard that Mr Peter King, the
Ship's carpenter, a strong made, vigorous man, was taken
suddenly and violently ill with cramp in his limbs and
stomach. He was put into a warm bath as soon as water
could be heated, and every remedy applied, without avail;
in one hour from his being first seized he was no more.
This quick death, added to the horrid land wind, gave me
a very unfavourable opinion of the East Indies.[13]

Mary Martha Sherwood, who was married to her army cousin Henry, made great play of her arrival off Madras in 1805 on a cloudless day where the shore 'appeared to be richly scattered with palaces'. Using a telescope, the passengers could see Indians moving about including 'a set of bearers carrying a palanquin' which confirmed her 'visions of oriental pomp and happiness, in which I had often indulged during my voyage. . . . How little did I then anticipate the thousand drawbacks from comfort which I was doomed to find in the new world to which I was hastening!'[14]

Another traveller, whose initial reaction was one of dread followed by wonder, was Reginald Heber, the newly appointed Bishop of Calcutta, who arrived off Calcutta in 1822. 'One of the first specimens of the manners of the country which have fallen under our notice, has been a human corpse, slowly floating past, according to the well-known custom of the Hindoos.'

Bishop Heber's first glimpse of living Indians occurred shortly afterwards when some boats arrived at the side of their vessel bearing fish and fruit. The Bishop observed that they 'were all small slender men, extremely black, but well made, with good countenances and fine features, certainly a handsome race . . .' He later concluded that 'the deep bronze tint is more naturally agreeable to the human eye than the fair skins of Europe, since we are not displeased with it even in the first instance, while it is well known that to them a fair complexion gives the idea of ill health, and of that sort of deformity which in our eyes belongs to an Albino'. His next comment was more original.

> The second observation was, how entirely the idea of indelicacy, which would naturally belong to such figures as those now around us if they were white, is prevented by their being of a different colour from ourselves. So much are we children of association and habit, and so instinctively and immediately do our feelings adapt themselves to a total change of circumstances; it is the partial and inconsistent change only which affects us.[15]

Until the 1830s, the journey to India could take anything up to six months. The advent of steam, coupled with judicious connections and travel overland from Suez, reduced the passage to India to about a month. William Howard Russell, the first and greatest foreign correspondent of *The Times*, who rushed out to cover the events of the Mutiny in 1857, reflected on the hitherto lengthy journey as he approached Calcutta.

The water rapidly became more turbid as we advanced, and speedily assumed the pea-soup hue which distinguishes the streams of great rivers. No land was visible in the morning; but soon after twelve o'clock a faint shadowy outline was seen on the horizon. Many ships and barks were edging along under full sail, for which there was but little wind; but the captain was more particularly interested in a fine handy brig, which lay, with her topsails aback, right in our course. Three similar brigs were anchored, or lying-to, almost in a line with her. This was our 'pilot' vessel; and at the word, all the old Indians, men and women, crowded to the forecastle. The quarter-boat was lowered from the brig, and made towards our ship. Long ago, before steam was, it was the great event of the voyage to receive the pilot on board, and to hear the news he had brought, and read the letters which he had on board for the Calcutta-bound passengers. Some not very old men who were with us spoke of the intense excitement which prevailed the moment the pilot came in view, as productive of very strange effects. And, indeed, how could it be otherwise, when one thinks that life passed as rapidly then as it does now, and that some four or five long months had intervened since the outward-bound had received their receipt, probably three or four months old? What great events in the smallest household can be marshalled in the space of a few weeks! Even with all the acceleration of our present route there are few who have not felt, in India, that half the earth's circumference divides them from those they love, and that 'distance' is as yet a perceptible ingredient in the cup of sorrow, and doubt, and anxiety, which separation fills so copiously. The wife heard, perhaps, that the husband she expected to have folded in her arms had been for months lying in his grave. In the district to which the old civilian was about to repair, in the hope of giving a last strong shake to the pagoda tree, all trace of British rule might have been swept away in a flood of Mahrattas or Pindarees for the time. There was scarcely a letter opened which did not contain a shock, a surprise, or a wonder, influencing, perhaps, the whole life of the recipient.[16]

After the Mutiny, and as a consequence, the East India Company was abolished and from 1858 the British Crown took over direct administration of the Indian Empire. The flow of arrivals to India increased considerably, with Edward Lear joining the list of artists intent on recording Indian scenery. He set off in October 1872, having overcome his reservations about leaving his new house in San Remo, which he confessed 'seems a kind of giddiness which it rather humiliates me to think of practising'. He had gained nearly £1,000 worth of commissions, including one from Lord Aberdare, who left the choice of the subject matter up to him. Lear's response was to write to him to ask 'Shall I paint Jingerry Wangerry Bang, or Wizzibizzigollyworryboo?' His gay mood was sustained by his first impressions upon arrival.

> Extreme beauty of Bombay harbour! At seven leave the 'India' in a steam tug. No trouble anywhere. Violent and amazing delight at the wonderful variety of life and dress here. Exquisite novelties, flowers, trees. Walk out with Giorgio [his Italian factotum], then in a phaeton to Breech Kandy and left cards for Mr Justice Melville. The way thither left me nearly mad from sheer beauty and wonder of foliage! O new palms! O flowers! O creatures! O beasts! Anything more overpoweringly amazing cannot be conceived. Colours and costumes and myriadism of impossible picturesqueness. These hours are worth what you will.[17]

India also made an initially favourable impression on E.M. Forster when he travelled out in 1912 to visit his close Indian friend and unrequited love, Syed Ross Masood. Forster was an entirely different type of Englishman from those to whom the Indian population was accustomed. Although he did not arrive with any particular literary plan, he was open-minded about the consequences of his journey and ultimately incorporated his experiences into *A Passage to India*. Soon after arrival at

Bombay, he set off on the 900-mile trip to Aligarh to stay with
Masood. In a letter to his mother, he described the journey as
'the most comfortable and also the most expensive' he had ever
undertaken.

> The moonlit country was beautiful, for we were crossing
> the hills; next morning it was not fine as scenery, but of
> course I was very excited. Sometimes it looked like Surrey-
> heaths with small hills, and 'blue distances'; but a 'blue
> distance' becomes very different when you see a camel
> walking across it or a palm tree growing against it, and
> a ploughed field over which women in crimson or blue are
> stalking, with beautiful pots of metal on their heads,
> becomes quite a new sort of ploughed field: I saw Bhopal,
> and Gwalior, which looks like a glorified Orvieto, rising
> sheer from the plain, and three magnificent elephants with
> hideous howdahs of red and green. But the railway sta-
> tions pleased me most – every sort of dress and undress
> running up and down, and the children with nothing on
> at all, bathing themselves solemnly under the drinking
> water tap. Sweets like greasy tennis-balls, messes of every
> colour, bread like pancakes, peacock-feather fans, plaster
> spaniel-dogs – every sort of thing was being sold, and
> there were Hindu sellers of food for the Hindus, so that
> they might not be defiled.[18]

The writer Robert Byron journeyed to the Subcontinent in
1929 as a special correspondent for the *Daily Express*. He, too,
called on imagery from the West in order to describe the
environment, unfavourably comparing Karachi to a vision of
an American city in the Mid-West. However, he was far more
interesting in his reflections on the unnatural gulf between the
ruler and the ruled.

> As I stepped from the aeroplane at Karachi on a hot
> August afternoon, the gaze of the assembled crowd turned
> in surprise to my hat; so that on the following morning
> I hastened to buy a topee. Its presence on my head,
> together with the sahib-formula of address employed by
> the taxi-driver, induced a sudden feeling of unreality.
> Stepping out of myself, I saw myself as a Russian film-

producer would have seen me, badged as an Englishman-
in-India, a brutal imperialist, a brawny exploiter . . . yet
scarcely: I tilted the topee uneasily. On our leaving the
shop, my companion suggested jocularly that we should
now see a little of India. Certainly India was not in sight;
the view was of asphalt and tram-lines, bounded by rectangular blocks of commercial buildings; the shops were
shut, passers-by few; Karachi groaned in silence beneath
an English Sunday. The taxi moved leisurely down the
main street, skirted a clock-tower encrusted with Gothic
pinnacles, then swerved into a tortuous lane. Silence and
Sunday were gone. A hive of humanity beset us, chafering
before the open-fronted shops and booths, hurriedly
removing their persons, chairs, and pipes from the narrow
roadway lest our progress should be impeded, idling, contemplative, or hastening on errands, bearing loads, chat-
tering, begging, rescuing their children; but one and all
turning, as at a right-dress command, their hundred pairs
of eyes in our direction. Without purpose or interest they
gazed; but they gazed, and their gaze was the only static
element in a cauldron of mobility. I gasped. I am not
untravelled. Many surprises have been my fortune in
foreign countries. But never has any thunderbolt fallen
upon me with quite the unexpectedness of an Indian
bazaar. 'Indian bazaar': the very words reek of the
obvious. And there the obvious was: the 'colour of the
East, the teeming millions'; the tiny humped cows
wandering at will; the awnings and trades, sweetmeats
and brassware; fakirs and sadhus, pockmarked, deformed,
bedaubed with dung; every feature, every stature that man
has evolved; hats, puggarees, shirts, waistcoats, *dhotis*,
lunghis, trousers, and *saris* of uncountable shapes, colours
and patterns; nose-rings, bangles, and anklets; painted
god-marks, teeth and gums stained red with pahn; the
fantastic emaciation of one, the astounding corpulence of
another; even the girl-mothers with their wizened babies;
every component of the multitude called echo in the
memory, an echo from nursery days and nursery literature. And yet, inside me, was something very, very
strange. For here was I in a position which I had never

conceived nor wanted, a ruler among the ruled. There
could be no doubt of it. It was written on every face, and
if mine proclaimed a doubt, the topee hid it. I experienced
a vague exaltation, an access of racial credit. Simultaneously a discomfort arose. I saw myself for the first
time as the white man grasping the earth, focus of the
earth's attention. And how should I, who am no stronger
than others, resist the assumption of my own superiority,
and preserve intact my desire for truth and proportion,
solace and palliative of existence, against this distortion-
mirror of complacence? I was disquieted, and my companion noticed it, though without divining the reason.
'Look at them', he said. 'It makes you realize what we're
up against here in India.' It did. It made me realize that
the thing we are up against existed in myself.[19]

Form was so important for the British Raj in India, especially
in these declining years of Empire, that Robert Byron was
banned from dining in the Sindh Club because he was not wearing a dinner-jacket, so he was obliged to eat in his room. These
rules were not seen as restrictive by many of the civil servants
and officers; rather they provided reassurance. Francis Yeats-
Brown, a young Sandhurst officer who was attached to the
King's Royal Rifle Corps, arrived in northern India at the turn
of the century. Within days, this teenage Harrovian was
someone of importance in the eyes of his servant.

I had only to shout *Quai Hai* to summon a slave, only to
scrawl my initials on a *chit* in order to obtain a set of furniture, a felt carpet from Kashmir, brass ornaments from
Moradabad, silver for pocket-money, a horse, champagne,
cigars, anything I wanted. It was a jolly life, yet among
these servants and salaams I had sometimes a sense of isolation, of being a caged white monkey in a Zoo whose
patrons were this incredibly beige race.
    Riding through the densely packed bazaars of Bareilly
City on Judy, my mare, passing village temples, cantering
across the magical plains that stretched away to the
Himalayas, I shivered at the millions and immensities and
secrecies of India. I liked to finish my day at the club, in
a world whose limits were known and where people

answered my beck. An incandescent lamp coughed its light over shrivelled grass and dusty shrubbery; in its circle of illumination exiled heads were bent over English newspapers, their thoughts far away, but close to mine. Outside, people prayed and plotted and mated and died on a scale unimaginable and uncomfortable. We English were a caste. White overlords or white monkeys – it was all the same. The Brahmins made a circle within which they cooked their food. So did we. We were a caste: pariahs to them, princes in our own estimation.[20]

While this vast artifice was a comfort to most of the serving officers, it was anathema to the new breed of arrivals for whom the Raj was a hollow sham. One visitor who felt like this was Robert Lutyens, the son of Sir Edwin, the architect responsible for designing much of New Delhi. Robert Lutyens flew out to India in 1937 to show the Maharaja of Jaipur his designs for a palace. The day after he arrived, he wrote to his mother, headlining his letter with

'Now that I have seen India, can't I come home again?'

Guest House, Jaipur, 3 November 1937

This northern part of the country mostly scrub desert, particularly in Jodphur, the roads only lined with tamerisk and pampas and banian trees, and others that look like laburnum, until you discover they are dripping in golden beans – it is more relentless than anything I had ever imagined. The villages are more pictorially beautiful and more alien than anything I had ever imagined. The country people – I have been motoring for two hundred miles, which is both a lot and a little – are of extraordinary personal beauty. Their clothes are the only colour in a nearly burnt-up land. And what colour!

In Europe we have dominated nature, unless her vengeance is still to come. Here nature is completely dominant and completely ruthless. The beauty, charm, chatter, friendliness of the people are so many symbols of capitulation. In its human element it is wholly inconsequent – trivial, lovely, resigned, and cruel in an impersonal, animal

way. Physically it is implacable and sinister, and unbeliev-
ably remote.

Too soon – far too soon I dare say – for such judge-
ments. I wouldn't have missed what I have seen today for
anything in the world. But I am not sure that I want to
see any more, or to see it again. What place have I – what
place have we here?

It is so incomparably strange – to me so frightening – that I cannot hope to give you a particle of my
impression. You can only see and wonder – I stared for
five hours driving until my eyes ached. The odd, yak-like
cattle (perhaps they are yak), and the odder sheep; the eter-
nally hovering hawk, and the stinging colour of the
women's saris; the ruined temple villages; the decay; the
stark unreality of human life (if it *is* human as we know
it in the West), its constant trivial enterprise; the vast
turbans of half-naked farmers; the dark cherub babies, and
the carriage, modesty and gentleness of the superbly
clothed peasant women; then – what I have just seen in
the dusk – the real Asiatic antiquity of the Jaipur bazaar –
none of these things can I hope to describe to you in a
letter, nor why this whole land of India – what little I
have seen of it – is intensely repugnant to me. We – that
is, we Europeans – might have come here to gaze and to
marvel. We had no right to trade and none whatever to
stay. The British influence – and it is very manifest
whenever you reach such places of brief refuge as this
Guest House; when you see the British-India architecture
of the Palace and the Clubs and hotels (and, good heavens!
the Mayo Boys' School at Ajmer); when you see the
hopeless effort of Englishmen to live comfortably, and
when you see the abominable vulgarity of the goods we
sell – the British influence, or its evidences, doesn't bear
looking at; it doesn't bear thinking about. Besides, the
Indian can't influence India. Nothing can. When God
thought of it he was stark raving mad![21]

Other new arrivals fell naturally into the white sahib role,
even after Independence. Nearly twenty years after Robert
Lutyens expressed his horror at what he had witnessed, Evelyn

Waugh wrote a tongue-in-cheek letter from Mysore to his wife
Laura.

There are cows wandering in all the gardens eating the
flowers. All the lower orders call me 'master' which I find
very familiar. I spent a dull Sunday in Bangalore . . . I met
an Englishman in the bar. I said I was coming here to look
at temples. He said: 'The Hindu religion is nothing but
Sex. But mind you they don't look on it as you & I do,
as something disgusting. *They* think it is beautiful' . . .
    An aged babu shaved my moustaches. He also took off
nearly all the hair on my head & then took my skull in
his hands and tried to crush it, then he tried to break my
neck & pinched my arms cruelly. Apparently that is all part
of getting one's hair cut in this strange land.
    The women here are all charmingly dressed and so
feminine they make all European women seem Lesbian.
The men are nearly all grotesque. The only dignified people are the servants.
    I am afraid that I caused offence in Bangalore because
an official came to greet me & conduct me to a palatial
official guest house but I found it was dry & moved
out. . . .[22]

Soon there was a new school of observers who made their
mark by emphasizing the grubby reality of India and especially
its nostril-wrenching stenches and other minor horrors that had
tended to be swept under the carpet by writers who spoke of
the Mysterious East. Arthur Koestler arrived in Bombay in
1960 and was not favourably impressed by his first experiences.

The sewers of Bombay had been opened by mistake, I was
told, before the tide had come in. The damp heat,
impregnated by their stench, invaded the air-conditioned
cabin the moment the door of the Viscount was opened.
As we descended the steps I had the sensation that a wet,
smelly diaper was being wrapped around my head by some
abominable joker. This was December; the previous day
I had been slithering over the frozen snow in the mountains of Austria. Yet, by the time we had crossed the
reclaimed marshes of the seven islands on which Bombay

is built, I had accepted the heat and was no longer aware of the smell.

An hour after leaving the aircraft, I was ushered into another air-conditioned environment: my hotel room. Its windows and shutters were hermetically closed against the outer atmosphere, its curtains drawn tight against the outer light. It was the peaceful interior of a bathyscape suspended in the sea. After a while I got accustomed to that too, and found it quite natural to live in an artificial atmosphere with artificial light, while the sun was blazing outside. However, each time I left my bathyscape and was hit by the steaming air with its heavy blend of smells, I felt the same shocked surprise as on the first occasion.[23]

Alan Ross, the poet and cricket enthusiast, lived in India as a child and wrote a poem about his first impressions.

The first addictive smell
And that curiously sated light
In which dhows and islands float
Lining the air with spices

The beginning and end
Of India, birth and death,
The bay curved as a kukri
And on Malabar Hill the vultures,
Like seedy waiters, scooping the crumbs off corpses.[24]

Sashti Brata, an Indian writer who left India in the 1960s, had to cope with both the initial numbing caused by the heat and poverty and also the gulf between his Westernized life and that of the teeming millions outside.

Every time I return to India, there is a sense of loss – imprecise, suspended, like a hole without a ring. Yet there is also a feeling of release, as if one had just escaped death by drowning. There is instant shock, even now, after twenty years of exile, in that first collision between West and East, in climbing down from a British Airways jumbo onto the sweating, indolent tarmac of Bombay airport. The fly-infested stalls, open sewers, reckless defiance of elementary hygiene, implode within my consciousness just as violently as they did exactly two decades ago, when I first revisited the country of my birth after two years in Britain.

But subtly, through a process of natural and unperceived mutation, the picture changes. Details become blurred, the landscape grows around one like a well-worn cloak. Beggars continue to exist, their mutilated limbs and oozing sores persist in objective reality, but with time, even within days, they no longer assault the eyes. Unmentionable phenomena register visually, but they get shunted to the side, till finally they are bleached out of conscious cognition.

One boards a taxi in Calcutta, and learns to ignore, even vehemently whoosh away, the eleven-year-old mother carrying a cretinous and skeletal baby in her arms, knocking on the window, tearfully begging for a penny. One puts on a Savile Row suit, and dines at the Bengal Club (the oldest in India) where eight-foot-tall oil portraits of Philip Mountbatten and Elizabeth Windsor adorn the main marble hall. Disease, squalor, and the unrelenting sun, even in winter, become familiar companions. One learns, perforce, to forget that there is another world, alternative visions, other ways for the human animal to survive.[25]

By the mid-1960s, interest in India had revived in the West, thanks to the advent of travellers on the Hippy Trail. At first, it was mainly Europeans and Americans heading east, ending their journeys in Kathmandu or even northern Thailand or Laos, where there was also that essential prerequisite of the hippy – cheap and potent marijuana.

The writer and poet Hugo Williams made the journey to India in 1965 at the beginning of its fame in the counter-culture.

I finished my letters and decided to look up my one contact in Delhi – a friend's friend, Buddy Isenberg: hash smoker, hipster and sometime sidekick of Allen Ginsberg. 'If you like I'll connect you to New Delhi,' my friend had said. And sure enough, when I rang up, Buddy said he would pick me up at the YMCA at six. I found him reading a paper in the lobby and we took a motor trishaw across Delhi to Jor Bagh. . . .

I had been two months in India, Buddy had been two
years. He spoke Hindi, had hitched all over the Subcontinent and Christmassed in the Taj Mahal with Allen
Ginsberg. He had photographs to prove it. Every temple
in India had a smoking room, he said, and all the holy
men were permanently 'turned on'. He'd spent many
happy hours smoking with them. They were all cool
cats – especially in Kashmir. Hashish grows wild up there
apparently – 'really wild, man' – and you could buy the
finished product in government stores . . .
    After dinner three people turned up 'to smoke a pipe of
peace'. There was a girl with straight fair hair wearing a
kurdah and pajamas introduced as 'The Light of Asia', an
English Buddhist with long, long hair and an American
jazz-lover with a crew cut. Buddy rolled reefers and put
on some Indian music and we settled down to a nice
anti-social.[26]

Patrick Marnham made the journey out in the late 1960s,
entering the Subcontinent through the North-West Frontier –
the same land route that invaders and travellers have used for
thousands of years. The perceptions of many of these self-styled
'travellers' about Indian culture were often as fanciful as those
of Strabo.

In the Delhi Coffee House the overlanders lay about like
beached fish, waiting for the rains to wash them out on to
the road again. While they waited they drank iced coffee
and swopped the usual poverty stories.
    'I met this Peace Corps worker who used to hear a baby
crying in one of the huts in his village. Finally he went
in and asked what was the matter and found that the
baby's eyes were bandaged. Underneath each bandage
there was a leech. The parents said they had put them there
because the child would one day have to be a beggar, and
they wanted him to be a good one, so they were making
him as ugly as possible. Isn't that a wild story?' . . .
    Before we left Delhi the Indian newspapers opened a
long series of investigations into the 'hippy phenomenon'.
Startled groups of tattered overlanders were approached in
the coffee house and invited to eyeball-to-eyeball confron-

tations with teams of sleuths from the *Statesman* or *The Times of India*. One such confrontation was organised by a Mr Naqui and it proved to be a small milestone in international misunderstanding.

Mr Naqui felt that this was the time to air a few of the unspoken questions about the appearance of this generation of filthy post-Imperialists in New Delhi, a city which had been constructed by their conquering forefathers. What did this anti-materialist philosophy have to offer India, and what was the connection between these international beggars and the European student revolt?

His visitors knew little of their imperial past, denied any community of interest with the Paris revolution of May 1968 and were bored by questions about how they lived without money. There were long pauses while neighbouring reporters pretended to be working and the atmosphere in the air-conditioned office grew strained. Finally discussion got round to girls. Why were there so few among the overlanders? An explanation about the number of attacks followed; the particular dangers of neighbouring Moslem countries were mentioned. Mr Naqui wanted this explained at greater length. 'Well. You know . . . Moslems . . .' said the spokesman. There was a pause. 'I am a Moslem,' said Mr Naqui. The meeting broke up.[27]

By the late 1960s and early 1970s, the trail had become crowded by new entrants from Australasia who were heading in the opposite direction. Young Japanese and Thai tourists, too, were curious to visit important Buddhist pilgrimage sites or seek out the Dalai Lama in the foothills of the Himalayas. There are still impoverished Westerners seeking enlightenment in the Subcontinent but their numbers are far less than in the 1960s.

There has been a middle-class Indian backlash against the occasionally mercenary behaviour of impoverished Westerners. Anita Desai, in her novel *Baumgartner's Bombay*, portrays an exchange between Baumgartner, a long-time resident, and Farrokh, owner of a seedy restaurant in Bombay. Farrokh is disgusted at the hippy who arrives and then slumps over one of his tables.

'He, he belongs to this new race – men who remain children, like pygmies, dwarfs. Yes, I know they are very tall – I know they are growing bigger and bigger, these jungly heathens of today. Eat and sleep and lie about in the sun all day, they grow like turnips you leave in the ground – *too* big. . . . why should I bend my back, dirty my hands? Hah? What for? For a kick from his boot – the boot in which he climbed Himalaya, I suppose. Already he has kicked his parents in the face, I think – rich parents, giving their son motor bike, motor car, watch, money, ticket to India, everything. Then what do they get? Boot in the face, goodbye and get off. Hah? That is how they come – to Afghanistan, to Nepal, to India. Tell their parents they don't want job, they don't want work. Tell them big big lies about Hindu gods, say they love Buddha, say they want to visit temples, live in ashrams. Yes, they visit temples and live in ashrams alright,' Farrokh sneered, 'but do they look at Buddha – or at Rama, or Krishna or any other god? I know what they do. *You* know what they do, Bommgarter *sahib*? Get drugs in these ashrams, drugs from those pundits and other people like them. *That* is why they come to India, and Nepal, and Afghanistan. I say let them take drugs – let them kill themselves – why not? I care? I just call police and tell them remove them, throw them into gaol, into city morgue. But what I don't like, Bommgarter *sahib*, is how they come to India, spoil Bombay, spoil Goa, spoil holy temples, spoil my restaurant. Why for? Have we invited them? No! Then why they come? And what do they give in return, hah? Do they pay my bill? No. When Rashid goes to them with the bill, then they pull out pockets, show the big holes, say, "No money, no pay". Just like that.' Farrokh slapped the table with his hand, making Baumgartner draw back. 'Just like that. And what you can do? Call police because boy has not paid bill for two rupees? No, you have to forget. Then they go to shop – I have seen them myself, picking up bread, picking up bananas, saying, "I am hungry, no money, no mummy-daddy no send money, please give me," and you know what kind of people we are in India, Bommgarter *sahib*, can we refuse food to anybody?'[28]

In the 1990s, vagrant Westerners have been overtaken in numbers by visiting 'NRIs' or Non-Resident Indians, affluent emigrants who now live in Europe and North America. As a group, the NRIs tend to be far more critical of Indian mores than visiting Westerners and, in turn, are more resented by local residents than the remnants of 1960s culture. Yet these latest arrivals to the Subcontinent are highly prized in the marketplace and their marriage advertisements in the weekend newspapers are eagerly read by prospective parents-in-law.

Despite the size of the Subcontinent, tourism is barely developed compared with the Far East. Beyond the established tourist routes in northern India, there are still numerous opportunities for new arrivals to encounter vibrant strands of the same culture that has confused and bewildered the rest of the world for the past two thousand years.

2
CLIMATE

In northern lands we can *feel* the earth gathering
herself together to 'go through it', steeling herself
for the freezing grip of winter. In India, this happens
in spring, when the hot weather sends out its first
herald. The fields were withdrawing into themselves
in dread – 'Now for it!' they seemed to say. 'It will
be awful – our only chance is to sleep through it.'

Edward Thompson, *An Indian Day*[1]

The climate of India has always been central to its culture – if
there are two poor monsoons in succession, tens of millions are
in danger of perishing. There is tension, dread and expectation
in northern India from early May until the start of the monsoon
a month later. In fact, there are two distinct monsoons – one
which sweeps up the south-west coast and the other which
makes its passage through the Bay of Bengal and across
Calcutta. In an ideal season, they intersect in northern India.
If they fail to do so, part of the countryside is blighted until
the following year. Such are the vagaries of the climate that
some districts of Rajasthan must wait three years between rains.
Then for many people the only hope is government employment on special drought-relief projects. Before Independence,
similar schemes were created by the more affluent princely
rulers. The thousands of labourers who helped build the
Maharaja of Jodhpur's extraordinary palace in the 1930s were
actually employed on famine relief.

Not surprisingly, the seasons play a major part in all aspects
of Indian life. The *Rig Veda*, the earliest known written work
in the world, composed between 1500 BC and 1000 BC, viewed
the weather cycle as the direct responsibility of Parjanya, the
personification of the rain-cloud whose three voices were
thunder, lightning and rain. This god was also responsible for
fertility and was held in great respect.

Summon the powerful god with these songs; praise Parjanya; win him over with homage. The bellowing bull, freely flowing with luscious drops, places his seed in the plants as an embryo.

He shatters the trees and slaughters the demons; he strikes terror into every creature with his enormous deadly weapon. Even the sinless man gives way before the god bursting with seed like a bull, when the thundering Parjanya slaughters those who do evil.

Like a charioteer lashing his horses with a whip, he makes his messengers of rain appear. From the distance arise the thunder-peals of a lion, when Parjanya makes the sky full of rain-clouds.

The winds blow forth, the lightnings fly, the plants surge up, the sky swells, the sun overflows. The sap of life quickens in every creature when Parjanya refreshes the earth with his seed.

By your law, the earth bends low; by your law, all animals with hoofs quiver; by your law, plants of all forms bloom. By these powers, Parjanya, grant us safe shelter.

Give us rain from heaven, O Maruts. Make the streams of the seed-bearing stallion overflow as they swell. Come here with your thunder, pouring down waters, for you are our father, the bright sky-god.[2]

What is especially attractive about the early Indian writings on nature is their exuberance and joy at the bountifulness of everything. The Gods may be feared for their infinite powers, but their deeds are worthy of celebration in song or in verse. In the fifth century AD, Kalidasa, the greatest dramatist of ancient India, composed a lengthy poem in celebration of the seasons, while in the following century, Subandhu wrote a particularly vivid account of the monsoon.

The rainy season had arrived. Rivers overflowed their banks. Peacocks danced at eventide. The rain quelled the expanse of dust as a great ascetic quells the tide of passion. The *chataka* birds were happy. Lightning shone like a bejewelled boat of Love in the pleasure-pool of the sky;

it was like a garland for the gate of the palace of paradise; like a lustrous girdle for some heavenly beauty; like a row of nail-marks left upon the cloud by its lover, the departing day.

The rain was like a chess player, while yellow and green frogs were like chessmen jumping in the enclosures of the irrigated fields. Hailstones flashed like pears from the necklaces of heavenly birds. By and by, the rainy season yielded to autumn, the season of bright dawns; of parrots rummaging among rice-stalks; of fugitive clouds. In autumn the lakes echoed with the sound of herons. The frogs were silent and the snakes shrivelled up. At night the stars were unusually bright and the moon was like a pale beauty.[3]

Marco Polo hardly mentioned the weather when he travelled through India in the thirteenth century. In describing what appears to have been the Malabar coast, he merely stated that

The climate is amazingly hot, which explains why they go naked. There is no rain except in the months of June, July, and August. If it were not for the rain in these three months, which freshens the air, the heat would be so oppressive that no one could stand it. But thanks to this rain the heat is tempered.[4]

Many of the early invaders of the Subcontinent complained about the climate, but as they usually came from central Asia they had a fair notion of extremes in temperature. Emperor Babur remarked that 'Compared with our countries it is a different world; its mountains, rivers, jungles, and deserts, its towns, its cultivated lands, its animals and plants, its peoples and their tongues, its rains, and its winds, are all different.'[5]

The first European residents in India were hopelessly ill-equipped to cope with the climate, chiefly because of their fixed ideas about dress. It was beneath contempt to wear what the local people did, so the Europeans persisted in going about in heavy clothing. However, François Bernier, the French physician to Emperor Aurangzeb, had a keen awareness of the appropriateness of Indian behaviour when dealing with the conditions of the Subcontinent. He also defended Indian cities against European criticism that they were inferior to those in the West. Delhi's beauties, he asserted, stemmed from the adaptions necessary for a city exposed to a hot climate.

> The heat is so intense in Hindoustan, that no one, not even the King, wears stockings; the only cover for the feet being babouches, or slippers, while the head is protected by a small turban, of the finest and most delicate materials. The other garments are proportionably light. During the summer season, it is scarcely possible to keep the hand on the wall of an apartment, or the head on a pillow. For more than six successive months, everybody lies in the open air without covering – the common people in the streets, the merchants and persons of condition sometimes in their courts or gardens, and sometimes on their terraces, which are first carefully watered. Now, only suppose the streets of St Jacques or St Denis transported hither, with their close houses and endless stories; would they be habitable? or would it be possible to sleep in them during the night, when the absence of wind increases the heat almost to suffocation? Suppose one just returned on horseback, half dead with heat and dust, and drenched, as usual, in perspiration; and then imagine the luxury of squeezing up a narrow dark staircase to the fourth or fifth storey, there to remain almost choked with heat. In the Indies, there is no such troublesome task to perform. You have only to swallow quickly a draught of fresh water, or lemonade; to undress; wash face, hands, and feet, and then immediately drop upon a sofa in some shady place, where one or two servants fan you with their great pankhas or fans.[6]

The Reverend James Ovington, at the end of the seventeenth century, described the devastating effect of the monsoon on the tiny European population which was still largely contained in the trading posts scattered around the Indian coast. In his *Voyage to Suratt* published in 1690, he observed that September and October were 'very pernicious to the health of Europeans'. He pointed out that in these 'two moons more of them die, than generally in all the year besides. For the excess of earthy vapours after the rains ferment the air, and raise therein such a sultry heat, that scarce any is able to withstand the feverish effect it has upon their spirits, nor recover themselves from those fevers and fluxes into which it cast them.' He added that a proverb had emerged that 'Two Mussouns are the age of man'. If proof were needed, of the twenty-four passengers who had survived the journey with him to Bombay, only four were alive after the monsoon. Similar figures can be found for all the other early European settlements in the Subcontinent, a third of all residents perishing in some years. In one eight-year period in the nineteenth century, three Governors-General and two of their wives died from disease and stress brought on by the climate. As a category, bishops fared no better, with no less than four Bishops of Calcutta going to meet their maker prematurely in the years between 1822 and 1831.

Of greater threat to the local population than epidemics was famine. If the monsoon failed twice, there was precious little chance that those living on the margins would survive until the next season. Before the advent of a comprehensive rail network throughout the Subcontinent, there was no effective way to shift large amounts of grain rapidly. Peter Mundy, a Cornish traveller, journeyed through the worst affected areas in 1630. At one town he and his companions had great difficulty in finding a location to pitch their tents 'by reason of the number of dead bodyes that lay scattered in and about the Towne'. Eventually, the only place that they could find that was not similarly afflicted was the local graveyard. The following day, while waiting for their servants to bargain for provisions,

> our noses were infested and our bodyes almost infected with a most noysome smell, which after search, wee found to come from a great pitt, wherein were throwne 30 or 40 persons, men, women and children, old and younge confusedly tumbled in together without order or coveringe, a miserable and most undecent spectacle. No less lamentable was it to see the poor people scraping on the dunghills for food, yea in the very excrements of beasts, as horses, oxen, etc., belonging to travellers, for grain that perchance might come undigested from them, and that with great greediness and strife among themselves, generally looking like anatomies with life, but scarce strength enough to remove themselves from under men's

feet, many of them expiring, others new dead . . . From
Surat to this place, all the highway was strewed with dead
people, our noses never free from the stink of them,
especially about towns; for they drag them out by the
heels, stark naked, and all ages and sexes, till they are out
of the gates, and there they are left, so that the way is half
barred up . . .

These gruesome descriptions are interspersed with comments
about the location of the town and what the 'better sort' built
their dwellings from, but such comments are overwhelmed by
the human miseries he witnessed.

In this place, men and women were driven to that
extremity by hunger that they sold their children for 12s.
6d., yea and to give them away to any that would take
them . . .
    Women were seen to roast their children; men
travelling in the way were laid hold of to be eaten and
having cut away much of his flesh, he was glad if he could
get away and save his life, others killed outright and
devoured. A man or woman no sooner dead but they were
cut in pieces to be eaten.[7]

Conditions were hardly any better a century and a half later,
when William Hickey observed the effects of famine around
Calcutta in the 1780s.

This year a dreadful scarcity of grain prevailed, the crops
having failed throughout the Provinces of Bengal and
Behar, from which circumstances the laborious poor
became distressed for food to supply their families. In consequence of this the British inhabitants of Calcutta, with
their accustomed benevolence, entered into a voluntary
subscription for their relief, whereby so large a sum was
raised as to enable them to feed upwards of twenty
thousand men, women, and children daily. Six different
stations were fixed upon in opposite directions for
delivering out rice, ghee and other articles of provisions,
two English gentlemen attending at each station to
superintend the proper distribution; this continued about
four months when such immense crowds of miserable

creatures were drawn to the Presidency by the hope of relief that Government became alarmed and were under the unpleasant necessity of issuing orders to stop the further delivery of rice, etc., after a certain day therein specified, of which public and written notices were proclaimed and stuck up all over the country and every possible precaution was taken to prevent a further influx of people to the Capital; but nothing could stop the unhappy, famished wretches from rushing in crowds to Calcutta, the neighbourhood of which became dreadful to behold. One could not stir out of doors without encountering the most shocking objects, the poor, starved people laying dead and dying in every street and road. It was computed that for many weeks no less than 50 died daily, yet this patient and mild race never committed the least act of violence, no houses or go-downs were broken into to procure rice, no exclamations of noisy cries made for assistance; all with the gentle resignation so peculiar to the natives of India, submitting to their fate and laying themselves down to die. Everything in the power of liberal individuals was done for their relief; indeed, one must have been less than a man, almost Buonaparte, to have witnessed such horrible scenes of misery without feeling the bitterest pangs and exerting every nerve to alleviate them.[8]

By the middle of the nineteenth century, the combination of railways, steamship travel and better roads meant that surplus food could be dispatched to afflicted areas. There has never been a complete crop failure throughout the entire Subcontinent – there has always been a surplus in one or other region. The last major famine occurred during the Second World War and was eloquently described by Jawaharlal Nehru. He himself never suffered any direct effects from it as he was imprisoned at Ahmadnagar Fort in Maharastra with a number of other prominent nationalist politicians.

Famine came, ghastly, staggering, horrible, beyond words. In Malabar, in Bijapur, in Orissa, and above all, in the rich and fertile province of Bengal, men and women and little children died in their thousands daily for lack of food. They dropped down dead before the palaces of Calcutta, their corpses lay in the mud-huts of Bengal's innumerable villages and covered the roads and fields of its rural areas. Men were dying all over the world and killing each other in battle; usually a quick death, often a brave death for a cause, death with a purpose, death which seemed in this mad world of ours an inexorable logic of events, a sudden end to the life we could not mould or control. Death was common enough everywhere.

But here death had no purpose, no logic, no necessity; it was the result of man's incompetence and callousness, man-made, a slow creeping thing of horror with nothing to redeem it, life merging and fading into death, with death looking out of the shrunken eyes and withered frame while life still lingered for a while. And so it was not considered right or proper to mention it; it was not good form to talk or write of unsavoury topics. To do so was to 'dramatize' an unfortunate situation. False reports were issued by those in authority in India and in England. But corpses cannot easily be overlooked; they come in the way.[9]

Despite the constant reminders of the need for Europeans to respect the exigencies of the Indian climate, many presumed they had mastered the perils of both the weather and the sanitary arrangements. Victor Jacquemont, a brilliant young French botanist, was one of many who believed they had achieved immunity. Jacquemont arrived in Calcutta in 1829 with a sheaf of introductions to everyone from the Governor-General, Lord William Cavendish-Bentinck, downwards. He intended to spend seven years on a scientific mission to investigate the natural history of India on behalf of the Royal Museum of Natural History in Paris. He wrote to a friend in France a few weeks after his arrival of his success in combating the effects of the climate on the banks of the Hoogly River near the Botanical Gardens.

In this beautiful spot, I gradually accustomed myself to the sun of this country. Undoubtedly it is powerful, and certainly raises unwholesome exhalations from a soil which is nothing but mud imperfectly dried, and filled with the remains of insects and worms without number; but I believe the danger of exposure to it greatly exaggerated. Though I flatter myself I have been very prudent, I ought, according to the Indians, to have been dead ere this. It is true that, according to the physicians who have most experience of this climate, and whose great skill I willingly allow, my constitution is wonderfully adapted to its prominent features.[10]

His optimism was tragically misplaced. Three years later, while collecting specimens near Bombay, he suffered an agonizing death from an abscess on the liver. Europeans did not succumb to disease in such huge numbers after the Mutiny as they had in the early days, but there was still a persistent fear that anything could happen there without much warning. Queen Victoria, in a letter to Lady Canning, her former Mistress of the Bedchamber, observed that 'if it was not for the heat and the insects, how much I would like to see India.'

Lady Canning, wife of Lord Canning, the Governor-General during the Mutiny, typified the futile attempt by the well-intentioned Memsahib to survive in the Subcontinent without troubling the hordes of local inhabitants nominally employed at Government House as servants. Just weeks after her arrival, Lady Canning complained, before the onset of the hot season, about having to live with so many 'odious punkahs' – 'I doubt if I shall ever have it pulled at night.' The punkah consisted of a large piece of canvas stretched across the ceiling which created a breeze through the rippling effect of a punkah-wallah pulling cords at one end of it. Less than a month later, in April, she began to comprehend the unrelenting power of the heat and humidity. She confessed that she now slept to perfection, thanks to this 'indulgence'. 'Now I am completely vanquished on the punkah point.' Her husband also learned to cope with the rigours of the Calcutta climate, especially between March and early June.

By shutting up every chink of window from $7\frac{1}{2}$ a.m., and the venetians outside, and by keeping heavy mats hung up against the outer doors into the court and garden ('compound' here called) just as you see them in Italian churches, we manage to keep the air inside the house pretty cool all day long, and, with the punkahs going, one's room is very endurable. But any attempt to go out, even in a carriage, makes one gasp, and dissolve immediately, and an open window or door lets in a flood of hot air, as though one were passing the mouth of a foundry. At 6 p.m. windows and venetians and doors are thrown open, and in comes the strong wind, blowing one's paper off the table (which is performed by the punkah at other times) and making the chandeliers swing, and their glass drops jingle, all night long. But even at night, if one gets out of the draught (which we never do, for we dine in a gale which blows up the corners of the tablecloth, and sends the bills of fare and lists of the tunes across the table, unless a fork is put on them; we sit in a gale, and we sleep in a gale), one becomes what Shelburne would call *nadando en sudor* in an instant.[11]

Sadly, both Lord and Lady Canning were eventually to fall victim to diseases contracted in India. In November 1861, Lady Canning was busy sketching flowers and rare orchids south of Darjeeling when she contracted what was termed 'jungle fever' – probably malaria. Although rushed to Calcutta for treatment, she died less than a fortnight later at the age of 44. She was buried on the banks of the Ganges near Government House at Barrackpore. Lord Canning never recovered from the shock of her sudden death and arranged for a lamp to be kept burning next to her grave, under which he would sit every night reading and re-reading her private papers until he suffered from a mental collapse. He returned to London the following March in poor health and died three months later at the age of 49. He was buried in Westminster Abbey but Lady Canning's remains are still at Barrackpore under a copy of the original headstone – the original now rests in the north portico of St John's Church, Calcutta.

Such tragedies did not deter the bulk of the English residents. A straightforward approach to the rigours of the climate was recommended by Flora Steel, in her classic *The Complete Indian Housekeeper and Cook*, first published in 1888 and still selling in large numbers nearly half a century later. 'The fact is, many people make the climate of India into a Frankenstein monster, and straightaway become alarmed at their creation . . . The gist of the whole lies in this – Don't give into it, and it will give in to *you*.' The modern Indian approach to heat control relies on a strange contraption called a desert cooler, which is a blend of the technology of Heath Robinson and a Sopwith Camel. An enormous fan whirs over a foetid pool of water and then blasts it through a rotting screen of damp hay. The precursor to this uniquely Indian invention was the thermantidote, which applied the same principles, but was propelled not by an electric motor but by a coolie's arm. Today the Indian élite and the Western community often resort to air-conditioning during the hot season but a combination of poor technology and daily power-cuts of one to two hours during the hottest period of the day ensures that the modern Indian resident fares much worse than those relying on punkahs and thermantidotes a century ago.

Miss Steel preferred these elaborate contraptions (especially Johnson's self-watering machine) to punkahs, as the latter were, she declared, really only capable of keeping away the mosquitoes. 'The presence of a punkah rope on a coolie's hand seems positively to have a soporific effect on him, whereas the handle or treadle of a thermantidote acquires an impetus of its own, and asserts its intention of going around, will-he nill-he.' In addition, the thermantidote-turner was actually outside the house, which meant 'there [was] less temptation to burst out on the offender and slay him on the spot' if he malfunctioned. If anyone was still pigheaded enough to doubt Miss Steel's logic, she added that 'Even if this homicidal mania does not seize on you, a thermantidote prevents the possibility of spoiling your boots and shoes by throwing them at the coolie's head.'[12]

Amongst the European population, soldiers suffered from the heat more than housewives because of their officers' insistence that they maintain standards by retaining their canvas jackets and thick twill trousers. Large numbers succumbed to heatstroke and dehydration. Private Frank Richards of the Royal Welch Fusiliers provides a vivid account of the suffering experienced by ordinary foot-soldiers in the hot season at the turn of the century.

We were all covered from head to foot with prickly heat rash, which itches intolerably, and quite a number of men were troubled with boils and water-blisters. Water-blisters, caused by the heat, would sometimes rise on a man's face and when they burst his skin would be in a nice condition for a few days. I also remember thirty men being in hospital at the same time with water-blisters on their privates. By the end of the first half of the summer, even without the help of water-blisters, the whole battalion had faces like whitewashed walls.[13]

No matter what precautions are taken to deal with the heat, it remains an obsessive topic from March until June. Alan Ross, who lived in India immediately before Independence, touches on the torpor and dread induced by the weather.

This listlessness of the Indians, often contrasted with the energy of the Europeans, was a constant feature of my own mother's conversation. A mixture of resentment and indifference exaggerated it in the case of servants on whose behaviour most European women based their generalizations. Yet, after a lifetime in India, the same complaining and vigorous Europeans tended to be as debilitated as the servants they harried. My father, after forty years in India, left at a week's notice, suddenly unable to face another monsoon and the lowering effects of amoebic dysentery. Indians, often equally exhausted by the climate, had no such options.[14]

Another generation on, Patrick Marnham also observed the growing tension in the Subcontinent at the approach of the monsoon.

The air in Northern India in the weeks before the monsoon is as tangible as the other elements. It is as hot as fire, as thick as water. It becomes an effort to part it. It burns you and soaks you at the same time. If you step into it from an air-conditioned building, the impression is of a physical blow; the heat rises from the ground and strikes. If you remain still, it enfolds you gently; if you try to move through it, it gains a malignant confidence and seizes you.

A nation which has to occupy itself in such a climate, which has to plan and build and exercise power and observation and change its mind and start again, might well

expect to find survival hard. As we approached Delhi
along the Ganges there was an impression of a listless
people, waiting for the rain, on a brown earth, in a grey
light, under a thick cloud of yellow dust that blanketed
sunlight and shadows alike.[15]

The arrival of the monsoon is one of nature's worse-kept
secrets. There is a sense in the air of impending drama – you
know that the enervating heat simply cannot last for ever. To
add to the unpleasantness of the heat, there are frequent dust
storms which give the entire landscape a curious amber light.
More than 90 per cent of India's rainfall comes in the months
of July, August and September. Indian finance ministers
concede that the economy is affected far more by the quality
of the monsoon than by anything they can do with their annual
budgets.

One of the earliest descriptions in English of the monsoon
comes from the Reverend Edward Terry, Sir Thomas Roe's
second chaplain during his embassy to Emperor Jahangir's court
at Agra in the early seventeenth century.

At Surat, and to Agra and beyond, it never raines but one
season of the yeere, which begins neare the time that the
sunne comes to the Northerne Tropicke, and so continues
till his returne backe to the Line. These violent raines are
ushered in, and take their leave, with most fearfull
tempests of thunder and lightning, more terrible than I
can expresse, yet seldome doe harme. The reason in Nature
may be the subtiltie of the aire, wherein there are fewer
thunderstones made then in such climates where the aire
is grosse and cloudy. In those three moneths it raines every
day more or lesse, sometimes one whole quarter of the
moone scarce with any intermission; which abundance of
raine, with the heat of the sunne, doth so enrich the
ground (which they never force) as that, like Egypt by the
inundation of the Nilus, it makes it fruitfull all the yeere
after. But when this time of raine is passed over, the skie
is so cleere as that scarcely one cloud is seene in their
hemisphere the nine moneths after. And here the good-
nesse of the soyle must not escape my pen; most apparent
in this, for when the ground hath beene destitute of raine

nine moneths, and lookes like to barren sands, within seven dayes after the raine begins to fall it puts on a green coate.[16]

Almost exactly two centuries later, another English minister, the Reverend John Hobart Caunter, described the arrival of the monsoon in almost Biblical language.

As the house which we occupied overlooked the beach, we could behold the setting in of the monsoon in all its grand and terrific sublimity. The wind, with a force nothing could resist, bent the tufted heads of the tall, slim coconut trees almost to the earth, flinging the light sand into the air in eddying vortices, until the rain had either so increased its gravity, or beaten it into a mass, as to prevent the wind from raising it. The pale lightning streamed from the clouds in broad sheets of flame, which appeared to encircle the heavens as if every element had been converted into fire, and the world was on the eve of a general conflagration, whilst the peal, which instantly followed, was like the explosion of a gun-powder magazine, or the discharge of artillery in the gorge of a mountain, where the repurcussion of surrounding hills multiplies with terrific energy its deep and astounding echoes . . . So heavy and continuous was the rain that scarcely anything, save those vivid bursts of light which nothing could arrest or resist, was perceptible through it. The thunder was so painfully loud, that it frequently caused the ear to throb; it seemed as if mines were momentarily springing in the heavens, and I could almost fancy that one of the sublimest fictions of heathen fable was realized at this moment before me, and that I was hearing an assault of the Titans. The surf was raised by the wind and scattered in thin billows of foam over the esplanade, which was completely powdered with the white feathery spray. It extended several hundred yards from the beach; fish, upwards of three inches long, were found upon the flat roofs of houses in the town during the prevalence of the monsoon, either blown from the sea by the violence of the gales, or taken up in the water-spouts, which are very prevalent in this tempestuous season . . .

During the extreme violence of the storm, the heat was occasionally almost beyond endurance, particularly after the first day or two, when the wind would at intervals entirely subside, so that not a breath of air could be felt, and the punkah afforded but a partial relief to that distressing sensation which is caused by the oppressive stillness of the air, so well known in India whilst the monsoon prevails. . . .

There are no doubt many parts of the world where, during the presence of hurricanes, the wind is more impetuous than during these periodic visitations in India: but in none, I will venture to say, does the rain pour in such a mighty deluge, and in no place can the thunder and lightning be more terrific.[17]

E.M. Forster spent some time in central India in the early 1920s working as a private secretary and tutor to the Maharaja of Dewas Senior, an eccentric but relatively enlightened homosexual princeling. In *The Hill of Devi* he too recorded the onset of the monsoon.

The first shower was smelly and undramatic. Now there is a new India – damp and grey, and but for the unusual animals I might think myself in England. The full monsoon broke violently, and upon my undefended form. I was under a little shelter in the garden, sowing seeds in boxes with the assistance of two aged men and a little boy. I saw black clouds and felt some spots of rain. This went on for a quarter of an hour, so that I got accustomed to it, and then a wheel of water swept horizontally over the ground. The aged men clung to each other for support. I don't know what happened to the boy. I bowed this way and that as the torrent veered, wet through of course, but anxious not to be blown away like the roof of palm leaves over our head. When the storm decreased or rather became perpendicular, I set out for the palace, large boats of mud forming on either foot. A rescue expedition, consisting of an umbrella and a servant, set out to meet me, but the umbrella blew inside out and the servant fell down.

Since then, there have been some more fine storms, with lightning very ornamental and close. The birds fly about with large pieces of paper in their mouths. They are late, like everyone else, in their preparations against the rough weather, and hope to make a nest straight off, but the wind blows the papers around their heads like a shawl, and they grow alarmed and drop it. The temperature is now variable, becomes very hot between the storms, but on the whole things have improved. I feel much more alert and able to concentrate. The heat made me feel so stupid and sleepy, though I kept perfectly well.[18]

There is in fact one place which exceeds all others on earth for the ferocity of its monsoon – Cherrapunji in Meghalaya, north-east India. This town holds the so-far-unchallenged distinction of being the wettest place on earth, with upwards of 400 inches of rain a year, rising to 800 inches in some years. Alexander Frater spent several months following the Indian monsoon and gathering material for his book, *Chasing the Monsoon*. After starting on the beach at Kerala and travelling up the coast through Goa to Bombay and then to Delhi, he finally ended up in Cherrapunji in time to witness the daily deluge during the monsoon season.

A fountain of dense black cloud came spiralling over the hills, then rose steeply into the sky. It formed a kind of tent, apex high overhead, sides unrolling right to the ground. It was very dark inside but I could just discern, trooping towards us, an armada of shadowy, galleon-like vessels with undersides festooned with writhing cables of water. They gave off thundery rumbles and a noise like discharging hydrants, the rain descending in hissing vertical rafts of solid matter that lathered the earth and made the spokes of the [poet's] umbrella, under which I had taken shelter, bend like saplings.[19]

During the nineteenth and early twentieth century, by the time the monsoon was underway, the annual exodus of Raj residents to the hills had already begun, with the women and children leading the way in early April. Simla was first settled in 1816 by some junior officers who had fought in the Gurkha Wars. Within a few years it became renowned as a safe haven from the heat of the plains and gradually established itself as the preferred hill station of fashionable India. It is situated on a ridge at the southern edge of the Himalayas, which are visible along the entire northern horizon. It also had the unassailable advantage of being the summer residence of the Viceroy, so that other hill stations could not compete in terms of prestige and influence.

In 1830, Simla was a town of only sixty wooden houses scattered over the peaks of low-lying mountains in what was then the Punjab. Victor Jacquemont considered it 'the resort of the rich, the idle and the invalid' where 'the luxury of the Indian capital has established itself, and fashion maintains its tyrannical sway'. Jacquemont stayed with the amiable Captain in Charge, who rarely had to put more than an hour aside for official duties.

> We gallop an hour or two in the morning on the magnificent roads which he has constructed, often joining some elegant cavalcade, among which I meet some of my Calcutta acquaintances. On our return we have an elegant and *recherché* breakfast; then I have the entire and free disposal of my day, and that of my host, whenever I think proper to put it in requisition, to view men and things. At sun-set fresh horses are [brought] to the door, and we take another ride, to beat up the most friendly and lively of the rich idlers and imaginary invalids whom we may chance to meet. They are people of the same kind as my host, bachelors and soldiers, but soldiers employed in all kinds of departments: the most interesting people in India to me. We sit down to a magnificent dinner at half-past seven, and rise at eleven. I drink hock, claret and champagne only, and at dessert Malmsey; the others, alleging the coldness of the climate, stick to port, sherry and Madeira. I do not recollect tasting water for the last seven days; nevertheless, there is no excess, but great cheerfulness every evening . . .
>
> Is it not curious to dine in silk stockings at such a place, and to drink a bottle of hock and another of champagne every evening – delicious Mocha coffee – and to receive the Calcutta journals every morning?[20]

Emily Eden, the sister of Lord Auckland the Governor-General, was full of admiration for the civilized nature of life in the hills. After attending the Queen's Ball of the 1839 season in Simla, she exclaimed in wonder:

Twenty years ago no European had ever been here, and there we were, with the band playing the 'Puritani' and 'Masanielo', and eating salmon from Scotland, and sardines from the Mediterranean, and observing that the chef's *potage à la julienne* was perhaps better than his other soups . . . and all this in the face of those high hills, some of which have remained untrodden since the Creation, and we 105 Europeans being surrounded by at least 3,000 mountaineers, who, wrapped up in their hill-blankets, looked on at what we call our polite amusements, and bowed to the ground if a European came near them. I sometimes wonder they do not cut all our heads off and say nothing more about it.[21]

One of the earliest novelists to satirize the place was Sir Henry Cunningham, who later became a senior judge in Madras. In his novel, *Chronicles of Dustypore*, a tale of modern Anglo-Indian society published in 1875, he lambasted the general level of ignorance and racism of the average British soldier in a fictional hill station which he called 'Elysium'.

There is something in the air of the place which bespeaks the close neighbourhood of the Sovereign rule, the august climax of the official hierarchy. Servants, brilliant in scarlet-and-gold, are hurrying hither and thither. Here some Rajah, petty monarch of the surrounding ranges or the flat plains below, attended with his mimic court and tatterdemalion cavalry, is marching in state to pay his homage to the 'great Lord Sahib'. Here some grand lady, whose gorgeous attire and liveried retinue bespeaks her sublime position, is constrained to bate her greatness to the point of being carried, slung like the grapes of Escol, on a pole, and borne on sturdy peasants' shoulders, to pay a round of the ceremonious visits which etiquette enjoins upon her. Officers, secretaries, aides-de-camp come bustling by on mountain ponies, each busy on his own behest. The energetic army of morning callers are already in the field. A dozen palanquins gathered at Madame Fifini's, the Elsyian 'Worth', announce the fact that as many ladies are hard at work within, running up long bills for their husbands, and equipping themselves for conquest at the next Government House 'at home'. Smartly-furnished shops glitter with all the latest finery of Paris and London, and ladies go jogging along on their bearers' shoulders, gay enough for a London garden-party in July. In the midst of all, the solid basis on which so huge a structure of business, pomp and pleasure is erected, clumps the British Private, brushed, buttoned and rigid, with a loud, heavy tread which contrasts strangely with the noiselessly moving crowd around him, and bespeaks his conscious superiority to a race of beings whom, with a lordly indifference to minute ethnological distinctions, he designates collectively as 'Moors.'[22]

Simla was later scandalized by its sharp portrayal by Rudyard Kipling in *Plain Tales from the Hills*. Kipling wrote with an appealing cynicism verging on ennui and for years after was considered by English residents as a bounder for having so accurately described the wife-swapping and general poor behaviour of the Simla set. One contemporary joke had it that it was impossible to sleep in Simla because of the din made by the grinding of axes.

Later viceroys, such as Lord Curzon, could not stand the place, so far removed from the normal problems of imperial rule and so obsessed with the minutiae of the social round. In 1912, Sir Edwin Lutyens, the recently appointed architect of the Viceroy's Palace in New Delhi, thought it 'inconceivable and consequently very English! – to have a capital as Simla is, entirely of tin roofs . . . if one was told monkeys had built it all one could only say "What wonderful monkeys – they must be shot in case they do it again." '[23]

Since Independence, the decline of Simla has become more marked. Grand Indians still go there in the summer, but what remains of the Mall and other remnants of the Raj have been horrendously overbuilt by grasping developers. There are still some exquisite places, such as Wildflower Hall and the Chapslee Hotel which are packed with social and hunting memorabilia, but most streets have succumbed to the pressure of population and commerce. Through some bureaucratic sleight of hand, the Indian Army have taken over the Gaiety Theatre, which was for decades the centre for amateur theatricals in the hills. One Indian friend of mine who visited the town recently thought a new town sign should be erected on its outskirts, saying 'Welcome to Simla – India's slum in the sky'.

There were a number of other notable hill stations dotted around northern India and several in the south, in the Nilgiri Hills. The most interesting of the latter is Ootacamund, popularly known as Ooty, which still serves as the hot season retreat for Tamil Nadu and Kerala. Although it too is afflicted by careless overdevelopment, enough of its charm is intact to make it well worth a visit. The Ooty Club it the best maintained club in India and has a further claim to fame as the place where snooker was invented more than a century ago. The explorer Richard Burton did not find Ooty to his taste when he recuperated there in the 1840s.

> What a detestable place this Ootacamund is during the rains! From morning to night, and from night to morning, gigantic piles of heavy wet clouds, which look as if the aerial sprites were amusing themselves by heaping misty black Pelions upon thundering purple Ossas, rise up slowly from the direction of the much-vexed Koondahs; each, as it impinges against the west flank of the giant Dodatetta, drenching us with one of those outpourings that resemble nothing but a vast aggregation of the biggest and highest douche baths. In the interim, a gentle drizzle, now deepening into a shower, now driven into sleet, descends with vexatious perseverance. When there is no drizzle there is a Scotch mist: when the mist clears away, it is succeeded by a London fog. The sun, 'shorn of his rays,' spitefully diffuses throughout the atmosphere a muggy warmth, the very reverse of genial. Conceive the effects of such weather upon the land in general, and the mind of man in particular! The surface of the mountains, for the most part, is a rich and reddish mould, easily and yet permanently affected by the least possible quantity of water. Thus the country becomes impassable, the cantonment dirty, every place wretched, every one miserable.[24]

Kashmir has always had an immense pull on the Indian and English imagination. Even a brief visit is enough to explain the cause of this – the Vale of Kashmir is a place of glorious natural beauty. This explains why, as the nineteenth-century *Indian Cyclopaedia* puts it, 'From all times the valley has been the retreat from the heats of India for the conquering races', though one might quibble with the encyclopaedia's other observation, namely that 'Probably owing to the circumstance that the valley has so often been the resort of pleasure-seekers, the morals of the people are not at a high standard.' Mr E.F. Knight, the unashamedly prejudiced author of *Where Three Empires Meet*, held a similarly cynical view of the inhabitants of the Vale.

> As a rule, an Englishman coming for the first time to this country takes a great fancy to these plausible, handsome Kashmiris, finding them clever, cheery, and civil, and it is not until he has been some time in the country that he discovers that these are among the most despicable creatures on earth, incorrigible cheats and liars, and cowardly to an inconceivable degree . . . [The Kashmiri] will presume on any kindness that is shown him until, at last, going too far, he is brought to reason by the thrashing he has long been asking for. I believe a Kashmiri likes a beating and the consequent luxury of a good howl; for he certainly neglects all warning, and persists in some offensiveness until what he knows will be the inevitable chastisement comes.[25]

In recent years, Kashmir has undergone a debilitating civil conflict, mainly because both India and Pakistan claim the state as their natural adjunct. While the majority of the residents are Muslim, there are also large numbers of Hindus who can trace their ancestry back for thousands of years. The Nehru family left only two centuries ago to seek their fame and fortune in the rich plains below. Jawaharlal Nehru wrote movingly of one of his visits to Kashmir before Independence.

> Like some supremely beautiful woman, whose beauty is almost impersonal and above human desire, such was Kashmir in all its feminine beauty of river and valley and lake and graceful trees. And then another aspect of this magic beauty would come to view, a masculine one, of hard mountains and precipices, and snow-capped peaks

and glaciers, and cruel and fierce torrents rushing down to the valleys below. It has a hundred faces and innumerable aspects, ever-changing, sometimes smiling, sometimes sad and full of sorrow. The mist would creep up from the Dal Lake and, like a transparent veil, give glimpses of what was behind. The clouds would throw out their arms to embrace a mountain-top, or creep down stealthily like children at play. I watched this ever-changing spectacle, and sometimes the sheer loveliness of it was over-powering and I felt faint. As I gazed at it, it seemed to me dream-like and unreal, like the hopes and desires that fill us and so seldom find fulfilment. It was like the face of the beloved that one sees in a dream and that fades away on awakening.[26]

The future of the woodlands around the foothills of the Himalayas is now jeopardized by deforestation and population growth. Well-run campaigns by conservation groups eager to preserve what little remains of India's forests have brought home to decision makers that in future more respect will have to be shown to the environment. But no matter what steps are taken or progress is made, the dependence of the Subcontinent on the monsoonal cycle will remain as strong as ever.

3

MUTINY AND PARTITION

[I]n spite of myself, I was obliged to witness the amputation of a dooly-bearer's thigh. I have seen quite enough of those sights, one way or other, but I never beheld greater courage or endurance than was displayed by this man, who appeared to be only twenty years of age – a slight, tall, dark-coloured Hindoo. His thigh was horribly shattered by a round-shot. His large eyes moved inquiringly about as the surgeons made their preparations, but he never even moaned when, with a rapid sweep of the knife, the principal operator had cut the flesh through to the broken splintered bone. . . . In two or three minutes the black leg was lying on the floor of what had once been the Begum's boudoir . . . in two or three minutes more the dusky patient, with a slow shiver, passed away quietly to the other world. Some of my friends in camp would deny he had any soul, or, as one of them put it, 'If niggers have souls, they're not the same as ours.'

William Howard Russell, *Mutiny Diary*[1]

On New Year's Day, 1903, Lord Curzon, the Viceroy of India, orchestrated the greatest ever pageant in the British Empire – the Delhi Durbar. The ostensible reason for this spectacle was the accession of Edward VII as King-Emperor of India but it was more significant as a display of the power and success of the British Raj in the Subcontinent. Everyone was there to pay homage to the Indian Empire (Curzon forbade the singing of 'Onward Christian Soldiers' during the Durbar church services because of his slight twinge of unease at the line 'Crowns and Thrones may perish, Kingdoms rise and wane'). A vast horseshoe amphitheatre was constructed in Mogul style with Saracenic arches and cupolas tipped in gold. The tens of

thousands of spectators included the Viceroy and all the important Indian princes and senior officials on whom the Empire
depended for its smooth running. Curzon described the brilliant
spectacle and his masterly scheme to inaugurate the celebrations.

Out on the plain, through the two points of the horseshoe, could be seen in the near distance the serried ranks
of the massed battalions, in close formation, 40,000
strong; and behind them was a tall mound, packed from
foot to summit with thousands of native spectators. In the
centre of the amphitheatre the imperial flag floated at a
height of 100 feet in the air. Round its base were massed
the bands of twelve regiments that had won glory in the
campaigns of the Mutiny, nearly half a century before.
The dais, in the inner hollow of the horseshoe, sur-
mounted by a domed pavilion directly copied from a
building of Akbar at Agra, awaited its Royal and
Viceregal occupants. At the sound of the bugle a sudden
hush fell upon the whole assembly.

Then was seen a spectacle that will never be forgotten
by those who witnessed it, that brought tears to the eyes
of strong men and a choking in every throat. Preceded by
a military band, there walked into the arena, in irregular
formation, with no attempt at parade or symmetry, a
group, a knot, a straggling company, of old or elderly
men. Nearly all were grey-headed or white-haired, many
were bowed with years, and were with difficulty supported by their comrades or by younger officers who conducted them round. In front marched a little knot of
Europeans, headed by a splendid veteran, Colonel A.R.
Mackenzie, C.B. Some were in stained and dilapidated
uniforms, others in every variety of civil dress; but there
was not a bosom that did not glitter with the medals that
both explained their presence and bespoke their glory.

Behind them walked, and in some cases tottered, a
cluster of Sikh veterans, many with long white beards,
clad entirely in white. The entire procession consisted of
between 300 and 400 men, of whom the great majority
were Indians, and a small minority of less than 30, Europeans and Eurasians.

They were the veterans of the Mutiny, the survivors of that great drama of mingled tragedy and heroism, the officers and non-commissioned officers who had borne a part in the immortal episodes of Delhi and Lucknow, the men but for whom the Imperial Durbar would never have been held.

As they made their way slowly round the broad track of the arena, to which none had hitherto been admitted but themselves, the entire audience, European and Indian, rose to their feet and greeted them with long and tumultuous cheering; but when the proud strains of 'See the Conquering Hero comes', to which the veterans had entered, and in response to which they drew themselves erect and marched with firm step, were succeeded by the wailing pathos of 'Auld Lang Syne', there was audible sobbing both of men and women, and many in that vast audience broke down. One brave old fellow, quite blind, was led by a younger comrade: he turned his sightless orbs towards the cheering, and feebly saluted. It was his last salute; for the excitement was too much for him, and on the morrow he died.[2]

Less than two miles away from the Durbar site is the highest point of Delhi, the Ridge, a scrub-covered rocky outcrop that forms the northern extreme of the great Aravalli range which stretches all the way from south-west Rajasthan. Perched precariously on the most commanding spot is an ugly Victorian spire, the Mutiny Monument, which would look more at home in Bognor Regis. Solid brass plaques painstakingly list the dead and wounded from the various British and loyal Indian regiments, partly obscured by latter-day Hindi graffiti, ranging from the obscene to 'Bhawanna, I am sure that you loves me!'

In 1972, a new plaque was attached to the monument which declares

The 'enemy' of the inscriptions on this monument were those who rose against colonial rule and fought bravely for national liberation in 1857.

In memory of the heroism of these immortal martyrs for Indian freedom.

This is a far cry from what the Mutiny was all about but one should be grateful that, in the best Indian tradition, the detritus of the previous conqueror is preserved and then emended by successive rulers.

By early 1857, British soldiers certainly had portents of the unrest in the army in northern India, prompted initially by rumours that the grease used on the new cartridges for the Enfield rifle was in fact an amalgam of cow and pork fat, thus cunningly spurring fears amongst both Hindus and Muslims that they would be permanently contaminated simply by loading their weapons and then forcibly converted to Christianity. The spark that fired the entire Mutiny occurred in Meerut, a nondescript garrison town just north of Delhi. Colonel George Monro Carmichael-Smyth, commander of the 3rd Light Cavalry Brigade, publicly humiliated eighty-five of his soldiers who had refused even to touch the new bullets by stripping them of their rank on a parade-ground and marching them in fetters to prison. An 18-year-old English soldier, John Mac-Nabb, thought his Colonel's behaviour foolish and wrote to his mother immediately after the incident.

> There was no necessity to have a parade at all or to make any fuss of the sort just now. No other Colonel thought of doing such a thing, as they knew at this unsettled time their men would refuse to be the first to fire these cartridges . . . The men themselves humbly petitioned the Colonel to put the parade off till this disturbance in India had gone over, in fact pointing out to him what he ought to have seen himself. He . . . sent for the [acting] Adjutant and asked him what he advised. Fancy a Colonel asking his Adjutant. He ought to be able to make his own mind up . . . if he is fit to command a regiment.[3]

The next day several Indian regiments attempted to massacre their English officers while they were attending church in Meerut. Indian sepoys had cut the main telegraph lines to Delhi, although the postmaster's sister did have time to dispatch a cable to her aunt in Agra advising her not to pay a visit to Meerut as the sepoys had just risen in revolt. Several English soldiers and residents, including Cornet MacNabb but not Carmichael-Smyth, were murdered. Without any further ado, a number

of the Indian regiments headed for Delhi. No attempt was
made by Major-General 'Bloody Bill' Hewitt, the Meerut
commander-in-chief, to pursue them.

Communications were understandably not as rapid then as
they are now, but word still spread quickly throughout Northern India. Field Marshal Lord Roberts, who later became
commander-in-chief of the Indian and ultimately the British
army, was then serving as a young officer in Peshawar. Spies
had warned the officers there that the 35th Native Infantry
intended to revolt. Shortly afterwards, the men were ordered
to fall in and two of them were discovered to have loaded
weapons – a sure sign that they intended to create trouble. A
drum-head court martial was called.

> The brigadier thought it desirable that the Court-Martial
> should be composed of Native, rather than British,
> officers, as being likely to be looked upon by the prisoners
> as a more impartial tribunal, under the peculiar cir-
> cumstances in which we were placed. . . . The prisoners
> were found guilty of mutiny, and sentenced to death.
> Chamberlain decided that they should be blown away
> from guns, in the presence of their own comrades, [this]
> being the most awe-inspiring means of carrying the
> sentence into effect. A parade was at once ordered. The
> troops were drawn up so as to form three sides of a square;
> on the fourth side were two guns. As the prisoners were
> being brought to the parade, one of them asked me if they
> were going to be blown from guns. I said, 'Yes'. He made
> no further remark, and they both walked steadily on until
> they reached the guns, to which they were bound, when
> one of them requested that some rupees he had on his per-
> son might be saved for his relations. The Brigadier
> answered: 'It is too late!' The word of command was
> given; the guns went off simultaneously, and the two
> mutineers were launched into eternity.
>
> It was a terrible sight, and one likely to haunt the
> beholder for many a long day; but that was what was
> intended. I carefully watched the sepoys' faces to see how
> it affected them. They were evidently startled at the swift
> retribution which had overtaken their guilty comrades,

but looked more crest-fallen than shocked or horrified, and we soon learnt that their determination to mutiny, and make the best of their way to Delhi, was in no wise changed by the scene they had witnessed.[4]

There were only 14,000 British troops in the Subcontinent at the time of the Mutiny and perhaps 300,000 Indian troops. However, there were large areas where the troops remained loyal to the Crown and ultimately these together with fresh troops from Britain were used to rout the revolt.

The first significant victory over the rebels occurred in Delhi, where the old city was finally taken by British, Sikh and Gurkha troops in September 1857, at a cost of more than 2,000 troops killed, wounded or missing. But the most heroic and protracted fighting took place at Lucknow, where the Residency was being besieged by the Nawab of Oudh's forces.

The author J.G. Farrell portrayed the events at Lucknow in his novel *The Siege of Krishnapur*, leavening the full horrors of the siege with farcical dark humour. The Collector attempts to make a tactical withdrawal from certain rooms in the fictional Residency:

A barricade of flagstones prised up from the floor had been erected for a final stand and the Collector, snatching a moment to look back towards it, was dismayed to see that the other party was already behind it, thus leaving himself and his men exposed on the flank. He bellowed at the Sikhs to retreat and as they stumbled back under a cross-fire from the other side of the hall, two of them fell dead and another mortally wounded. Once again there was a flurry of bodies from the doorway they had been defending and another charge. It was now time for the Collector to play his last card.

All this time he had been keeping a reserve force waiting in the library. This 'veteran assault force' (as he called it) was composed of the only men left from the cantonment community whom he had not yet made use of, the few elderly gentlemen who had managed to survive the rigours of the siege. Their joints were swollen with rheumatism, their eyes were dimmed with years, to a man they were short of breath and their hands trembled; one old gentleman believed himself to be again taking part in the French wars, another that he was encamped before Sebastapol. But never mind, though their blue-veined old hands might be trembling their fingers could still pull a trigger. It was this force which the Collector now threw into the engagement, though he had to shout the order more than once as their leader, Judge Adams, was rather deaf. From the library they staggered forth with a querulous shout of 'Yah, Boney!' Shotguns and sporting rifles went off in their hands. The hall chandelier crashed to the ground and shot sprayed in every direction. For a moment, until the old men had been dragged back to the barricade, all was chaos. The veteran assault had not been a success.[5]

In reality, there was little humour and even less mercy shown to the mutineers after the siege was lifted. William Howard Russell, the special correspondent of *The Times*, recounted that one mutineer was burned on a fire while some Englishmen looked on, saying they dared not interfere because their Sikh soldiers were so incensed at the loss of some of their men in an earlier encounter. Russell's description of the storming of the Nawab's palace, or Kaiserbagh, in Lucknow, is one of the best descriptive pieces from the Mutiny.

It was one of the strangest and most distressing sights that could be seen; but it was also most exciting. Discipline may hold soldiers together till the fight is won; but it assuredly does not exist for a moment after an assault has been delivered, or a storm has taken place . . . The buildings which surround the courts are irregular in form, for here and there the lines of the quadrangle are broken by columned fronts and lofty porticos before the mansions of the ministry, or of the great offices of the royal household, which are resplendent with richly gilt-roofs and domes. Here and there the invaders have forced their way into the long corridors, and you hear the musketry rattling inside; the crash of glass, the shouts and yells of the combatants, and little jets of smoke curl out of the closed lattices. Lying amid the orange-groves are dead and dying sepoys; and the white statues are reddened with

blood. Leaning against a smiling Venus is a British soldier
shot through the neck, gasping, and at every gasp bleeding
to death! Here and there officers are running to and fro
after their men, persuading them or threatening in vain.
From the broken portals issue soldiers laden with loot or
plunder. Shawls, rich tapestry, gold and silver brocade,
caskets of jewels, arms, splendid dresses. The men are wild
with fury and lust of gold – literally drunk with plunder.
Others are busy gouging out the precious stones from the
stems of pipes, from saddle-cloths, or the hilts of swords,
or butts of pistols and firearms. Some swathe their bodies
in stuffs crusted with precious metals and gems; others
carry off useless lumber; brass pots, pictures, or vases of
jade and china.[6]

Queen Victoria maintained an especially keen interest in the
fate of India, saying to Lord Canning just before he left to
become Viceroy in 1856, 'Look after my poor Indians.' Lady
Canning remained a confidante of the Queen and received long
letters from her during the Mutiny, in which the Queen bent
over backwards not to believe any of the more outrageous
stories of the perfidy of her once loyal forces.

Dear Lady Canning,
I cannot tell you *how* thankful I am for your writing to
me so regularly by every mail or what a pleasure & satisfaction it is to me to receive your letters which (without flat-
tery) are universally considered as the *best* which are
received from India, & I hope you will continue writing
to me by every mail as long as Affairs are not restored to
what they were, before this dreadful mutiny . . .
    Thank God – the accounts are much more cheering &
those of Lucknow are a *very great* relief. The continued
arrival of Troops will I trust be of great use, & that no
further mutinies & atrocities will take place. As regards
the latter I should be very thankful if you & Lord Canning
could ascertain *how* far these are true. Of course the *mere*
murdering – (I mean shooting or stabbing) innocent
women & children is very shocking in itself – but in *civil*
War this will happen, indeed I fear that many of the awful
insults &. to poor children & women are the inevitable

accompaniments of such a state of things – & that the ordinary sacking of Towns by Christian soldiers presents spectacles & stories which if published in Newspapers would raise outbursts of horror & indignation: Badajoz & St Sebastian I fear were two examples which would equal much that has occurred in India and these the Duke of Wellington could not prevent – & they were the acts of British Soldiers, not of *black* blood, I mention this not as an *excuse* but as an explanation of what seems so dreadful to our feelings. Some of these stories are certainly untrue – as for instance that of Colonel & Mrs Farquarson who were said to be sawn asunder and has turned out to be a sheer invention, no such people existing in India! What I wish to know is whether there is any *reliable evidence* of eye witnesses – of horrors, like people having to eat their children's flesh – & other unspeakable & dreadful atrocities which I could not write? Or do these not rest on *Native* intelligence & witnesses whom one cannot believe implicitly? So many fugitives have arrived at Calcutta that I'm sure you could find out to a great extent how this *really* is.

I am delighted to hear that that most loyal excellent veteran hero Sir Colin Campbell is well & that you like him; I was sure you would, for it is impossible not to do so – & we never for a moment credited the shameful lies of disagreement between him & Lord Canning. If he is still with you say everything most kind to him. I am glad to hear that he does not share that indiscriminate dislike of all brown skins which is very unjust – for the inhabitants have, it appears, taken no part in this purely Military Revolution – & while summary punishment must alas! be dealt out to the mutinous sepoys – I trust he will see that great forebearance is shown towards the innocent & that women & children will not be touched by *Christian* soldiers. . . .

Recruiting is going on quite wonderfully lately; last week *2165* men were obtained! The Militia have come out very readily & the Country has again shown the very best spirit. Generally it is not at all animated by a spirit of revenge or violence against the people of India with the

exception of a few newspapers who hold very unchristian
language.

Yours Affectionately VR[7]

Not surprisingly, the Mutiny left deep scars. Subedar Sita
Ram, a Brahmin soldier who was supposed to have spent most
of his life in the Bengal Army, recounted that things were never
again the same for the Indian soldiers. This he blamed partly
on the 'Padre Sahibs' who discouraged the new officers from
fraternizing with their men at nautches, evenings of singing and
dancing. Young officers also confided to Sita Ram that they did
not know what to say to their men, something that had never
been the case in the early days.

The officers of the Royal Army since the Mutiny do not
treat us in the same fashion as they used to do. I am fully
aware of the execration my unworthy brethren deserve for
their brutal conduct during the Mutiny, but surely this
should come from their own officers, and not from officers
of the Royal Army. Even when it was known that I had
served with the force which relieved Lucknow, I can
nevertheless remember being called a 'damned black pig'
by more than one officer of the Royal Army. And yet I
can recall that officers of the 13th and 41st Foot, when I
made chappatis for them in Kabul, told me 'Jack Sepoy is
a damned good fellow!' I have not served 48 years with
English officers without knowing the meaning of all this.
It can largely be attributed to hastiness of temper, and who
can struggle against fate? I was always good friends with
the English soldiers, and they used to treat the sepoy with
great kindness. And why not – did we not do all their
work? We performed all their guard duties in the heat.
We stood sentry over their rum-casks. We gave them our
own food. Well, English soldiers are a different breed
nowadays. They are neither as fine nor as tall as they used
to be. They can seldom speak one word of our language
except to abuse us, and if they could learn polite expressions as quickly as they can learn abusive ones, they would
indeed be apt scholars.[8]

Exactly a century earlier, in 1757, an equally decisive campaign had been fought on Indian soil by British troops which culminated in the Battle of Plassey. The number of troops involved at Plassey, in west Bengal, was somewhat smaller – Robert Clive only commanded 3,000 men against the Nawab of Bengal's force of around 50,000, including his French allies.

A midday monsoonal downpour drenched the powder of the Nawab's cannons, but had little effect on Clive's as he covered his ammunition and guns with tarpaulins. While he changed his drenched clothes in the grove where his men were sheltering, another officer decided to move ahead, still unaware of the other army's problem with their artillery. When Clive eventually caught up with him, he realized that there was indeed little resistance and so took advantage of the situation to press his advantage home.

That night, after the main force of the Nawab had withdrawn from the battlefield, Clive dispatched the following message to Calcutta.

> Gentleman – This morning at one o'clock we arrived at Placis [Plassey] Grove and early in the morning the Nabob's whole army appeared in sight and cannonaded us for several hours, and about noon returned to a very strong camp in sight, lately Roydoolub's, upon which we advanced and stormed the Nabob's camp, which we have taken with all his cannon and pursued him six miles, being now at Doudpoor and shall proceed for Muxadavad tomorrow. Meer Jaffeir, Roydoolub, and Luttee Cawn gave us no other assistance than standing neutral. They are with me with a large force. Meer Muddun and five hundred horse are killed and three elephants. Our loss is trifling, not above twenty Europeans killed and wounded.[9]

The importance of Plassey has been played down by modern historians but the fact remains that it was the decisive battle which led to the ultimate conquest of the Subcontinent by Britain, at the expense of not only the considerable array of Indian rulers, but also the rival European colonial powers.

A few years before the Battle of Plassey, Clive had carried off a masterly victory at Arcot in southern India against Chanda Sahib, the Nawab of the Carnatic. However, it was not until early in the nineteenth century that the south was cleared by the British of all major military opposition.

The most colourful of the Indian opponents to British rule during this period was Tippoo Sultan, the Nawab of Mysore. At the height of his power, Tippoo had an army of 100,000 men, the most formidable in India, thanks to their expert training by the French in conventional military manoeuvres. Tippoo was perhaps the most charismatic of all Indian rulers, and was especially revered for never making any alliance with the British against other Indian rulers. However, he was a Muslim bigot who in his youth gained pleasure by wounding and killing sacred bulls in Hindu temples. He did not endear himself to Christians either by personally circumcizing an English soldier. Arthur Wellesley, the future Duke of Wellington and younger brother of Richard, the Governor-General, finally defeated Tippoo in 1799 at the Battle of Seringapatam, an island just north of Mysore. During the battle, Tippoo Sultan fell from the ramparts and was killed in combat – the exact spot is now marked by a small cairn. An English traveller, Francis Buchanan, journeyed through the area a few years later.

> No individual claimed the honour of having slain the Sultan, nor did any of either party know that he had fallen in the gateway. The assailants were, indeed, at that time too much enraged to think of any thing but the destruction of their enemy . . . Meer Saduc, the favourite of the Sultan, fell in attempting to get through the gates. He is supposed to have been killed by the hands of Tippoo's soldiery, and his corpse lay for some time exposed to the insults of the populace, none of whom passed without spitting on it, or loading it with a slipper; for to him they attributed most of their sufferings in the tyrannical reign of the Sultan . . .[10]

The East India Company felt a degree of remorse at the brave stand of Tippoo Sultan and his slaying. Richard Wellesley wrote that 'The dreadful fate of Tippoo Sultan cannot be contemplated without emotions of pain and regret.' Near the site of his death, Tippoo's glorious teakwood summer-house remains intact. His family mausoleum, which was partly paid for by East India Company funds, is one of the most haunting in the entire Subcontinent, fresh flowers and a tiger-striped dhurrie still covering it.

The British method of ruling the Subcontinent differed little from that employed by Alexander the Great in central Asia – a skilful combination of direct rule and satrapies. Pliant nawabs and maharajas were installed and provided with English Residents who ensured that their interests never strayed far from those of the Raj. A number of remarkable individuals and adventurers also fostered British encroachment and conquest. Some of these soldiers of fortune, such as Colonel William Gardner, fought for various maharajas against their native rivals before forming irregular regiments which came under the control of the East India Company. There were others who were part and parcel of the British military establishment who still lived in the style of oriental potentates. Sir David Ochterloney, or 'Looney-Akhtar' as he was known, was the most splendid of them all, formerly Delhi Resident and victor of the 1815 Nepalese Wars. Sir David was granted a baronetcy and was allegedly considered for a peerage but was ruled out because of his flamboyant personal life. He kept a harem of upwards of a dozen Indian wives, whom he would parade at sunset in Delhi single-file on elephant-back. The equally remarkable Bishop Heber, the Anglican Bishop of Calcutta, encountered Sir David near the end of his days in Rajasthan.

Jan 27. 1825. We passed Sir David Ochterlony and his suite on his road to Bhurtpoor. There certainly was a very considerable number of led horses, elephants, palanqueens, and covered carriages, belonging chiefly, I apprehend, (besides his own family) to the families of his native servants. There was an escort of two companies of infantry, a troop of regular cavalry, and I should guess forty or fifty irregulars, on horse and foot, armed with spears and matchlocks of all possible forms; the string of camels was a very long one, and the whole procession was what might pass in Europe for that of an eastern prince travelling. Still, neither in numbers nor splendour did it at all equal my expectation. Sir David himself was in a carriage and four, and civilly got out to speak to me. He is a tall and pleasing-looking old man, but was so wrapped up in shawls, kincob, fur and a Mogul fur cap, that his face was all that was visible. I was not sorry to have even this glimpse of an old officer whose exploits in India have been so distinguished . . . He is now considerably above seventy, infirm, and has been often advised to return to England. But he has been absent from thence fifty-four years; he has there neither friend nor relation, – he has been for many years habituated to eastern habits and parade, and who can wonder that he clings to the only country in the world where he can feel at home? Within these few days I had been reading Coxe's Life of Marlborough, and at this moment it struck me forcibly how little it would have seemed in the compass of possibility to any of the warriors, statesmen, or divines of Queen Anne's time, that an English General and an English Bishop would ever shake hands on a desert plain in the heart of Rajpootana!'[11]

Ochterloney died five months later and is buried in Meerut. His house still stands in Old Delhi, but is now part of the Delhi Institute of Technology, while in Calcutta he is best remembered by the imposing Ochterloney Monument on the Maidan.

During the time of the Raj, there were never more than 100,000 or so British troops in the entire Subcontinent, but their impact went far beyond that of mere numbers. Entire families served in India for generations and built up vast connections and knowledge. Edward Thompson, a missionary and poet with considerable experience of India, wrote about such characters in *An Indian Day*, pubished in 1927. 'Vishnugram' is a remote district in Bengal, where Vincent Hamar is being sent as a judge after being considered too sympathetic to the Indian nationalist cause. *En route*, he shares his rail carriage with two archetypal English officers.

> 'Akbar! I've seen his Taj at Delhi. Why didn't he do another one here? I say, sir, that *is* a top-hole bit of work, isn't it?'
>
> 'Shut up, Tommy. You let the Raj down, every time you speak. A happy barbarian' – the Major smiled at Hamar – 'he's not deep in anything but polo and shooting.'
>
> 'Oh, I say sir!'

Hamar joined in the general laugh; in that moment, all three men liked each other. Major Henderson, taking the *Gazetteer* leant across – the train was jolting, and it was hard to hear – and introduced himself. His pose dropped from him, and his manner was pleasant and cordial.

He was about a couple of years older than Hamar, who was thirty-four or so. His face, furrowed with quizzical lines, was attractively discontented. Keen on a score of things, and finding life full of interest everywhere, Major Henderson amused everyone he met by keeping up a slightly pained, querulous tone about everything. He spoke of Indians, and of everything Indian, as if their presence on the planet distressed him physically. Yet he bought every book about India, he read largely about Indian history, customs, religion even literature, he patiently went on pilgrimage to even the lesser sites, and he returned after every furlough, in spite of offers of excellent billets at home.

'No one has a steadier grouse at life than Henderson,' said the Colonel. 'But I never met a chap who enjoyed it more. He's like our quarter-master sergeant, who curses the canteen beer, but sups all he can lay his hands on.'

Hamar looked at him, and then at the athletic philistine opposite. He knew both types; the former naturally generous and sympathetic, but warped by long listening to mess politics and mess philosophy – the latter stupid, self-satisfied, energetic and kind. Both of them impossible people, of course, whatever the Major had once had it in him to become – impossible in their talk, incredibly circumscribed in attitude and opinions, ill-informed and bigoted in training and ideas. But in practice often queerly tolerant, and breaking out in unexpected ways. You never knew where they might not shame you by some instinctive decency, when your careful thinker and scrupulous official would be ineffably mean, in his just, righteous fashion.[12]

George Orwell depicted a rather less sympathetic type of English officer in *Burmese Days*, portraying the classic type of soldier who couldn't see the point of India except that it was a vast park for his enjoyment of various sports, preferably those that involved horse-riding or killing game of some description.

Verall had come out to India in a British cavalry regiment, and exchanged into the Indian Army because it was cheaper and left him greater freedom for polo. After two years his debts were so enormous that he entered the Burma Military Police, in which it was notoriously possible to save money; however, he detested Burma – it is no country for a horseman – and he had already applied to go back to his regiment . . . He knew the society of those small Burma stations – a nasty, poodle-faking, horseless riffraff. He despised them.

They were not the only people whom Verral despised, however. His various contempts would take a long time to catalogue in detail. He despised the entire non-military population of India, a few famous polo players excepted. He despised the entire Army as well, except the cavalry. He despised all Indian regiments, infantry and cavalry alike. It was true that he himself belonged to a native regiment, but that was only for his convenience. He took no interest in Indians, and his Urdu consisted mainly of swear-words, with all the verbs in the third person singular.[13]

In the course of the book, one Englishman complains when a riot is put down without violence. 'But why don't they use their rifles, the miserable sons of bitches? They could slaughter in bloody heaps if they'd only open fire. Oh, God, to think of missing a chance like this!'[14]

Such a chance was to occur just after the First World War, when the old Imperial order was ended by the brutal act of an English officer who ordered his troops to fire without warning on a prohibited meeting in the Punjab. The event is now known as the Amritsar Massacre. In his official report attempting to justify the killing of 379 people and wounding of more than 1,200 others, Brigadier Dyer wrote

I entered the Jallianwala Bagh by a very narrow lane which necessitated leaving my armoured cars behind. On entering I saw a dense crowd, estimated at about 5,000 (those present put it at 15,000 to 20,000); a man on a raised

platform [was] addressing the audience and making gesti-
culations with his hands.

I realized that my force was small and to hesitate might
induce attack. I immediately opened fire and dispersed the
mob. I estimated that between 200 and 300 of the crowd
were killed. My party fired 1650 rounds.

I returned to my headquarters about 1800 hours. At
2200 hours, accompanied by a force, I visited all my
pickets and marched through the city in order to make sure
that my order as to inhabitants not being out of their
homes after 2000 hours had been obeyed. The city was
absolutely quiet and not a soul was to be seen. I returned
to headquarters at midnight. The inhabitants have asked
permission to bury the dead in accordance with my orders.
This I am allowing.

(Signed) R. E. H. Dyer, Brigadier-General. Commanding
45th Brigade.[15]

The Lieutenant-Governor of the Punjab, Sir Michael
O'Dwyer, promptly returned the simple terse message: 'Your
action correct and Lieutenant-Governor approves.' There was
no concern about the wounded or the consequences elsewhere,
although a complete news blackout was imposed on the
massacre. (Ironically, more than two decades later, Sir Michael
was shot dead in London by a Sikh nationalist.) The Indian
Government set up an inquiry into the massacre which divided
on racial grounds, although it did ultimately censure Brigadier
Dyer. The House of Lords, however, voted in his favour and
a large subscription was raised. More important, the massacre
led Mohandas Karamchand Gandhi, a lawyer who advocated
passive resistance to British rule, to declare that 'co-operation
in any shape or form with this satanic government is sinful'.
Several months later, an interesting encounter took place in a
railway carriage.

Towards the end of that year [1919] I travelled from
Amritsar to Delhi by the night train. The compartment
I entered was almost full and all the berths, except one
upper one, were occupied by sleeping passengers. I took
the vacant upper berth. In the morning I discovered that

all my fellow-passengers were military officers. They conversed with each other in loud voices which I could not help overhearing. One of them was holding forth in an aggressive and triumphant tone and soon I discovered that he was Dyer, the hero of Jallianwala Bagh, and he was describing his Amritsar experiences. He pointed out how he had the whole town at his mercy and he had felt like reducing the rebellious city to a heap of ashes, but he took pity on it and refrained. He was evidently coming back from Lahore after giving his evidence before the Hunter Committee of Inquiry. I was greatly shocked to hear his conversation and to observe his callous manner. He descended at Delhi station in pyjamas with bright pink stripes, and a dressing gown.[16]

The writer was Jawaharlal Nehru, one of the key members of the Congress Party which was seeking self-rule for the Indian population.

After this initial catalytic role, the British army in India did not play an important part in the Independence movement. Its next major task was to depart after Partition with the minimum of fuss. The trauma of the forcible carving up of India into a secular state and a religious breakaway (Pakistan) resulted in the killing of hundreds of thousands of innocent civilians, both Muslim and Hindu.

One senior British civil servant who has written at length about Partition is Sir Penderel Moon, an Indian Civil Service officer who spent much time in the Punjab and continued as a senior civil servant in Independent India.

Most civilized societies have been liable to occasional pogroms. What occurred in the Punjab in 1947 was qualitively a not uncommon phenomenon; but it was unusual in so far as it affected so many people simultaneously over such a wide area and resulted in such a very heavy death toll. In India the nearest well-authenticated precedent to frenzy on such a scale is afforded by the Mutiny. The parties to the conflict at that time were different, Hindus and Muslims being ranged on one side and Christians of all kinds – European, Eurasian and Indian – on the other; but the passions aroused were much the same and caused the adherents of all three religions alike to sink to the crudest savagery. The mutineers set the standard by shooting their British officers and then murdering their wives and children. This roused in the British such a burning spirit of revenge that British troops, when they got the opportunity, slaughtered 'niggers' indiscriminately without regard to guilt or innocence, age or sex. These ferocious reprisals provoked further outrages by the sepoys, including the hideous massacre of women and children at Cawnpore, and this in turn stimulated the British to more fearful acts of vengeance. Thus one atrocity or the report of it led to another and prompted the irrational massacre of quite innocent persons. A young English Assistant Commissioner, whose sister had undoubtedly been murdered in Delhi by the mutineers, believed that she had first been stripped naked and outraged. The thought of this so worked upon his feelings that on the recovery of Delhi by the British, 'he had put to death', according to his own admission, 'all he had come across, not excepting women and children'. The less sophisticated Punjabi, inflamed by similar provocations, real or rumoured, perpetrated in 1947 many like insensate deeds of violence, though he has probably left no such clear written record of his vengeful exploits.[17]

Even today, many Indians still feel bitter about the haste with which the British departed from the Subcontinent after the Second World War. Most people now forget the lasting impact that Partition had on an entire generation. Dhiren Bhagat, a talented young writer who was tragically killed in a road accident in 1988, touched on this in an article he wrote for *The Spectator* the previous year.

I am a child of partition. My parents were two of the approximately 10 million refugees partition created and like most of the 10 million they lost almost everything they had. Most important, they lost Lahore and with Lahore, they lost the Punjab. (Used to the broad spaces of Lahore they could not settle in the claustrophobic, largely rural society of East Punjab.) They went to Bombay where they met, they became part of the Punjab

Diaspora of 1947 that has gone almost entirely unremarked among the movements of our time.[18]

His mother, who still lives in Bombay, recounted her terror at the time of Partition in the same article.

The emotions of the period, the tremendous bewilderment is hard for me to describe in words . . . That summer I was to appear for my final BA examination. There were riots all over Lahore, in fact there was so much arson and looting that one did not know if one would be able to sit for exams or not. We had to read at night by a kerosene light. Even to go and sit the exam was such a frightening experience because you never knew what would happen to you on the way. We were living in constant fright of the 'enemy' as it was called coming and attacking our homes. At night I remember somebody or other sitting in a quiet corner on top of the house and keeping vigil to see if there were mobs coming in our direction.

I remember distinctly a couple of nights when we heard mobs running across the fields with slogans like *Allah ho Akbar* and I remember how frightened we used to be. My little sister Giota was once hidden by Daddy in a tandoor [clay oven] outside the house and told not to make the slightest noise.

The older girls, Minnie and myself, were considered more responsible. We were given Molotov cocktails and told to stand on the balconies and to throw these on the Muslims from above if they tried to come in. At one point Minnie and I were given a small bottle of poison by Daddy with strict instructions that this was to be used by us as an *absolute last resort*.[19]

The horrors that took place in the frenzied period between the announcement of Partition and the ultimate transfer of the populations led to some of the worst massacres of civilians in the twentieth century. *The Times* Special Correspondent wrote at length about the role of the Sikhs in the violence even after the Independence celebrations.

MUSLIMS BUTCHERED BY ARMED MOBS OF SIKHS
BREAKDOWN OF CIVIL ADMINISTRATION

Punjab 25 August, 1947

As a reminder that this communal war is not one-sided, a train loaded with Sikh refugees from West Punjab was attacked by a Muslim mob west of Ferozepur yesterday and arrived with 25 dead bodies on board and more than 100 passengers with stabbing wounds of varying degrees of seriousness. Three small girls in one compartment had been hacked to death . . .

'A thousand times more horrible than anything we saw during the war,' is the universal comment of experienced officers, British and Indian, on the present slaughter in east Punjab. The Sikhs are on the warpath. They are clearing eastern Punjab of Muslims, butchering hundreds daily, forcing thousands to flee westwards, burning Muslim villages and homesteads, even, in their frenzy, burning their own too. This violence has been organized from the highest levels of Sikh leadership, and it is being done systematically, sector by sector. Some large towns, like Amritsar and Jullundur, are now quieter, because there are no Muslims left. In a two hours' air reconnaissance of the Jullundur district at the week-end I must have seen 50 villages aflame . . . The Sikhs will tell you that this is retaliation for what the Muslims did to the Sikhs in Rawalpindi in March – which was retaliation for Hindu massacres of Muslims in Bihar, which was retaliation for Noakhali, which was retaliation for Calcutta. So it goes back, violence begetting violence. But even India has never seen anything worse than this present orgy, which has already sullied the name of the Sikh, synonymous in two world wars with martial valour. Only most determined efforts on the part of the leaders can end this madness.

There are very few fictional accounts of Partition that are still available. One of the best-known novels is by Khushwant Singh, a Sikh and a veteran writer and columnist who now lives in Delhi.

The summer before, communal riots, precipitated by reports of the proposed division of the country into a

Hindu India and a Muslim Pakistan, had broken out in
Calcutta, and within a few months the death roll had
mounted to several thousand. Muslims said the Hindus
had planned and started the killing. According to the
Hindus, the Muslims were to blame. The fact is, both
sides killed. Both shot and stabbed and speared and
clubbed. Both tortured. Both raped. From Calcutta, the
riots spread north and east and west: to Noakhali in East
Bengal, where Muslims massacred Hindus; to Bihar,
where Hindus massacred Muslims. Mullahs roamed the
Punjab and the Frontier Province with boxes of human
skulls said to be those of Muslims killed in Bihar. Hundreds of thousands of Hindus and Sikhs who had lived for
centuries on the Northwest Frontier abandoned their
homes and fled towards the protection of the predominantly Sikh and Hindu communities in the east. They
travelled on foot, in bullock carts, crammed into lorries,
clinging to the sides and roofs of trains. Along the way –
at fords, at crossroads, at railroad stations – they collided
with swarms of Muslims fleeing to safety in the west. The
riots had become a rout. By the summer of 1947, when
the creation of the new state of Pakistan was formally
announced, ten million people – Muslims and Hindus and
Sikhs – were in flight. By the time the monsoon broke,
almost a million of them were dead, and all of northern
India was in arms, in terror, or in hiding.[20]

There are still no hard facts about how many died during Partition. Even Sir Penderel Moon could not rely on anything but
intelligent guesswork to estimate the full extent of the killings
during Partition.

During and immediately after the disturbances it was
freely stated that millions had lost their lives. Even a later
and more sober estimate made by an Indian High Court
Judge puts the figure at about half a million. An English
journalist, Andrew Mellor, thinks that the number killed
is unlikely to have been less than two hundred thousand
and may well have been far more. The other extreme
is represented by an estimate, attributed to Nehru, that
twenty to thirty thousand people had been killed in the

Punjab. My own guess, based on some rough calculations originally made in December 1947, is not widely different from that of Andrew Mellor. Slightly varying his conclusion I would say that the number killed is unlikely to have been more than two hundred thousand and may well have been appreciably less. This, though lower than most estimates, is an enormous total for civilian casualties in time of peace.[21]

4

THE RULERS

Where the land is kingless the cloud, lightning-wreathed and loud-voiced, gives no rain to the earth.

Where the land is kingless the son does not honour his father, nor the wife her husband.

Where the land is kingless men do not meet in assemblies, nor make lovely gardens and temples.

Where the land is kingless the rich are unprotected, and shepherds and peasants sleep with bolted doors.

A river without water, a forest without grass, a herd of cattle without a herdsman, is the land without a king.

Ramayana[1]

Chandragupta Maurya can lay claim to the title of the first Indian emperor, having expelled the remnants of Alexander the Great's army from northern India in 326 BC. He also achieved the goal that eluded the British 2,000 years later, that of controlling all territory as far north as Herat and Kabul. This required the creation of an enormous army of between 400,000 and 600,000 men plus tens of thousands of horses, camels and elephants. The splendour and sophistication of Chandragupta's empire is revealed in the detailed accounts of court life by Megasthenes, the Greek ambassador to Chandragupta's court at Pataliputra on the site of modern Patna in Bihar. Megasthenes' records are probably the most accurate before those of the Chinese Buddhist pilgrims who visited India six centuries later.

The care of the king's person is entrusted to women, who also are bought from their parents. The guards and the rest of the soldiery attend outside the gates. A woman who kills the king when drunk becomes the wife of his successor. The sons succeed the father. The king may not sleep during the daytime, and by night he is obliged to change his couch from time to time, with a view to defeating plots against his life.

The king leaves his palace not only in time of war, but also for the purpose of judging causes. He then remains in court for the whole day, without allowing the business to be interrupted, even though the hour arrives when he must needs attend to his person – that is, when he is to be rubbed with cylinders of wood. He continues hearing cases while the friction, which is performed by four attendants, is still proceeding. Another purpose for which he leaves his palace is to offer sacrifice; a third is to go to the chase, for which he departs in Bacchanalian fashion. Crowds of women surround him, and outside of this circle spearmen are ranged. The road is marked off with ropes, and it is death, for man and woman alike, to pass within the ropes. Men with drums and gongs lead the procession. The king hunts in the enclosures and shoots arrows from a platform. At his side stand two or three armed women. If he hunts in the open grounds he shoots from the back of an elephant.[2]

In 1837, James Prinsep, a young British scholar, deciphered the rock inscriptions of Ashoka, Chandragupta's grandson, thus solving the centuries-old mystery of what the various edicts scattered throughout India actually meant. Until then, knowledge of Ashoka had been sketchy, and it was not until 1915, with the deciphering of another inscription, that he was finally identified.

There is no known likeness of Ashoka, but he clearly took his duties as king very seriously indeed as the following rock edict shows.

I am never complacent in regard to my exertions or the dispatch of people's business by me. I consider it my only duty to promote the welfare of all men. But exertion and prompt dispatch of business lie at the root of that. There is verily no duty which is more important to me than promoting the welfare of all men. And whatever effort I make is made in order that I may discharge the debt which I owe to all living beings, that I may make them happy in this world, and that they may attain heaven in the next world.[3]

After the death of Ashoka, the Mauryan kingdom fragmented and came under further pressure in the north-west from fresh waves of invaders from central Asia. Southern India absorbed some influences from the Indo-Aryans, but was still ruled by three indigenous kingdoms who frequently fought each other. Although central and northern India were now ruled by several different kingdoms, society did not collapse. The process of urbanization continued and scholarship flourished.

The laws of Manu, composed some time in the first two centuries AD, stressed the divine nature of the king and the unbearable chaos that awaited any civilization that was kingless.

> When the world was without a king
> and dispersed in fear in all directions,
> the Lord created a king
> for the protection of all.
>
> He made him of eternal particles
> Of Indra and the Wind,
> Yama, the Sun and Fire,
> Varuna, the Moon, and the Lord of Wealth.
>
> And, because he has been formed
> of fragments of all those gods,
> the king surpasses
> all other beings in splendour.
>
> Even an infant king must not be despised,
> as though a mere mortal,
> for he is a great god
> in human form.[4]

In the latter half of the fifth century, there occurred a new phase of invasions from central Asia, starting with the Huns. It was during this time that several separate kingdoms emerged, some of which were to remain intact for hundreds of years. In

AD 712, Arab rulers reached as far as Sind and in the eleventh century Turkish invasions of India led by Mahmud of Ghazni became almost annual affairs, aimed at plundering the fertile plains of the Punjab and the proverbial riches of India's temples.

By the end of the twelfth century, Islam had triumphed in northern India. Turkish Muslim invaders based in Afghanistan eventually formed the Sultanate of Delhi which controlled a vast area of the Gangetic plain. These invaders showed very little interest in the local inhabitants except as a source of profit. As one later historian put it, 'the blood-stained annals of the Sultanate of Delhi are not pleasant reading'. Ibn Battuta, a Muslim theologian from Tunis, who stayed in India from 1333 to 1347, has left a vivid record of the rulers of the period. He commented with particular interest on the extent to which order was rapidly imposed by the Muslim invaders.

When the new arrival reaches the town of Multan, which is the capital of Sind, he stays there until an order is received from the sultan regarding his entry and the degree of hospitality to be extended to him. A man is honoured in that country according to what may be seen of his actions, conduct, and zeal, since no one knows anything of his family or lineage. The king of India, Sultan Muhammad Shah, makes a practice of honouring strangers and distinguishing them by governorships or high dignities of State. The majority of his courtiers, palace officials, ministers of state, judges, and relatives by marriage are foreigners, and he has issued a decree that foreigners are to be given in his country the title of '*Aziz* [Honourable]', so that this has become a proper name for them.

Every person proceeding to the court of this king must have a gift ready to present to him, in order to gain his favour. The sultan requites him for it by a gift many times its value. When his subjects grew accustomed to this practice, the merchants in Sind and India began to furnish each newcomer with thousands of dinars as a loan, and to supply him with whatever he might desire to offer as a gift or to use on his own behalf, such as riding animals, camels, and goods. They place both their money and their persons at his service, and stand before him like attendants. When he reaches the sultan, he receives a magnificent gift from him and pays off his debt to them. This trade of theirs is a flourishing one and brings in vast profits. On reaching Sind I followed this practice and bought horses, camels, and white slaves and other goods from the merchants. I had already bought from an Iraqi merchant in Ghazna about thirty horses and a camel with a load of arrows, for this is one of the things presented to the sultan.[5]

The relative order of the Sultanate of Delhi was abruptly shattered in 1398 when Tamerlane (Timur) invaded northern India and sacked Delhi. His name may sound romantic in comparison with that of Genghis Khan but there was little to choose between them when it came to brutality. Tamerlane, who was to control an empire just as vast as his notorious predecessor, left a remarkably frank account of his bloody conquest. Before entering Delhi itself, he held a meeting with his senior princes.

At this court Amir Jahan Shah and Amir Sulaiman Shah, and other amirs of experience, brought to my notice that, from the time of entering Hindustan up to the present time, we had taken more than 100,000 infidels and Hindu prisoners, and that they were all in my camp. On the previous day, when the enemy's forces made the attack upon us, the prisoners made signs of rejoicing, uttered imprecations against us, and were ready, as soon as they heard of the enemy's success, to form themselves into a body, break their bonds, plunder our tents, and then to go and join the enemy, and so increase his numbers and strength. I asked their advice about the prisoners, and they said that on the great day of battle these 100,000 prisoners could not be left with the baggage, and that it would be entirely opposed to the rules of war to set these idolaters and foes of Islam at liberty. In fact, no other course remained but that of making them food for the sword. When I heard these words I found them in accordance with the rules of war, and I directly gave my command for the *Taqachis* to proclaim throughout the camp that every man who had infidel prisoners was to put them to death, and whoever neglected to do so should himself be executed and his property given to the informer.[6]

Tamerlane left India in less than three months, carrying enormous amounts of booty back to Samarkand, seventy elephants being required to transport the plundered jewellery alone. He installed a new sultan to rule Delhi, but in 1451 the Lodis from Afghanistan took advantage of the declining fortunes of the dynasty and replaced it. The Lodi tombs are still to be seen in New Delhi's tranquil and picturesque Lodi Gardens.

The Lodi kings were in turn ousted by Babur, the first of the Mogul emperors, who, in a series of deft alliances with dissatisfied rulers, managed to conquer most of northern India before his death in 1530. His son Humayun lost out in family rivalries to his brothers in the 1540s before being restored to power in 1555, but he died before completing his task of recovering the whole of his former empire and was succeeded by his teenage son, Akbar.

It took several years for Akbar to consolidate his position and then to expand his influence to encompass the remaining territorial possessions of rival rulers. Akbar possessed all the necessary skills, despite being illiterate, to expand and unify his kingdom, winning support from the troublesome Rajputs of Rajasthan by marrying the daughter of the Maharaja of Jaipur. He also won favour by using senior Rajput generals in his army and appointing Hindus to high positions in his growing imperial bureaucracy. By the time the English merchant Ralph Fitch arrived in Agra in the 1580s, Akbar had created an impressive capital.

Agra is a very great citie and populous, built with stone, having faire and large streets, with a faire river running by it, which falleth into the Gulf of Bengala. It hath a faire castle and strong, with a very faire ditch. Here bee many Moores and Gentiles. The king is called Zelabdim Echebar; the people for the most part call him the Great Mogor. From thence we went to Fatepore, which is the place where the king kept his court. The towne is greater then Agra, but the houses and streetes be not so faire. Here dwell many people, both Moores and Gentiles. The king hath in Agra and Fatepore (as they doe credibly report) 1,000 elephants, thirtie thousand horses, 1,400 tame deere, 800 concubines: such store of ounces [cheetahs], tigers, buffles, cocks and haukes, that is very strange to see. He keepeth a great court, which they call Dericcan [Persian for Palace]. Agra and Fatepore are two very great cities, either of them much greater than London and very populous. Between Agra and Fatepore are 12 miles [in fact 23 miles], and all the way is market of victuals and other things, as full as though a man were still in a towne, and so many people as if a man were in a market. They have many fine cartes, and many of them carved and gilded with gold, with two wheeles, which be drawen with two little bulls about the bigness of our great dogs in England, and they will runne with any horse, and carie two or three men in one of these cartes; they are covered with silke or very fine cloth, and be used here as our coaches be in England. Hither is great resort of marchants from Persia and out of India, and very much marchandise of silke and cloth, and of precious stones, both rubies, diamants, and pearls. The king is apparelled in a white cabie [muslim tunic] made like a shirt tied with strings on the one side, and a little cloth on his head coloured oftentimes with red or yealow. None comes into his house but his eunuches which keepe his women.[7]

Akbar's legacy was the creation of an administrative framework which survived for another century and a half. His son Jahangir succeeded him in 1605 and proved to be a ruthless ruler. In his own memoirs, he devotes considerable space to his love of and fight with the grape.

I had not drunk it till I was 15 years old, except when in the time of my infancy two or three times my mother and wet-nurses gave it by way of infantile remedy . . . At the time when the camp of my revered father had been pitched in order to put down the disturbance of Yusufza's Afghans at the fort of Attock . . . one day I had mounted to go out to hunt. When I had moved about a good deal and the signs of weariness had set in, a gunner of the name of Ustad Shah Quli, a wonderful gunner out of those under my revered uncle Mirza Muhammad Hakim, said to me that if I would take a cup of wine it would drive away the feeling of being tired and heavy. It was in the time of my youth, and as I felt disposed towards it I ordered Mahmud, the Ab-dar [cupbearer], to go to the house of Hakim 'Ali and bring me an intoxicating draught. He sent me the amount of one and a half cups of yellow wine of a sweet taste in a little bottle. I drank it, and found its quality agreeable. After that I took to drinking wine, and increased it from day to day until wine made from grapes ceased to intoxicate me, and I took to drinking arrack and by degrees during nine years my potions rose to twenty cups of doubly distilled spirits, fourteen during the daytime and the remainder at night. . . . In that state of matters no one had the power to forbid me, and matters went to such a length that in the crapulous state from the excessive trembling of my hand I could not drink from my own cup, but others had to give it to me to drink until I sent for Hakim Human, brother of Hakim Abu-I-fath, who was one of the most intimate with my revered father, and informed him of my state. He, with excessive sincerity, and unfeigned burning of heart, said to me without hesitation, 'Lord of the world, by the way in which you drink spirits, God forbid it, but in six months matters will come to such a pass that there will be no remedy for it.' As his words were said out of pure good-will, and sweet life was dear to me, they made an impression on me, and from that day I began to lessen my allowance . . .[8]

William Hawkins, the British captain who formalized trading links between Jahangir and the British, has left a vivid account of life at Jahangir's court.

When hee rideth on progresse or hunting, the compasse of his tents may bee as much as the compasse of London and more; and I may say that of all sorts of people that follow the campe there are two hundred thousand, for hee is provided as for a citie. This king is thought to be the greatest emperour of the East for wealth, land, and force of men, as also for horses, elephants, camels, and drome-daries. As for elephants of his owne and of his nobles, there are fortie thousand, of which the one halfe are trayned elephants for the warre; and these elephants of all beasts are the most understanding. . . . He hath also infinite numbers of dromedaries, which are very swift, to come with great speed to give assault to any citie; as this kings father did, so that the enemies thought he had beene in Agra when he was at Amadavar, and he came from Agra thither in nine daies upon these dromedaries with twelve thousand choyce men . . . My selfe, in the time that I was one of his courtiers, have seene many cruell deeds done by him. Five times a weeke he commandeth his brave elephants to fight before him; and in the time of their fighting, either comming or going out, many times men are killed or dangerously hurt by these elephants. But if any be grievously hurt which might very well escape, yet neverthelesse that man is cast into the river, himselfe commanding it, saying: dispatch him, for as long as he liveth he will doe nothing else but curse me, and therefore it is better than he dye presently. I have seen many in this kind . . .

He is exceeding rich in diamants and all other precious stones, and usually weareth every day a faire diamant of great price; and that which he weareth this day, till his time be come about to weare it again he weareth not the same; that is to say, all his faire jewels are divided into a certaine quantitie or proportion to weare every day.[9]

Within a century, Hawkins' compatriots were actually controlling the Subcontinent. Even before Shah Jehan had completed the Taj Mahal in 1648, Madras had been settled by the British and Bombay was pushed into the modern age when it was given to Charles II as part of Catherine de Braganza's dowry by the Portuguese in 1661. Job Charnock, an obscure East India Company clerk, founded Calcutta in 1690. The creeping British control of the Subcontinent was consolidated by the middle of the eighteenth century. Warren Hastings, the controversial Governor-General of Bengal in the 1770s, who later successfully fought a seven-year impeachment trial in the House of Lords, presented the orthodox view of the civilizing nature of Western intervention.

Every accumulation of knowledge, and especially such as is obtained by social communication with people over whom we exercise a dominion founded on the rights of conquest, is useful to the state: it is the gain of humanity: in the specific instance which I have stated, it attracts and conciliates distant affections; it lessens the weight of the chain by which the natives are held in subjection; and it imprints on the hearts of our countrymen the sense and obligation of benevolence. Even in England, this effect is greatly wanting. It is not very long since the inhabitants of India were considered by many as creatures scarcely elevated above the degree of savage life; nor, I fear, is that prejudice yet wholly eradicated, though surely abated. Every instance which brings their real character home to observation will impress us with a more generous sense of feeling for their natural rights, and teach us to estimate them by the measure of our own. But such instances can only be obtained in their writings; and these will survive when the British dominion in India shall have long ceased to exist, and when the sources which it once yielded of wealth and power are lost to remembrance.[10]

Ram Mohan Roy, the nineteenth-century Bengali thinker responsible for conveying modern Western thought to the Indian intellectual élite, gave a surprisingly sympathetic hearing to the British conquest of India.

In the year 1712, the star of the Moghul ascendancy inclined towards descent, and has since gradually sunk below the horizon. The princes oftender consulted their own personal comfort than the welfare of the state, and relied for success on the fame of their dynasty, rather than on sound policy and military valour. Not only their crowns, but their lives also, depended on the good will of the nobles, who virtually assumed independence of the sovereign power, and each sought his own individual aggrandisement . . .

The Marquis of Cornwallis [who had surrendered to George Washington at Yorktown in 1781], a straightforward honest statesman, assumed the reigns of government in Bengal in 1786. He succeeded not only in consolidating the British power in its political relations in those remote regions, but also in introducing in 1793, material changes in every department, particularly in the revenue and judicial systems. These changes, approximating to the institutions existing in England, are calculated to operate beneficially, if regularly reduced to practice.[11]

The reality of colonial power was also well understood even at the time by some of the toilers in the field. The Abbé Dubois was a French Catholic who spent more than thirty years in India, mainly in the south, before returning to France in the 1820s. He was praised by many contemporaries for his classic book, *Description of the Character, Manners and Customs of the People of India, and of their Institutions, Religious and Civil.* Dubois was granted a pension by the East India Company and in later life became convinced that it was futile to attempt to convert Hindus to Christianity.

The European Power which is now established in India is, properly speaking, supported neither by physical force nor by moral influence. It is a piece of huge, complicated machinery, moved by springs which have been arbitrarily adapted to it. Under the supremacy of the Brahmins the people of India hated their government, while they cherished and respected their rulers; under the supremacy of Europeans they hate and despise their rulers from the bottom of their hearts, while they cherish and respect their government . . .

If it be possible to ameliorate the condition of the people of India I am convinced that this desirable result will be attained under the new *régime*, whatever may be said by detractors who are ready to find fault with everything. Whatever truth indeed there may be in the prejudiced charges, engendered by ignorance and interested motives, which are brought against the new order of things, and which are perhaps inseparable from every great administration, I for one cannot believe that a nation so eminently distinguished for its benificent and humane principles of government at home, and above all for its impartial justice to all classes alike – I for one cannot believe that this nation will ever be blind enough to compromise its own noble character by refusing participation in these benefits

to a subject people which is content to live peaceably under
its sway.

At the same time I venture to predict that it will attempt
in vain to effect any very considerable changes in the social
condition of the people of India, whose character, principles, customs, and ineradicable conservatism will always
present insurmountable obstacles.[12]

Lord William Cavendish-Bentinck purchased the manuscript
of the Abbé Dubois's book when he was Governor of Madras
from 1803 to 1807. In 1828, he was appointed Governor-
General, based in Calcutta. The second son of the Duke of
Portland, he was an evangelical and liberal-minded ruler who
believed his role was to 'secure and improve the condition of
all classes, to bring into life the vast dormant resources which
undoubtedly exist and to found a British Empire in India not
less solid or less worthy of admiration by all Asiatic nations than
Britain has been to the European world.'

He undertook considerable reform of the legal system and,
after a thorough investigation, abolished suttee, the Hindu
practice of sacrificing widows on the funeral pyres of their
husbands. He also set up a special agency for the supression of
thuggee, the name given to the practice of gangs of thieves who
robbed travellers on the roads after first strangling them with
a noose. And he opened up all posts in the East India Company
to any inhabitant of British India, regardless of race or religion.
Victor Jacquemont, who arrived in Calcutta in 1829 with an
armful of introductions, described dining with Lord William
at Government House:

Everything around was royal and Asiatic: the dinner completely French, and exquisite delicious wines served in
moderation, as in France, but by tall servants with long
beards, in white gowns with turbans of scarlet and gold.
Lord William asked me to take wine, a compliment which
I immediately returned, begging the honour of taking
wine with my fair neighbour, who was conversing with
me on a variety of agreeable topics, and offered to act as
my Cicerone. To give our appetites time to revive for the
second course, an excellent German orchestra, led by an
Italian, performed several of the finest symphonies of

Mozart and Rossini, and in a most perfect manner. The distance from which the sound proceeded, the uncertain light flickering between the columns of the neighbouring room, the brilliancy of the lights with which the table was illuminated, the beauty of the fruit which covered it in profusion, and the perfume from the flowers by which its pyramids were decorated, and perhaps also the champagne, made me find the music admirable. I experienced a sort of intoxication, but it was not a stupid intoxication. I chatted with Lady William in French on art, literature, painting, and music, while I answered, in a regular English speech, the questions put by her husband concerning the internal politics of France . . .[13]

Lord William felt that despite his various reforms, he had failed to bridge the enormous social gulf between the rulers and the ruled. He had no illusions about European comprehension of India.

The result of my own observation during my residence in India is that the Europeans generally know little or nothing of the customs and manners of the Hindus. We are all acquainted with some prominent marks and facts, which all who run may read; but their manner of thinking, their domestic habits and ceremonies, in which circumstances a knowledge of the people consists, is, I fear, in great part wanting to us. We understand very imperfectly their language. They perhaps know more of ours; but their knowledge is by no means sufficiently extensive to give a description of subjects not easily represented by the insulated words in daily use. We do not, we cannot, associate with the natives. We cannot see them in their houses and with their families. We are necessarily much confined to our houses by the heat; all our wants and business which would create a greater intercourse with the natives is done for us, and we are in fact strangers in the land.[14]

On his return to England, Lord William told a House of Commons committee that British rule was worse than that of the Moguls, who had at least gone as far as intermarrying with

Indians and considering themselves to be part of the country. Instead, he believed that the Raj had been 'cold, selfish and unfeeling; the iron hand of power on one side, monopoly and exclusion on the other.'

In a letter to her mother in the 1850s, Lady Canning expressed her own reservations about living in such a gilded cage.

It is quite a mistake to suppose that the society here is *bad*. Even flirting is very rare & of the mildest description, & I really believe hardly any woman but *me* goes out riding without her husband. It is really a very proper place; its greatest sin is its intense dullness, with some frivolity – of a dull kind too. People here are not inclined to toady; on the contrary, they are rather independent & more like republicans; but still the influence & example of the Governor-General is very great, & 'Government House' is looked up to as the authority for everything to a degree which is astonishing. People, you say, tell you that I have done good & have influence. I am not in the slightest degree aware of it, & not conscious that I have done anything but lead a more idle & selfish life than I ever did before in all my days. But that it should ever be *said* rather shows what I mean of the way this establishment is the centre of everything. Gossiping & evil-speaking is very common, I am told; so if there is bad to tell, it comes out soon enough. No one is intimate enough to gossip to me, so I cannot speak from experience.[15]

Queen Victoria was acutely aware of the danger of imperial smugness, and in a surprisingly forthright letter written in 1899 to her Prime Minister, Lord Salisbury, she outlined what she thought were important attributes for the new Viceroy. The person under consideration was George Curzon.

The future Viceroy must really shake himself more and more free from his red-tapist, narrow-minded Council and entourage. He must be more independent, must *hear for himself* what the *feelings* of the Natives really are, and do what he thinks right, and not be guided by the *snobbish* and vulgar overbearing and offensive behaviour of many

of our Civil and Political Agents, if we are to go on
peacefully and happily in India, and to be liked and beloved
by high and low, as well as respected as we ought to be,
and not trying to trample on the people and continually
reminding them and make them feel that they are a conquered people. They must of course *feel* that we are
masters, but it should be done kindly and not offensively,
which alas! is so often the case. Would Mr Curzon feel
and do this?[16]

Jawaharlal Nehru, the Harrow and Cambridge-educated
nationalist politician, was Independent India's first and greatest
prime minister. Because of his early associations with the
British, he was also more acutely aware of the problems the
British had in dealing with Indians during the Raj.

For many generations the British treated India as a kind
of enormous country-house (after the old English fashion)
that they owned. They were the gentry owning the house
and occupying the desirable parts of it, while the Indians
were consigned to the servants' hall and pantry and kitchen. As in every proper country-house there was a fixed
hierarchy in those lower regions – butler, house-keeper,
cook, valet, maid, footman, etc. – and strict precedence
was observed among them. But, between the upper and
lower regions of the house there was, socially and
politically, an impassable barrier. The fact that the British
Government should have imposed this arrangement upon
us was not surprising; but what does seem surprising is
that we, or most of us, accepted it as the natural and
inevitable ordering of our lives and destiny. We developed
the mentality of a good country-house servant.[17]

V.S. Naipaul elaborates on this theme in his first book about
India, *An Area of Darkness*, published in 1964. It brought a
remorseless logic to its analysis of Independent India and for
many years was considered to be 'anti-national' by the more
blinkered Indian nationalists.

The outer and inner worlds . . . coexist; the society only
pretends to be colonial; and for this reason its absurdities
are at once apparent. Its mimicry is both less and more

than a colonial mimicry. It is the special mimicry of an old country which has been without a native aristocracy for a thousand years, and has learned to make room for outsiders. But only at the top. The mimicry changes, the inner world remains constant: this is the secret of survival . . . Yesterday the mimicry was Mogul: tomorrow it might be Russian or American; today it is English.[18]

Jan Morris is another writer who believes that the Anglomania of India and its lingering nostalgia for much of its British heritage is a bad thing.

It is popular still, even among many Indians, to view with complacency the continuing Britishness of the Indian system, despite all odds. Only the British-founded Civil Service, they say, could have brought India through so many troubles. Only the British-inspired Indian Army could have preserved its security. And is it not gratifying, Britons especially like to say, to see pictures of old white Governors still *in situ* on official walls, or better still, group portraits of Staff College course members above the mantelpieces of New Delhi Communists?

I take an opposite view. . . . the inescapable relics of British method seem to me to debilitate this Asian nation, set beside the styles and loyalties of China or Japan. Of course it is aesthetically interesting to see the remains of the Raj still apparent among the crumbled castles, the deserted capitals, the mosques and temples of their predecessors. They add a new and often elegant dimension to the inconceivable richness of India. The stunning Victorian buildings of Bombay, towering there in their flamboyant mixture of Gothic, Muslim and Hindu, ecclesiastic and secular, commanding and conciliatory, will one day join the Taj and the ruins of Fatehpur Sikri, I do not doubt, as symbols on tourist posters. And few experiences of modern travel are more historically suggestive than a drink on the terrace of the Adyar Club in Madras, gleaming white above the Adyar River, with its green gardens all around and the garden bench mounted high in its classical cupola to catch the fresh breezes off the sea – the perfect English colonial house, still comfortable in the

English kind, still graced by touches of English eccentricity, but long ago left high and dry among its tennis courts by history's shifting course.

But as to Britishness in less substantial forms, it seems to me an Indian curse. Systems which may have been progressive in Edwardian times still linger on, ever more bedraggled and outdated. The powerful Federal Government at the centre, once an instrument of imperial stability, remains an instrument of reaction, for ever preserving the *status quo*, stifling always, one after the other, the movements for change which bubble down the years from Assam to Kashmir. If there has not been a revolution in India, sweeping away to a fresh start, it is because the ghosts of the British are lingering still around the halls of the Indian Government.[19]

The writer R.K. Narayan has also reflected on the relationship between Englishmen and the Subcontinent.

The Englishman preferred to leave the Indian alone, carrying his home on his back like a snail. He was content to isolate himself as a ruler, keeper of law and order and collector of revenue, leaving Indians alone to their religion and ancient activities. He maintained his distance from the native all through . . .

How did a little island so far away maintain its authority over another country many times its size? It used to be said by political orators of those days that the British Isles could be drowned out of sight if every Indian spat simultaneously in that direction. It was a David-Goliath ratio, and Britain maintained its authority for nearly two centuries. How was the feat achieved? Through a masterly organisation, which utilized Indians themselves to run the bureaucratic and military machinery. Very much like the *Kheddah* operations in Mysore forests, where wild elephants are hemmed in and driven into stockades by trained ones, and then pushed and pummelled until they realize the advantages of remaining loyal and useful, in order to earn their ration of sugar cane and rice. Take this as a symbol of British rule in India.

The Indian branch of the army was well trained and

disciplined, and could be trusted to carry out imperial orders. So was the civil service. Instead of taking the trouble to understand India and deal directly with the public, Britain transmuted Indians themselves into Brown Sahibs. After a period of training at Oxford and Cambridge, first-class men were recruited for the Indian Civil Service. They turned out to be excellent administrators. They were also educated to carry about them an air of superiority at all times and were expected to keep other Indians at a distance.

I had a close friend in the ICS who could not be seen or spoken to even by members of his family living under the same roof, except by appointment. He had organized his life in a perfect colonial pattern, with a turbaned butler knocking on his door with tea in the morning. Black tie and dinner jacket while dining with other ICS men, even if the table were laid in a desert; dropping visiting cards in 'Not at Home' boxes brought by servants when they formally called on each other. At home, when he joined the family gathering, he occupied a chair like a president, laughed and joked in a measured way; the utmost familiarity he could display was to correct other people's English pronunciation in an effort to promote Oxford style.

The ICS manual was his Bible that warned him against being too familiar with anyone. He was advised how many mangoes he could accept out of a basket that a favour-seeker proffered; how far away he should hold himself when a garland was brought to be slipped over his neck. It was a matter of propriety for an average visitor to leave his vehicle at the gate and walk down the drive; only men of certain status could come in their cars and alight at the portico.

The ICS was made up of well-paid men, above corruption, efficient and proud to maintain the traditions of the service, but it dehumanized the men, especially during the national struggle for independence. These men proved ruthless in dealing with agitators, and may well be said to have out-Heroded Herod. Under such circumstances, they were viewed as a monstrous creation of the British.

An elder statesman once defined the ICS as being neither Indian nor Civil nor Service. When Nehru became the Prime Minister, he weeded out many of them.[20]

It is a common mistake to think that the colonialists were unaware of this poisonous state of affairs. Philip Mason, one of the most intelligent entrants into the Indian Civil Service in the late 1920s, remained in the ICS until Independence, and then worked briefly for the Nizam of Hyderabad.

I certainly did not stop to think of the corrupting influence of authority. After all, it was for exercising authority that I had been trained at school. But it is hard to convey the authoritarian atmosphere of India, the expectation that anyone would do whatever you told him. It was not an importation; it was native. Persian poetry, Indian folk-lore, Rajput legends, are full of tales of kings, and the good king is the strong king who will not suffer rebellion or anarchy, whom everyone obeys. At another level, the countryside in which I worked was steeped in the tradition of man's mastery over man. In the last chapter, I used the word 'henchman', a term both vague and archaic, but one that seems right because the idea for which it stands is foreign to Western society today. It was not only a matter of landlord and tenant; in every village, there would be people who owed someone else an allegiance, usually hereditary, which had little to do with land. It might be a professional allegiance, the priest and the barber and the washerman gave professional services to a patron, a protector, but they gave and received much more – total service on one side, total protection on the other. It was the same with landless labourers; each family had an overlord who gave them food, clothing and protection and in return they would turn out as ploughmen, messengers, beaters at a shoot, witnesses in a law suit, retainers in an affray – any task the protector thought suitable to their degree – again an archaic word but right because the idea is archaic. Master and man, protector and henchman, everyone you spoke to in a village fitted somewhere in this pattern. And it was not a relationship that could be casually dissolved but one that both parties were born into and would pass to their children.

It was impossible not to be affected by this network of hereditary authority, just as it was almost impossible not to be affected by the idea of caste. We – young men like myself, straight from Oxford or Cambridge – were superimposed on top of this system, like an additional caste, as patrons or protectors above the whole network. You would find that a junior official had mysteriously attached himself to you and become your henchman because you had given him a word of praise or encouragement; not only that, but everywhere, anywhere, at a word or a gesture, you could summon temporary henchmen who would do anything you told them.[21]

While the civil service continued in the twentieth century along its straight and predominantly honest path, the pressure for self-government grew stronger. Even in 1921, the non-cooperation movement, which was spearheaded by Gandhi, had a considerable impact on official thinking. The 27-year-old Prince of Wales, during his official visit in 1921–2, wrote a private letter to Lord Reading, the Viceroy, outlining his misgivings over his tour of the Subcontinent.

I must tell you at once that I am not at all happy about the results of the tour as far as it has gone. £25,000 of English money and goodness knows how many lakhs of rupees are being spent over it, and I must honestly say that I have not as yet been able to justify the expenditure.

The ostensible reason for my coming to India was to see as many of the natives as possible and to get as near to them as I could. At least I presume it was the main reason, and I looked upon that as my duty. Well, I am afraid that I have not had many opportunities of doing this, either in British India or in the Native States.

Of course you know only too well how much my visits to British Indian cities have been boycotted by Gandhi and his disciples, and it has been obvious to me that the non-co-operators have prevented thousands of natives from turning out to see me. You will no doubt have had reports from Bombay, Poona, Ajmer, Lucknow,

Allahabad, Benares and Patna. The cases of each have been the same – hartals [the closing of shops and offices as a mark of protest] and more or less emptied streets.

I do not so much worry about the native populations ignoring my visits to their cities, because only very few of them understand, and given the smallest lead, they follow like sheep; but I must say I was very angry and felt very insulted when at the University of Lucknow, Allahabad, and Benares practically all the students (in the case of Allahabad *all* the students) refused to meet me or attend the University functions. At Benares it was quite a big ceremony, conferring of honorary degrees etc. and it would have been humorous if it had not been so sad this way they tried to 'kid' me by filling up the empty students' seats with High School boys, boy scouts and Europeans. I suppose they hoped I would never get to hear of what had been done, or realise what a b.f. they had made of me!!![22]

Later, he wrote an even gloomier letter to Edwin Montagu, the Secretary of State for India, in which he concluded that 'India is no longer a place for a white man to live in.'

This was a view also held by Jawaharlal Nehru, but for vastly different reasons. In the 1920s, Jawaharlal Nehru emerged as a leading figure in the Congress Party, which had become the most important political grouping in the country since its formation in 1885. During the First World War, Congress leaders began to call for self-government – a goal that became more urgent after the Amritsar Massacre in 1919. While Nehru and other Congress leaders made their way through straightforward political pressure, Mahatma Gandhi was using different tactics to achieve the same goal. He courted arrest in order to shame the British into granting self-government. Verrier Elwin, a brilliant theology student who went to India in the 1920s and became an ardent supporter of the Congress Party, gave an interesting portrait of the moment when a British policeman came to arrest Gandhi for breaking the law in one way or another.

We started up and I saw what I shall never forget – a fully uniformed Commissioner of Police at the foot of Bapu's bed, and Bapu just waking, a little bewildered, looking old, fragile and rather pathetic with the mists of sleep still on his face.

'Mr Gandhi, it is my duty to arrest you.'

A beautiful smile of welcome broke out on Bapu's face and now he looked young, strong and confident. He made signs to show that he was keeping silence.

The Commissioner smiled and with great courtesy said, 'I should like you to be ready in half an hour's time.'

It was five minutes past three. Bapu looked at his watch and the Commissioner said, 'Ah, the famous watch!' And they both laughed heartily. Bapu took a pencil and wrote, 'I will be ready to come with you in half an hour.'

The Commissioner laid his hand on Bapu's shoulder with a gesture so full of affection that I thought it was an embrace, until I realised that it was the formal token of arrest. Bapu then cleaned his teeth and then retired for a moment. The door was guarded, and all of us who were on the roof sat round in a circle. I looked out on to the road where some had been keeping all-night vigil and where a little crowd, very quiet and orderly, had collected, but there were no special police precautions . . . Everyone in turn touched his feet, and when I said good-bye he pulled my ear with a smile. He was in very good spirits: he might have been going to a festival rather than a jail.[23]

While the Congress Party was open to all who believed in Indian independence, it failed to appeal to the Muslim minority. In the nineteenth century, Muslims comprised about a quarter of the population but only 10 per cent of Congress delegates in 1899 were Muslim. This dwindled to an even smaller fraction in the early years of the twentieth century as Muslims feared that the goal of Congress was merely to replace the British Raj with a Hindu Raj. In 1907, a group of prominent Muslims created the All-India Muslim League, which put an end to Congress hopes of representing both Hindus and Muslims. By 1940, Mohammed Ali Jinnah, as leader of the Muslim League, was openly advocating the creation of Pakistan as a Muslim state, as shown in his most famous speech delivered at the annual meeting of the Muslim League in Lahore.

It is extremely difficult to appreciate why our Hindu friends fail to understand the real nature of Islam and Hinduism. They are not religions in the strict sense of the word, but are, in fact, different and distinct social orders, and it is a dream that the Hindus and Muslims can ever evolve a commonality, and this misconception of one Indian nation has gone far beyond the limits and is the cause of most of your troubles and will lead India to destruction if we fail to revise our notions in time. The Hindus and Muslims belong to two different religious philosophies, social customs, literatures. They neither intermarry nor interdine together, and, indeed, they belong to two different civilizations which are based mainly on conflicting ideas and conceptions. Their aspects on life and of life are different. It is quite clear that Hindus and Mussalmans derive their inspiration from different sources of history. They have different epics, different heroes, and different episodes. Very often the hero of one is a foe of the other and, likewise, their victories and defeats overlap. To yoke together two such nations under a single state, one as a numerical minority and the other as a majority, must lead to growing discontent and final destruction of any fabric that may be so built up for the government of such a state . . .

Whereas under the plea of the unity of India and one nation, which does not exist, it is sought to pursue here the line of one central government, we know that the history of the last twelve hundred years has failed to achieve unity and has witnessed, during the ages, India always divided into Hindu India and Muslim India. The present artificial unity of India dates back only to the British conquest and is maintained by the British bayonet, but termination of the British regime . . . will be the herald of the entire break-up with worse disaster than has ever taken place during the last one thousand years under Muslims. Surely that is not the legacy which Britain would bequeath to India after one hundred and fifty years

of her rule, nor would Hindu and Muslim India risk such a
catastrophe.[24]

Nehru had met Lord Linlithgow, who was appointed
Viceroy in 1936, during one of his visits to Britain in the 1930s.
In the first weeks of the Second World War he wrote to him
in surprisingly friendly terms in a vain effort to ensure some sort
of British commitment to eventual freedom for India so that
he might feel able to collaborate actively on the side of Britain
in the war.

> This letter, written in the train to Wardha, has grown
> long. But I want to add a few words to it and tell you
> how much I desire that the long conflict of India and
> England should be ended and that they should cooperate
> together. I have felt that this war, with all its horrors, has
> brought this opportunity to our respective countries and
> it would be sad and tragic if we were unable to take
> advantage of it. None of us, in India or England, dare
> remain in the old grooves or think in terms of past
> conditions. But events are moving so fast that some-
> times I fear that they will overtake our slow moving
> minds. There are all the elements of a Greek tragedy in
> the world situation today and we seem to be pushed along
> inevitably to a predestined end. You told me that I moved
> too much in the air. Probably you are right. But it is often
> possible to get a better view of the lie of the land from
> the heights than from the valleys. And I have wandered
> sufficiently on the solid earth of India and mixed with
> the people who labour there to think of India in earthly
> terms.
>   May I say how much I appreciate your friendly courtesy
> to me? It was a pleasure to meet you for a second time,
> and whenever chance offers an opportunity for this again,
> I shall avail myself of it. But whether we meet or, as you
> once said, look at each other from a distance over a gulf
> that has not been bridged, we shall do so, I earnestly trust,
> with no trace of unfriendliness, and realizing the dif-
> ficulties which encompass us and which compel us to pur-
> sue different paths.[25]

This was the only time between the Amritsar Massacre and the arrival of Lord Mountbatten twenty-seven years later that Nehru managed any personal warmth in his dealings with the highest British officials. It proved futile. Later, Nehru said that Linlithgow was a man 'heavy of body and slow of mind, solid as a rock and with almost a rock's lack of awareness'.

Field Marshal Archibald Wavell, Linlithgow's successor as Viceroy in 1943, was an altogether more compassionate individual but was overwhelmed by the scheming and backstabbing that went on during his rule. He had released Congress leaders from detention in an endeavour to reach a political agreement but was undermined by the prevarication of the new Labour government. Ultimately, Wavell was too much of a soldier to play the necessary games of bluff and deceit at which his successor Lord Mountbatten showed himself to be so expert. Wavell was a highly literate man, and wrote an amusing poem to show his frustration at getting to the bottom of Indian politics.

> I picked up Alice through the Looking Glass one evening shortly before the end of the Mission and wrote the parody below; I put it down here, but doubt whether it is really worth preserving.

JABBER-WEEKS
(from Phlawrence through the Indian Ink)
Twas grillig; and the Congreelites
Did harge and shobble in the swope;
All Jinsy were the Pakstanites,
And the spruft Sikhs outstrope.

Beware the Gandhiji, my son,
The satyagraha, the bogy fast,
Beware the Djinnarit, and shun
The frustrious scheduled caste.

He took his crippsian pen in hand,
Long time in draftish mood he wrote,
And fashioned as his lethal brand
A cabimissionary note.

And as he mused with pointed phrase,
The Gandhiji, on wrecking bent,
Came trippling down the bhangi ways,
And woffled as he went.

Ek do, Ek do, and blow on blow
The pointed phrase went slicker snack;
And, with the dhoti, Ghosh and goat, he
Came chubulating back.

And hast thou swozzled Gandhiji!
Come to my arms, my blimpish boy!
Hoo-ruddy-ray! o Labour day,
He shahbashed in his joy.

Twas grilling; and the Congreelites
Did harge and shobble in the swope,
All jinsy were the Pakstanites,
And the spruft Sikhs outstrope.

'It's very interesting', said Phlawrence a little wearily,
'but it's rather hard to understand.'

'So is nearly everything in this country,' answered
Hobson-Jobson. 'Shall I explain some of the difficult
words to you?'

'Yes, please,' said Phlawrence.

'Well, grillig is in the hot-weather at Delhi, when
everyone's brains are grilled before 2 pm and don't get
ungrilled till 2 am. Congreelites are animals rather like
conger eels, very slippery, they can wriggle out of anything they don't like. Harge is a portmanteau word, it
means to haggle and argue; to shobble is to shoft and wob-
ble; a swope is a place open to sweepers. Pakstanites are
rather fierce noisy animals, all green, they live round mosques and can't bear Congreelites. Spruft means spruce and
puffed up; outstrope means that they went round
shouting out that they weren't being fairly treated and
would take direct action about it.'

'That seems a lot for one word to mean,' said
Phlawrence.

'The Sikhs don't quite know what it does mean yet,'
said Hobson-Jobson.

'Well, anyway, the Gandhiji seems to have been swozzled, whatever that means,' said Phlawrence, 'And I expect that was a good thing.'

'But he wasn't,' said Hobson-Jobson, 'they found out afterwards that he had swozzled everyone else.'

'Thank you very much for your explanation,' said Phlawrence after a pause, 'but I am afraid it is still very difficult.'[26]

Independence was finally granted in August 1947, with Nehru as the first prime minister of India and Jinnah as governor-general of the new state of Pakistan. Nehru rose to the occasion with a speech delivered just minutes before Independence was granted.

Long years ago we made a tryst with destiny, and now the time comes when we shall redeem our pledge, not wholly or in full measure, but very substantially. At the stroke of the midnight hour, when the world sleeps, India will waken to life and freedom. A moment comes, which comes but rarely in history, when we step out from the old to the new, when an age ends, and when the soul of a nation long suppressed finds utterance. It is fitting that at this solemn moment we take the pledge of dedication to the service of India and her people and to the still larger cause of humanity.[27]

The haste with which Independence was granted has been ascribed to many factors, including Lord Mountbatten's desire to be back in London by 20 November so he could attend the Royal Wedding of Princess Elizabeth and Philip Mountbatten. W.H. Auden provided another answer in the following poem.

In seven weeks it was done, the frontiers decided.
A continent for better or worse divided.
The next day he sailed to England, where he quickly forgot
The case, as a good lawyer must.

> Return he would not,
> Afraid, as he told his Club, that he
> might get shot.[28]

Nehru remained as prime minister until his death in 1964. Despite various failings, he towered over his colleagues and was considered by many to be the *de facto* leader of the Third World.

James Cameron, the veteran foreign correspondent, valued him as a leader and as a friend and wrote a moving portrait of him.

I think Jawaharlal Nehru was the most important man I ever met. Scores of intelligent and well-intentioned Indians have derided me for this, citing for me the vast fallibilities of the man and the national catastrophe of his decline. All this is true. As a national leader Nehru was cursed by his imagination. He was paralysed by his intellectual evaluation of alternatives. He was, to coin a platitude, such a genuine giant among pigmies; it fed his pride and made possible his eternal equivocations. His achievement as the first prime minister of this enormous shapeless nation was so great that we who so respected him maintained the momentum of our affection far too long, after his vacillations and arbitrary impatience turned him – certainly against his own will – into an almost purposeless tyrant, torn by arrogance and love. In the end, he was surrounded by courtiers, chosen by caprice for their past loyalty or personal influence, never for the quality of their basic policies, almost always because ridding himself of them would have reflected on his own judgement. Thus in his final days was Jawaharlal Nehru surrounded by incompetents and sycophants and corrupt men; he denounced religious sectarianism and yet closed his eyes to its flagrant exploitation in his party's interests; he knew only too well the dangers of corruption in his circle and remained silent while it flourished around him. He was a hopeless administrator, and refused to be relieved of the irritating and time-consuming detail of administration. So obsessed was he with the vision of the future that he could not bring himself to envisage or accept the dismaying futilities and dishonesties all around him.

He was cursed with two strangely incompatible attributes: compassion and vanity. Thus, in the end he could reign but never could bring himself to rule. And he was to me the most admirable, and potentially the most valuable, public man I have ever known, and I mourned at his death.[29]

Nehru's daughter, Indira Gandhi, later became Prime Minister and when she was assassinated in 1984 by her Sikh bodyguards, her son Rajiv Gandhi was appointed as her successor. So engrained is dynastic rule in India that immediately after Rajiv's assassination in 1991, the Congress (I) Party unilaterally appointed his widow as the new party president, even though she despised politics and made every effort to keep the rest of the family out of the public eye. It was only after a considerable time that party stalwarts realized that her refusal to take up the Nehru mantle was final. However, the party stalwarts have not lost hope of changing her mind and even if they fail to do so there is still the possibility that Priyanka, the Gandhis' daughter, might assume the role in the future.

5

RELIGION

Hinduism – whatever Hinduism may be – is so vast, so elastic, so eclectic, so accommodating to the believers in one God, ten thousand gods or no gods at all, embodying everything from the most elaborate envisionments of the Brahmin mind to a granite phallus in a cave, is yet held together by two primary concepts: *karma*, the reward or punishment in the next life for the behaviour in this; and *dharma*, the obligation to accept one's condition and perform the duties appropriate to it. This is intrinsic to the whole principle of caste. Not only every individual but every *thing* has this attribute. It is the *dharma* of the wind to blow, and that of the rain to fall; it is the *dharma* of a stone to be hard and a leaf to be soft. It is likewise the *dharma* of a brahmin to be respected, and that of a sweeper to be despised. There is no getting away from it. The sacred Bhagavadgita, which cannot properly be questioned, says: 'Even should one's *dharma* seem to be mad, its performance brings blessing more than the assumption and pursuit of another's *dharma*.'

James Cameron, *An Indian Summer*[1]

India was the birthplace of Hinduism, Buddhism, Jainism and Sikhism and of myriad spiritual schisms and offshoots which remain in a constant state of evolution and erosion. Indeed, life in the Subcontinent still appears to be more affected by religious factors than anywhere else. India's religious festivals are the largest and most spectacular in the world and on most days of the week some important festival is being celebrated by thousands of worshippers. More than 80 per cent of India's population are nominally Hindu and there are an estimated 90 to 100 million Muslims plus significant Christian and Sikh minorities and small pockets of Jews and Zoroastrians or Parsees.

The origins of Hinduism are now thought to predate even the Indus valley civilization, which was at its peak between 2500BC and 1500BC. Archaeologists have yet to decipher the Indus valley script but from the evidence of statues and other artefacts, it is likely that one of the main deities worshipped there was a precursor of Shiva, one of the three primary gods of Hinduism. The mingling of the numerous elements which came to be identified as Hindu took place in the following centuries as indicated in the devotional hymns which are still an integral part of the Hindu religion. In fact, Hinduism can lay claim to being the world's oldest religion that has been practised continuously. The 'Hymn of Creation', composed some time before 1200BC, is one of the oldest surviving records of philosophical doubt.

Then even nothingness was not, nor existence.
There was no air then, nor the heavens beyond it.
What covered it? Where was it? In whose keeping?
Was there then cosmic water, in depths unfathomed?

Then there was neither death nor immortality,
nor was there then the torch of night and day.
The One breathed windlessly and self-sustaining.
There was that One then, and there was no other.

At first there was only darkness wrapped in darkness.
All this was only unilluminated water.
That One which came to be, enclosed in nothing,
arose at last, born of the power of heat.

In the beginning desire descended on it –
that was the primal seed, born of the mind.
The sages who have searched their hearts with wisdom
know that which is is kin to that which is not.

And they have stretched their cord across the void,
and know what was above, and what below.
Seminal powers made fertile mighty forces.
Below was strength, and over it was impulse.

But, after all, who knows, and who can say
whence it all came, and how creation happened?
The gods themselves are later than creation,
so who knows truly whence it has arisen?

Whence all creation had its origin,
he, whether he fashioned it or whether he did not,
he, who surveys it all from highest heaven,
he knows – or maybe even he does not know.[2]

The first categorization of the Hindu population along
caste lines appears in the *Rig Veda*, which provides a mythic
explanation for the entire system. In fact, it was a sophisticated form of closed shop which enabled the paler-skinned
Aryans to keep the darker-skinned local inhabitants at arms'
length.

When the gods made a sacrifice with the man as their
victim . . .
When they divided the Man, into how many parts did
they divide him?
What was his mouth, what were his arms, what were
his thighs and his feet called?
The brahmin was his mouth, of his arms were made the
warrior.
His thighs became the vaishya [merchant and
agricultural caste], of his feet the shudra [labourers and
other low-caste people] was born.
With Sacrifice the gods sacrificed to Sacrifice, these
were the first of the sacred laws. These mighty beings
reached the sky, where are the eternal spirits, the gods.[3]

Sacrifice to the Gods in return for their favours remained
central to early Aryan beliefs. The next phase of Hindu thought
is represented in the *Upanishads*, a collection of 108 specu-
lative treatises composed between 800 BC and 600 BC. The
Upanishads go beyond the *Rig Veda*'s concern with sacrifice and
first touch on the doctrine of transmigration – not just of
human souls but of all forms of life – and the belief that one's
conduct, or *karma*, determines the direction that one's reincar-
nation will take. These developments are shown beautifully in
the early *Isa Upanishad*.

Behold the universe in the glory of God: and all that lives and moves on earth. Leaving the transient, find joy in the Eternal: set not your heart on another's possession.

Working thus, a man may wish for a life of a hundred years.

Only actions done in God bind not the soul of man.

There are demon-haunted worlds, regions of utter darkness. Whoever in life rejects the Spirit goes to that darkness after death.

The Spirit, without moving, is swifter than the mind; the senses cannot reach Him: He is ever beyond them. Standing still, He overtakes those who run. To the ocean of His being the spirit of life leads the stream of action.

He moves, and He moves not. He is far, and He is near. He is within all, and He is outside all.

Who sees all beings in his own Self, and his own Self in all beings, loses all fear . . .

May life go to immortal life, and the body go to ashes. Om. O my soul, remember past strivings, remember! O my soul, remember past strivings, remember!

By the path of good lead us to final bliss, O fire divine, thou god who knowest all ways. Deliver us from wandering evil. Prayers and adoration we offer unto thee.[4]

The teachings of the *Upanishads* were developed further in the *Bhagavad-Gita*, now the most revered holy book of Hindus. Debate about when it was written continues, with estimates ranging from 500 BC to 350 AD. The importance of the *Gita* is that it represents the transition of Hinduism from the sacrificial and ritualistic world of the *Vedas* to the realm of daily life on earth. Although the *Gita* is part of a much larger work, the *Mahabharata*, it stands by itself as a dialogue between the gods Krishna and Arjuna about the morality of undertaking a war that will lead to the destruction not only of Krishna's rival but also of members of his own family. The following is Krishna's rationalization of this state of affairs.

The wise grieve not for those who live; and they grieve not for those who die – for life and death shall pass away.

Because we all have been for all time: I, and thou, and those kings of men. And we all shall be for all time, we all for ever and ever.

As the spirit of our mortal body wanders on in childhood, and youth and old age, the Spirit wanders on to a new body: of this the sage has no doubts.

From the world of the senses, Arjuna, comes heat and comes cold, and pleasure and pain. They come and they go: they are transient. Arise above them, strong soul.

The man whom these cannot move, whose soul is one, beyond pleasure and pain, is worthy of life in Eternity.

The unreal never is: the Real never is not. This truth indeed has been seen by those who can see the true.

Interwoven in his creation, the Spirit is beyond destruction. No one can bring to an end the Spirit which is everlasting.

For beyond time he dwells in these bodies, though these bodies have an end in their time; but he remains immeasurable, immortal. Therefore, great warrior, carry on thy fight.

If any man thinks he slays, and if another thinks he is slain, neither knows the ways of truth. The Eternal in man cannot kill: the Eternal in man cannot die.[5]

The period between the seventh and fifth centuries BC was marked by spiritual ferment which also led to the emergence of two other religious strands now known as Jainism and Buddhism.

Jainism was responsible for the development of vegetarianism amongst Hindus in India for Jains believe that all forms of life are sacred. Mahatma Gandhi also adopted their belief in *ahinsa*, or non-violence. There are only three and a quarter million Jains remaining in India but they are far more influential than these numbers would suggest as many lay members of the faith are successful businessmen.

The other important schism occurred in the sixth century BC with the growth of Buddhism. Gautama, or Buddha, was the son of a minor chieftain in north-east India. According to the scriptures, he found enlightenment after six years of wandering and meditation. He preached 'the middle path' which hovered between the extreme asceticism of the Jains and the caste-ridden Hindu hierarchy. Instead, he advocated the eightfold path, which emphasized that suffering was central to existence. According to early Buddhist scriptures, the only way to break out of the cycle of rebirth is to attain *nirvana*, or complete release from the human condition by reaching a state of spiritual perfection. Although Buddhism later fragmented into various schools and spread throughout central and eastern Asia, its rejection of the notion of caste meant that its impact on India was immense. The most influential Buddhist writings on lay morality, which are more than 2,000 years old, sound remarkably modern.

> Husbands should respect their wives, and comply as far as possible with their requests. They should not commit adultery. They should give their wives full charge of the home, and supply them with fine clothes and jewellery as far as their means permit. Wives should be thorough in their duties, gentle and kind to the whole household, chaste, and careful in housekeeping, and should carry out their work with skill and enthusiasm.
>
> A man should be generous to his friends, speak kindly of them, act in their interest in every way possible, treat them as his equals, and keep his word to them. They in turn should watch over his interests and property, take care of him when he is 'off his guard' (i.e intoxicated, infatuated, or otherwise liable to commit rash and careless actions), stand by him and help him in time of trouble, and respect other members of his family.
>
> Employers should treat their servants and work people decently.[6]

Buddhism made its greatest inroads in India seventy years after Alexander the Great abandoned his quest to conquer India. The agent for the spread of Buddhism was Ashoka, the enigmatic ruler who became the first emperor of a unified India. Disgusted by the devastation caused by his annexation of the kingdom of Kalinga, he converted to Buddhism and spent the remainder of his forty-year reign attempting to promote religious tolerance and non-violence. One of the rock edicts Ashoka, or 'The Beloved of the Gods', erected in his empire showed the extent to which he was prepared to espouse religious tolerance.

> The Beloved of the Gods . . . honours members of all sects, whether ascetics or householders, by gifts and various honours. But he does not consider gifts and honours as important as the furtherance of the essential message of all sects. This essential message varies from sect to sect, but it has one common basis, that one should so control one's tongue as not to honour one's own sect or disparage another's on the wrong occasions; for on certain occasions one should do so only mildly, and indeed on other occasions one should honour other men's sects. By doing this one strengthens one's own sect and helps the others, whereas by doing otherwise one harms one's own sect and does a disservice to the others. Whoever honours his own sect and disparages another man's, whether from blind loyalty or with the intention of showing his own sect in a favourable light, does his own sect the greatest possible harm. Concord is best, with each hearing and respecting the other's teachings. It is the wish of the Beloved of the Gods that members of all sects should be learned and should teach virtue . . . Many officials are busied in this matter . . . and the result is the progress of my own sect and the illumination of righteousness.[7]

Within the next few centuries, Buddhism had spread so widely that Chinese pilgrims came to India to seek more accurate versions of their holy texts. The seventh-century pilgrim Hsuan Tsang spoke warmly of the Hindu holy men that he encountered on his travels.

> There are men who, far seen in antique lore and fond of the refinements of learning, are content in seclusion, leading lives of continence. These sink and float outside of the world, and promenade through life away from human affairs. Though they are not moved by honour or reproach, their fame is far spread. The rulers treating them with ceremony and respect cannot make them come to court. Now as the State holds men of learning and genius in esteem and the people respect those who have high

intelligence, the honours and praises of such men are conspicuously abundant, and the attentions private and official paid to them are very considerable. Hence men can force themselves to a thorough acquisition of knowledge. Forgetting fatigue, they expiate in the arts and sciences; seeking for wisdom while relying on perfect virtue they count not 1000 li [350 miles] a long journey. Though their family be in affluent circumstances, such men make up their minds to be like the vagrants, and get their food by begging as they go about. With them there is honour in knowing truth and there is no disgrace in being destitute.[8]

Although Buddhism continued to spread throughout the Far East, after the seventh century it began to decline within the Subcontinent for a variety of reasons. Some scholars think that in many cases it became indistinguishable from Hinduism and that its shunning of a priestly caste meant that there were no people to work as active exponents. With the coming of Islam in the eighth century, many monasteries and other centres of learning were destroyed by the invaders. While there was a certain degree of common ground between Hinduism and Buddhism, there was none between Islam and these faiths. This was borne out by Alberuni, the scholarly traveller from Khiva who visited northern India in the eleventh century.

The Hindus totally differ from us in religion, as we believe in nothing in which they believe, and vice versa. On the whole, there is very little disputing about theological topics among themselves; at the utmost, they fight with words, but they will never stake their soul or body or their property on religious controversy. On the contrary, all their fanaticism is directed against those who do not belong to them – against all foreigners. They call them *mleccha*, i.e., impure and forbid having any connection with them, be it by intermarriage, or any other kind of relationship, or by sitting, eating, and drinking with them, because thereby, they think, they would be polluted.[9]

Various sultanates were formed in northern India by Muslim invaders but it was not until early in the sixteenth century that a nominally Islamic empire ruled over the greater part of the Subcontinent. Despite their strong Islamic heritage, the Mogul emperors did not adopt a fundamentalist approach to their Hindu subjects. Akbar, who ruled as emperor from 1560 until 1605, was a remarkably tolerant ruler who went to considerable lengths to play down his Islamic heritage. High above the Buland Darwaza, or Gate of Victory, in Fatehpur Sikri, his now abandoned capital near Agra, there is the following inscription:

> Jesus Son of Mary (on whom be peace) said:
> The world is a bridge, pass over it,
> but build no houses on it. He who hopes for an hour
> may hope for eternity. The world endures but an hour.
> Spend it in prayer, for the rest is unseen.

Akbar went on to form an idiosyncratic blend of religious beliefs termed the 'divine faith' but it failed to bring Muslims and Hindus together and did not survive his death in 1605. Almost at the same time as the rise of the Mogul Empire, another movement began in the Punjab under the inspiration of Guru Nanak, the first of ten gurus who founded the Sikh religion. He too sought a separate path from the two major religious groups, stating in his writing that 'The age is like a knife. Kings are butchers. Religion hath taken wings and flown. In the dark night of falsehood I cannot see where the moon of truth is rising.' In a more specific text, he noted that 'Modesty and religion have disappeared because falsehood reigns supreme. The Muslim Mulla and the Hindu Pandit have resigned their duties, the Devil reads the marriage vows . . . Praises of murder are sung and people smear themselves with blood instead of saffron.'[10]

Guru Nanak rejected the pantheism of Hinduism as the following poem shows.

> There is One God.
> He is the supreme truth
> He, the Creator,
> Is without fear and without hate.
> He, the Omnipresent,
> Pervades the universe.

He is not born,
Nor does He die to be born again.
By His grace shalt thou worship Him.

Before time itself
There was truth.
When time began to run its course
He was the truth.
Even now, He is the truth
And evermore shall truth prevail.[11]

Although at an early stage of his life as a holy man he would state that 'There is no Hindu, there is no Mussalman', by the end of his life he was far more tolerant of them. As he approached his death, a dispute broke out about what to do with his body, the Hindus wanting to cremate it and the Muslims advocating burial. According to legend, neither were offended for his body simply vanished.

The enmity between Muslims and Hindus simmered for centuries and flared up during Partition, resulting in the deaths of hundreds of thousands of people and the creation of Pakistan. There are still occasional flare-ups between the two communities in independent India. The current flashpoint involves an interminable dispute about the siting of the Babri Masjid mosque in the holy city of Ayodhya in Uttar Pradesh. Scores of people were killed in 1989 after Hindu fanatics attempted to destroy the mosque on the grounds that it stands on the site of a destroyed Hindu temple commemorating the birthplace of the deity Ram.

In the nineteenth century, the British civil servant William Sleeman wrote of the innate hostility of the two faiths.

Though every mosque and mausoleum was a seat of learning, that learning, instead of being a source of attraction and conciliation between the Muhammadans and Hindoos, was, on the contrary, a source of perpetual repulsion and enmity between them – it tended to keep alive in the breasts of the Musalmans a strong feeling of religious indignation against the worshippers of idols; and of dread and hatred in those of the Hindoos . . . no man could well rise from the perusal [of the Koran] without the wish to serve God by some act of outrage against them [the idolators]. These buildings were, therefore, looked upon by the Hindoos, who composed the great mass of the people, as . . . religious volcanoes, always ready to explode and pour out their lava of intolerance and outrage upon the innocent people of the surrounding country.[12]

Some of the more intellectual foreigners who toured India in the nineteenth century, such as Victor Jacquemont, quickly grasped the reality of Indian life and beliefs behind the exotic displays in temples and festivals.

We adopt in Europe a completely false notion of the real intellectual habits of the Indian nations. We generally suppose them inclined to an aescetic and contemplative life; and, upon the faith of Pythagoras, we continue to look upon them as extremely occupied with the metamorphosis of their souls after death. I assure you, sir, that the metamorphosis is the last of their cares: they plough, sow, and water their fields, reap, and recommence the same round of labours; they work, eat, smoke and sleep without having either the wish or the leisure to attend to such idle nonsense, which would only make them more wretched, and the very name of which is unknown to the greater number of them.[13]

Generally speaking, the early Europeans in India were quite ignorant of Hinduism. One of the first parties of Portuguese soldiery in the early sixteenth century in Goa sat through a religious rite in the Hindu temple of Kali (the dark goddess) under the mistaken impression that it was the shrine of a local Black Madonna. Although there was scattered missionary activity from the arrival of St Francis Xavier in Goa in 1542, it was only in the nineteenth century that missionaries had a significant impact in India. Protestant Evangelicals were shocked at the idolatrous manifestations of Hinduism. The East India Company considered the missionaries and evangelists irritants as they aroused suspicion and hostility amongst many Hindus. The missionaries also spoke out against the poor living conditions of Indians, which the East India Company preferred to ignore. Some more independent-minded foreign observers, such as Richard Burton had contempt for the narrow-minded evangelical approach of some of the English missionaries. Burton viewed the behaviour of these earnest souls as something to joke about rather than to respect.

The rank climate of India, which produces such a marvellous development of vegetation, seems to have a similar effect upon the Anglo-Indian individuality. It shot up, as if suddenly relieved of the weight with which society controls it in England. The irreligious were marvellously irreligious, and the religious no less marvellously religious. The latter showed the narrowest, most fanatic, and the most intolerant spirit; no hard-grit Baptist could compare with them. They looked upon the heathen around them (very often far better than themselves) as faggots ready for burning. They believed that the Parsees adored the sun, that the Hindus worshipped sticks and stones, and that the Mohammedans were slaves to what they called 'the impostor Mahomet'. They were not more lenient to those of their own blood who did not run on exactly the same lines with them. A Roman Catholic, as they called him, was doomed to perdition, and the same was the case with all non-church-going Protestants. It is hardly to be wondered at if, at times, they lost their wits. One man, who was about the wildest of his day, and who was known as the 'Patel' (village headman) of Griffin-gaon (literally 'newly arrived Englishman in a village'), suddenly got a 'call'. He used to distinguish himself by climbing a tree every morning, and by shouting with all his might, 'Dunga Chhor-do, Jesus Christ, Pakro', meaning 'Abandon the world, and catch hold of the Saviour'. This lasted for years, and it ended in his breaking down in the moral line, and dying in a mad-house.[14]

The signal lack of success of the European Christians in converting the native population was freely admitted by many of them, not least by the Abbé Dubois.

For my part I cannot boast of my successes in this sacred career during the period that I have laboured to promote the interests of the Christian religion. The restraints and privations under which I have lived, by conforming myself to the usages of the country; embracing, in many respects, the prejudices of the natives; living like them, and becoming all but a Hindu myself; in short, by being made all things to all men, that I might by all means save some – all these have proved of no avail to me to make proselytes. During the long period I have lived in India in the capacity of a missionary, I have made, with the assistance of a native missionary, in all between two and three hundred converts of both sexes. Of this number two thirds were Pariahs or beggars; and the rest were composed of Sudras, vagrants, and outcasts of several tribes, who, being without resource, turned Christian in order to form connections, chiefly for the purpose of marriage, or with some other interested views.[15]

There is a hilarious account of this process of gaining what are termed 'Rice Christians' in *Untouchable*, by one of India's most important writers, Mulk Raj Anand.

'Who is *Yessuh Messih*, Sahib? Is he the God of the Sahibs?' Bakha asked, slightly afraid that he was bothering the white man too much. He knew from experience that Englishmen did not like to talk too much.

'He is the Son of God, my boy,' answered the Colonel, ecstatically revolving his head. 'And he died for us sinners:

He died that we might be forgiven,
He died to make us good,
That we might go at last to heaven,
Saved by his precious blood.'

Bakha was a bit bored by this ecstatic hymn-singing. But the white man had condescended to speak to him, to take notice of him. He was happy and proud to be in touch with a sahib. He suffered the priest and even reiterated his enquiry:

'Do they pray to *Yessuh Messih* in your *girja ghar*, Sahib?'

'Yes, yes,' replied the Colonel, breaking into the rhythm of a new hymn:

'Jesus, tender shepherd, hear me.
Let my sins be forgiven!
Let there be light,
Oh, shed Thy light in the heart of this boy.'

Bakha was baffled and bored. He did not understand anything of these songs. He had followed the sahib because the sahib wore trousers. Trousers had been the dream of his life. The kindly interest which the trousered man had shown him when he was downcast had made Bakha conjure up pictures of himself wearing the sahib's clothes, talking the sahib's language and becoming like the guard whom he had seen on the railway station near his village. He did not know who *Yessuh Messih* was. The sahib probably wanted to convert him to his religion. He didn't want to be converted. But he wouldn't mind being converted if he knew who *Yessuh Messih* was. The sahib, however, was singing, singing to himself and saying *Yessuh Messih* was the son of God. How could God have a son? Who is God? If God is like Rama, He has no son, for he had never heard that Rama had a son. It was all so puzzling that he thought of excusing himself by lying to the sahib that he had to go to work and couldn't come with him.[16]

One of the most bigoted of the early proselytizers was Henry Martyn, the first translator of the New Testament and the Prayer Book into Hindustani. The son of a Cornish coal-miner, Martyn opened the first church in Cawnpore in 1810 and spent what spare time he had in constant preaching to sceptical Indian congregations. His initial impressions of an evening service at a Hindu temple in Bengal were the catalyst for his translation of the New Testament.

As we walked through the dark wood which everywhere covers the country, the cymbals and drums struck up, and never did sounds go through my heart with such horror in my life. The pagoda was in a court, surrounded by a wall, and the way up to it was by a flight of steps on each side. The people to the number of about fifty were standing on the outside, and playing the instruments. In the centre of the building was the idol, a little ugly black image, about two feet high, with a few lights burning round him. At intervals they prostrated themselves, with their foreheads to the earth. I shivered at being in the neighbourhood of hell; my heart was ready to burst at the dreadful state to which the Devil had brought my poor fellow-creatures. I would have given the world to have known the language, to have preached to them.[17]

He despaired of ever achieving God's Will with these 'children of darkness' who responded to his hectoring 'with the smile of indifference'.

Among all the different people whom I have occasion to speak to, I know not which is most hardened. How shall it ever be possible to convince a Hindoo or Brahmin of any thing. These are people possessed by Satan, like the idols they worship, without any understanding. Truly, if ever I see a Hindoo a real believer in Jesus, I shall see something more nearly approaching the resurrection of a dead body, than any thing I have yet seen.

Later he admitted that 'Four years have I been in the ministry, and I am not sure that I have been the means of converting four souls from the error of their ways; why is this? The fault must be in myself.'[18]

Mary Martha Sherwood, another Evangelical, was horrified by heathenism, especially as practised in Benares. She saw the Hindu Gods portrayed there as 'horrible and disproportioned figures, similitudes of the gods of their depraved imaginations, painted on the walls of the buildings, or carved in stone or wood [that] seem to point out the more immediate presence in the place of the Prince of the Powers of Darkness.'

She was also taken aback by the swarm of beggars to whom Henry Martyn preached at Cawnpore.

Sometimes Mr Martyn's garden has contained as many as five hundred on a Sunday evening. No dreams or vision excited in the delerium of a raging fever could surpass these realities. They were young and old, male and female, bloated and wizened, tall and short, athletic and feeble, some clothed with abominable rags, some nearly without clothes, some plastered with mud, others with matted, uncombed locks streaming down to their heels, others with heads bald or scabby; every countenance being hard and fixed, as it were, by the continual indulgence of bad passions, the features having become exaggerated and the lips blackened with tobacco, or blood-red with the juice of the henna [an error – she meant *pan*]. These and such as these formed only the general mass of the people; there were among them still more distinguished monsters . . .

From time to time low murmurs and curses would arise in the distance, and then roll forward till they became so loud as to drown the voice of this pious one [Martyn], generally concluding with hissings and fierce cries. But when the storm left off he might be heard going on in the same calm tone, as if he were incapable of irritation.[19]

One contemporary English writer described Martyn's religious passion as 'erotic delirium' while others claimed he approached sainthood. He died of fever in Persia two years later shortly after completing a Persian translation of the New Testament for the Shah and was eulogized as 'the one heroic name which adorns the annals of the Church of England from the days of Elizabeth to our own'.

Other English writers in the nineteenth century criticized certain Hindu practices with more credibility. John Beames, a district officer in Orissa, described the wretched conditions to which some pilgrims were reduced by the exploitation of unscrupulous Hindu priests.

There is a class of brahmans attached to the temple of Jagannath (*vulgo* Juggernaut) called Pandàs, whose business it is to travel long distances all over India, extolling the virtues of pilgrimage to Jagannath, and inducing people to undertake it. The decaying zeal of the modern Hindu for pilgrimage is kept alive by these touters, who are naturally most successful with the women. It used to be a common sight to see a strong, stalwart Panda marching along the road, followed by a little troop of small, cowering Bengali women, each clad in her one scanty, clinging robe, her small wardrobe in a pal-leaf box on her head, with the lordly Panda's luggage on her shoulders. At night they put up at one of the chatties or lodging-houses which are found all along the road. Here his lordship reposes while his female flock buy his food and cook it, spread his couch, serve his dinner, light his pipe, shampoo his limbs, and even, if he so desire, minister to his lust.

When at length they reach Jagannath, the Panda leads his flock round to all the places of worship, sees them through all the ceremonies and, in collusion with the Parihàris, or temple priests, screws out of them all their money down to the last cowry, in fees and offerings. The ceremonies ended, he has done with them, and remorsely turns them adrift to find their way home, a distance perhaps of many hundred miles, as best they may. So far from their homes from which they have in many cases started surreptitiously, purloining their husbands' hoard of money, these wretched women have to tramp wearily back through the rain, for it is mostly for the Rath Jàtrà, in the rainy season, that they come. What with exposure, fatigue and hunger they die in great numbers by the road-side. Those whose youth and strength enable them to survive the journey are often too much afraid of their husbands' anger to return home, and end by swelling the numbers of prostitutes in Calcutta. *Tantum religio potuit suadere malorum!* ('To deeds so dreadful could religion prompt!')[20]

The importance of caste is another key aspect of Hinduism which confuses the non-believer. Despite the best efforts of the secular Constitution of India, which outlaws caste discrimination, it still dominates the lives of many Hindus. Indian Sunday newspapers contain thousands of personal advertisements from families seeking a spouse who conforms to the correct caste requirements for their son or daughter. The Abbé Dubois found much to admire in the caste system, seeing it as a crutch for the less privileged rather than as a monstrous burden.

For my part, having lived many years on friendly terms with the Hindus, I have been able to study their national life and character closely, and I have arrived at a quite opposite decision on this subject of caste. I believe caste division to be in many respects the *chef d'oeuvre*, the happiest effort, of Hindu legislation. I am persuaded that it is simply and solely due to the distribution of the people into castes that India did not lapse into a state of barbarism, and that she preserved and perfected the arts and sciences of civilization whilst most other nations of the earth

1. The progress of the Mogul Emperor Shah Alam II (reigned 1760–1806) along the banks of a river. Lucknow, *c.*1790. Despite his splendid trappings, Shah Alam was merely a useful figurehead for the East India Company. A century and a half earlier, William Hawkins had commented that when Emperor Jahangir 'rideth on progresse or hunting, the compasse of his tents may bee as much as the compasse of London and more.'

2. A party encamped by a palace near Garhwal, *c.*1840. The traveller François Bernier said the heat was so intense in India that 'for more than six successive months, everybody lies in the open air without covering – the common people in the streets, the merchants and persons of condition sometimes in their courts or gardens, and sometimes on their terraces, which are first carefully watered.'

3. *The East Offering Its Riches to Britannia in 1778, by Spiridoni Roma. Commenting on the relationship between Indians and the British Crown, Vi—————— to————— that 'The amount of —— of each —————— as we ——, but it should be done kindly, and not offensively,*

4. Landing at Madras. Coloured acquatint engraving by C. Hunt after a drawing by J. B. East, 1856. Madras was always the most difficult of the major cities at which to disembark because of the open sea. On arriving there in 1805, Mary Martha Sherwood said the shore 'appeared to be richly scattered with palaces' and that passengers could see Indians moving about including 'a set of bearers carrying a palanquin.'

5. An Indian woman committing suttee, *c.*1800. Suttee was abolished in 1829 but there are still occasional instances reported. In the sixteenth century, the English traveller Ralph Fitch reported that 'when the husbande dieth, his wife is burned with him, if shee be alive; if shee will not, her head is shaven, and then is never any account made of her after.'

6. A Bengal village, *c.*1870. The Indian writer and painter Prafulla Mohanti, who grew up in one of India's 700,000 villages, wrote that 'I saw the paddy fields change through the seasons, from vivid green to gold, the mango trees blossom, the sweet-scented flowers open out in the evening, the multi-coloured birds, the brilliant sunsets and sunrises. It was magic. I felt peaceful and at one with Nature.'

7. Maharaja Sindhia and courtiers, c.1870. Many of the Indian ruling families were creations of the British although some of the larger kingdoms had existed for centuries. Lord Curzon warned that 'if ever they be allowed to disappear, Indian society will go to pieces like a dismantled vessel in a storm.'

8. The interior of an Anglo-Indian home at Madura near Madras in the mid-1860s. Nearly a century earlier, writing about Madras, Eliza Fay wrote that 'many of the houses and public buildings are very extensive and elegant . . . I could have fancied myself transported into Italy, so magnificently are they decorated, yet with the utmost taste.'

9. An Englishman travelling by palanquin, c.1860. The orientalist Sir Richard Burton warned there was not 'much pleasure in the enjoyment of this celebrated Oriental luxury . . . After a day or two you will hesitate which to hate the most, your bearers' monotonous, melancholy, grunting, groaning chaunt, when fresh, or their jolting, jerking, shambling, staggering gait, when tired.'

10. A view of the bazaar leading to Chitpore Road, Calcutta, from J. B. Fraser's *Views of Calcutta, 1824–26*. Half a century later, Rudyard Kipling remarked of the city: 'What a dive – what a heavenly place to *loot* . . . adorned, docked, wharfed, fronted, and reclaimed by Englishmen, existing only because England lives, and dependent for its life on England.'

11. The Viceroy, Lord Curzon, with his wife on a shikar party, Hyderabad, 1902. It was the accepted practice in India until the 1960s for important guests to be taken tiger shooting.

remained in a state of barbarism. I do not consider caste to be free from many great drawbacks; but I believe that the resulting advantages, in the case of a nation constituted like the Hindus, more than outweigh the resulting evils. . . . Caste assigns to each individual his own profession or calling; and the handing down of this system from father to son, from generation to generation, makes it impossible for any person or his descendants to change the condition of life which the law assigns to him for any other. Such an institution was probably the only means that the most clear-sighted prudence could devise for maintaining a state of civilization amongst a people endowed with the peculiar characteristics of the Hindus.[21]

However, in the twentieth century caste is more likely to be associated with insurmountable privilege and the bigotry of those at the top of the caste pyramid. Mahatma Gandhi attempted, unsuccessfully, to eradicate the curse of untouchability on tens of millions of Indians. As early as 1921, he wrote the following powerful indictment of his caste-ridden compatriots.

I regard untouchability as the greatest blot on Hinduism . . . So long as the Hindus wilfully regard untouchability as part of their religion, so long as the mass of Hindus consider it a sin to touch a section of their brethren, Swaraj [self-government] is impossible of attainment . . . What crimes, for which we condemn the Government as satanic, have we not been guilty of toward our untouchable brethren? We are guilty of having suppressed our brethren; we make them crawl on their bellies; we have made them rub their noses on the ground; with eyes red with rage, we push them out of railway compartments – what more than this has British Rule done? What charge that we bring against Dyer and O'Dwyer may not others and even our own people, lay at our doors? We ought to purge ourselves of this pollution. It is idle to talk of Swaraj so long as we do not protect the weak and helpless, or so long as it is possible for a single Swarajist to injure the feelings of any individual.[22]

Despite the best intentions of Gandhi and the Indian Constitution, India is still run very much along caste lines, although growing numbers of exceptions are being made for the talented or enterprising. Only a Bengali, and perhaps only Nirad C. Chaudhuri, could write the following passage and not be lynched.

The Hindu regards himself as heir to the oldest conscious tradition of superior colour and as the carrier of the purest and almost exclusive stream of blood which created that colour, by whose side the Nazi was a mere parvenu. When with this consciousness and pride he encounters a despised *Mlechchha*, an unclean foreigner, with a complexion fairer than his, his whole being is outraged. His deep-seated xenophobia is roused. He is intolerably humiliated, and in the unforgiving envy and hatred he seeks to obliterate the foreigner's superiority by casting on it the shame of the most loathsome disease which can afflict a man. The demented creature tries to console himself with the illusion that if in this world there is a foreigner fairer than he, it is only because that foreigner is a leper.[23]

Shiva Naipaul, the younger brother of V. S. Naipaul, wrote savagely about the impact of caste in Bihar, the most reactionary and feudal state in India, where villagers who question the power of the Rajput caste are frequently murdered by hired gangs.

The havoc caste can wreak has been nowhere better demonstrated than in the relentless degradation imposed over the centuries on the millions of untouchables. No other tyranny has ever surpassed it in cruelty. To the pariah, the temples were forbidden; instruction of any kind was forbidden; the free use of the public highways was forbidden. He was not allowed to have in his possession – or to recite – the sacred scriptures. He had to live apart from other men and draw his water from separate wells. He was condemned to the most squalid tasks. His mere shadow was polluting and its heedless deployment could lead to his murder. Those more fortunate could sleep with a clear conscience because to suffer

thus was his *karma*, his punishment for wrongs committed during the whirl of many lifetimes. The untouchable
was a felon preordained by fate and the extremity of his
condition was an ethical necessity. At the other end of the
scale, crowning the sublunar Hindu chain of being, was
the Brahmin, the earthly god. Such was the nature of the
system that came to full flower in Bihar. Hindu education
in Bihar – a monopoly, needless to say, of the Brahmins –
was mainly religious and ritualistic and imparted only to
the chosen few. The picture that emerges is one of a people
increasingly mired in superstition of the grossest kind, in
proliferating caste taboos, in all the neuroses connected
with defilement remorselessly channelled through their
Brahminical preceptors.[24]

This obsession with personal purity that inevitably accompanies the belief in caste purity is nowhere better portrayed than
in V. S. Naipaul's brilliant account in his first Indian travel
book, *An Area of Darkness*, of Indian blindness when it comes
to defecation.

Indians defecate everywhere. They defecate, mostly,
beside the railway tracks. But they also defecate on the
beaches; they defecate on the hills; they defecate on the
river banks, they defecate on the streets; they never look
for cover. Muslims, with their tradition of purdah, can at
times be secretive. But this is a religious act of self-denial,
for it is said that the peasant, Muslim or Hindu, suffers
from claustrophobia if he has to use an enclosed latrine . . .
These squatting figures – to the visitor, after a time, as
eternal and emblematic as Rodin's Thinker – are never
spoken of; they are never written about; they are not mentioned in novels or stories; they do not appear in feature
films or documentaries. This might be regarded as part of
a permissible prettifying intention. But the truth is that
Indians do not see these squatters and might even, with complete sincerity, deny that they exist: a collective blindness
arising out of the Indian fear of pollution and the resulting
conviction that Indians are the cleanest people in the
world.[25]

Arthur Koestler made a particularly savage attack on Hinduism. He spent some time in the late 1950s interviewing Indian mystics and 'Godmen', finding virtually all of them wanting. In the introduction to his book, *The Lotus and the Robot*, he asserted that 'To look to Asia for mystic enlightenment and spiritual guidance has become as much of an anachronism as to think of America as the Wild West.'

India has never severed its ties with the magic world. The editorial columns of the great Indian dailies bear the imprint of the twentieth century, but the back of the page, except for the Linotype, could have been printed in the sixteenth. There, in the marriage advertisements, parents specify their sons's and daughter's religion, caste, colour, height, education, and 'powerful' or 'excellent' mahamsa. One or the other specification might be missing, but never the mahamsa, the horoscope. It is a decisive factor in the choice not only of the candidate, but also of the auspicious day and hour for consummating the marriage. In half a million villages, where eighty per cent of the population lives, every important activity and decision is still regulated by consulting the stars.

The reason is, simply, that although India is going through an Industrial Revolution of sorts, it has never gone through a Scientific Revolution of the kind which changed the structure of European thought in the seventeenth century, supplanting magical causation by physical causation. Before that turning point, Europe was almost as deeply immersed in astrology and other forms of magic thought as India still is. But in Europe, that transformation of thought preceded the transformation of society; in India it is the other way round. Underneath the power dams and steel works of the Second Five Year Plan lies the ancient soil; one only has to scratch it and the black magic comes oozing out with its slightly rancid smell.[26]

Koestler was also scathing about what he perceived as traditional Hindu family values, with the result that his book was suppressed in India.

The young male's unconditional submission to the will of
his father, and the hierarchic structure of the family, were
designed to mould him into the stable, traditional cast, to
undermine his initiative and independence; the family
household was a school of conformity, obedience, resignation. All decisions were made for him by his elders; they
chose his bride for him while he was a child or before he
was even born; his education, vocational choice and later
career would be decided for him, after more or less liberal
discussions, yet ultimately nevertheless by others. The
result was an ingrained reluctance to make decisions, a lack
of self-reliance and independence, a tendency to evade
responsibilities. As long as he lived in the joint household,
his behaviour must be a symbolic denial of the fact that
he had a wife, children, a life and a will and opinions of
his own; respect for the parents implied denial of his own
manhood. Strictly speaking, no Hindu could consider
himself grown up as long as his father was alive. All this
was often no more than polite pretence; yet to this day
a large number of Indians give that curious impression of
never having quite grown up, of a rather moving, child-
like quality, an arrested development not of the intellect
but of the character, which seems somehow blurred,
soft, undecided and vague, without proper contour and
individuality. In extreme cases, they indeed seem to have
no will and no personality of their own – eager for praise,
over-sensitive to criticism, smilingly irresponsible, always
ready to oblige, yet stubborn in an infantile way, shy,
prim, prudish and sexless. This impression is, of course,
more often than not completely misleading, for underneath the meek and gentle manner there may be a furnace
of repressed passions, leading to unexpected outbursts,
or to the chronic, nagging conflicts which plague the
undecided.

The pressures in the family work in the service of the
same idea of perfection which is proclaimed as the ultimate
goal in Hindu religious philosophy: the shedding of the
ego, its passions, appetites, ambitions, idiosyncrasies –
the elimination of individuality. The process of character formation in the family was a kind of de-boning

process, inspired by the model of shapeless, spineless non-individuals, drifting through the world of illusions towards the ultimate deep sleep of Nirvana. The result of this ideal is still much in evidence on the contemporary scene. It is at the root of the spiritual and social crisis, the tragic predicament of India.[27]

In the 1960s, hippies converged on the Subcontinent in great numbers, frequently in search of spiritual and sexual escape from their stultifying middle-class life in the West. They often attached themselves to gurus, or 'Godmen' as they are always referred to in the less reverential Indian press. These Godmen ranged from plump Indian teenagers who took vows of silence to Krishnamurti, perhaps the first Indian spiritual leader to make a major impact in the West. He was told at an early age by the Theosophists that he was the incarnation of Christ on earth – a position he later rejected. Although by no means a fraud in the manner of more recent Godmen, his reputation as an ascetic was damaged by recent allegations of his protracted sexual liaison with a Western disciple.

But the practice of relying on a guru for personal advice and prestige did not start in the twentieth century. Abbé Dubois wrote about the use of such people nearly two hundred years ago.

People of very high rank, such as kings or princes, have a *guru* exclusively attached to their households who accompanies them everywhere. They prostrate themselves daily at the guru's feet and receive from him the *prasadam* or gift, and the *asirvadam*, or blessing. When they travel the guru is always in close attendance; but if they are going to take part in a war or any other dangerous expedition, the holy man usually takes care to remain prudently behind . . .

Princes, from motives of ostentation, affect to keep their gurus in great splendour, with the result that the latter's extravagant pomp often exceeds their own. Besides giving them very valuable presents, they also endow them with land yielding large revenues. Hindu high priests never appear in public except in magnificent state. They like best to show off all their splendour when they are

making a tour in their districts. They either ride on a richly
caparisoned elephant or in a superb palanquin. Many have
an escort of cavalry, and are surrounded by guards both
mounted and on foot, armed with pikes and other
weapons. Bands of musicians playing all sorts of instruments precede them, and numberless flags of all colours,
on which are painted pictures of their gods, flutter in the
midst of the cavalcade. The procession is headed by
heralds, some of whom sing verses in the high priest's
honour, while the rest go on ahead and warn the passers-
by to clear the way and to pay the homage and respect that
are his due. . . . All along the route incense and other per-
fumes are burnt in the high priest's honour; new cloths
are perpetually spread for him to pass over; triumphal
arches called *toranams*, made of branches of trees, are
erected at short intervals; bevies of professional prostitutes
and dancing girls form part of the procession, and relieve
each other at intervals, so that the obscene songs and
lascivious dances may continue uninterruptedly. This
magnificent spectacle attracts great crowds of people, who
prostrate themselves before the guru, and, after having
offered him their respectful homage, join the rest of the
crowd and make the air ring with their joyful shouts.[28]

Paul Theroux visited an ashram in the early 1970s while on
his journey through Asia gathering material for his travel book,
The Great Railway Bazaar.

I had been interested in visiting an ashram ever since the
hippies on the Teheran Express had told me what
marvellous places they were. But I was disappointed. The
ashram was a ramshackle bungalow run by a talkative old
man named Gupta, who claimed he had cured many people
of advanced paralysis by running his hands over their legs.
There were no hippies in this ashram, though Mr. Gupta
was anxious to recruit me. I said I had a train to catch.
He said that if I was a believer in yoga I wouldn't worry
about catching trains. I said that was why I wasn't a
believer in yoga. Mr Gupta said, 'I will tell you a story.
A yogi was approached by a certain man who said he
wanted to be a student. Yogi said he was very busy and

had no time for man. Man said he was desperate. Yogi did
not believe him. Man said he would commit suicide by
jumping from roof if yogi would not take him on. Yogi
said nothing. Man jumped.

"Bring his body to me," said yogi. Body was brought.
Yogi passed his hands over body and after a few minutes
man regained his life.

"Now you are ready to be my student," said yogi. "I
believe you can act on proper impulses and you have
shown me great sincerity." So man who had been restored
to the living became student.'

'Have you ever brought anyone to life?' I asked.

'Not as yet,' said Mr Gupta.[29]

The biggest hoaxer of all was Mohan Chandra Rajneesh, alias
the Bhagwan, who before his expulsion from the United States
on a number of charges had amassed the world's largest private
collection of new Rolls Royces. His approach to the meaning
of life was through a deft blend of religious platitudes and the
joys of uninhibited, not to say random, sex. By the end of the
1970s, thousands of well-educated Westerners had flocked to
his ashram in Poona for spiritual nourishment, usually leaving
considerably poorer than they had arrived, although to this day
many still preach the virtues of their late Godman, who
generally preferred to observe other couples copulating rather
than perform the sacred act himself. Hugh Milne, his former
bodyguard, wrote a damning account of his practices, which
often bordered on the farcical. In the early stages of his career,
Milne had to drive to the Bhagwan's village to pick up a cow
which had been offered by some of the Bhagwan's distant
relatives to supply the ashram with milk.

At first they could not believe that seemingly sophisticated, sensible people like myself could think that 'Mohan'
was the true guru, and that we had given up everything
to follow him. They said with surprise: 'You are following *him*, our Mohan? Is it true? Other foreign friends are
also following him, not just yourself?' The family brought
out pictures of Mohan and said, still wonderingly, '*This*
Mohan, this is the one you are following? He is having
lady disciples also, is that so? And he is still doing the hyp-

nosis? He was experimenting terribly on all of us when we last met him.'[30]

According to Milne, drug-dealing was quietly condoned at Poona and some female sannyasis regularly went to the five-star hotels in Bombay to prostitute themselves to gain more money for the ashram. The Bhagwan finally fled from Poona to the United States with some senior aides in the specially disinfected first-class section of a jumbo jet. With the help of his continuing band of wealthy supporters, he created a huge commune in Oregon, without bothering to follow local planning laws. Before long, he was arrested on a variety of charges while attempting to flee the country in a private jet. Expelled from the United States, he returned to India, where he became obsessed with the Aids virus, and died at his original ashram in Poona.

New Godmen spring up all the time, with the occasional 'Godchild' just to add variety. In one instance in Southern India in 1991, an eight-year-old girl was paid hundreds of thousands of rupees by ignorant villagers who believed that they could be cured of a whole spectrum of physical and mental ailments merely by having her blow on their faces three times. Nevertheless, despite such instances of fraud and fakery, there are, throughout India, numerous ashrams where disciples live blameless lives.

The Khumbh Mela is the largest religious festival in the world. Each year, Melas are held at several sacred sites throughout India, but every twelfth year, several million people gather at Allahabad. The travel writer and Byzantine scholar Robert Byron attended the festival there in 1930.

For a year beforehand the authorities had been at work preparing for the pilgrims' advent, staking out encampments, making water available, drafting special police and other law-enforcing bodies, and above all providing for the prevention of those disastrous epidemics of cholera which always threaten these assemblies, and thence are spread over the whole country by the returning pilgrims . . . The object of the whole excursion is a triangular spit of land, two miles and more from base to apex, along whose sides the holy rivers of Ganges and Jumna flow to union at the summit. The scene which confronts the new arrival as he tops the sandy ridge that constitutes the base of the triangle and separates the river shores from the surrounding country, is that of a desert suddenly peopled. The sun, pallid through a haze of dust, beats threateningly upon an endless vista of temporary dwellings, amongst which the pilgrims in their millions pulsate and subside with the indeterminate movements of cheese beneath a microscope. From far away on the horizon come two gleams of water, one from the left, the other from the right, the holy rivers whose uniting receives every twelfth year the personal homage of twenty millions of people. Fleets of small boats, loaded to the water-line, dot their sacred flux. The apex of the two shores, the actual point of confluence, is hidden by a swarm of humanity, a mere shadow in the distance, beneath whose serried feet land and water have no margin.

Fantastic contrasts meet the eye. Over to the left, the pink iron skeleton of a railway bridge thrusts into the sky. Above it circles an aeroplane, giving ten rupee trips to view the crowd. Down the great central way, two miles of beaten sand, which leads through a street of curving masts and bright floating pennants to the confluence, there lumbers an elephant, resplendent in plush and golden sequins, and bearing aloft three ragged figures, wealthy zemindars [landowners], who have momentarily cast aside the trappings of this world. Moving in the opposite direction a car contains a wealthy lady, who feeds 500 *sadhus* [holy men] every day. The car is a cheap American vehicle. But above her head a disciple holds a cloth-of-gold umbrella; while another fans her with a peacock fan. In a miserable booth by the side of the central way, a jeweller has set up shop with furniture of solid silver and a chandelier of solid gold. Outside, the *sadhus*, exponents of destitution, clamour for the unwanted anna, exhibiting, if they are fortunate enough, the mutilated stumps of absent limbs. Monstrous creatures they are. A dropsical Falstaff, belly pouching over to conceal the strand of rope that is his only decency, straddles to the camera, his face broken by an ivory smile and a garland of rich yellow marigolds falling down over his dusky paps to the quiver-

ing navel beneath. Another, emaciated as the fasting Buddha at Lahore, chignon plastered with dung, body
smeared with ashes, salaams with a sword between his
teeth, ready to hire himself for miracles and horrors. A
third is only a head, a matted football on the sand that I
avoid by stepping quickly aside, remembering those fearful tales of African Bedouins who leave their prisoners to
die, buried to the neck, with food and water placed within
their sight. Farther on, a circle of admirers surrounds a
three-foot dwarf, a pug-nosed bearded Hindu Xit, strung
with wooden beads, and whirling on his podgy Chippen-
dale legs to the clash of tiny cymbals.

Accompanied by a Parsi, I made my way towards the
confluence. As the waters' edge came in sight, humanity
thickened in its effort to reach the sacredest point of all.
Family parties, holding hands like Alpine climbers in
terror of separation, jostled past. Out in the waters stood
countless immobile figures imbibing virtue. Beneath
tumbledown shacks on the sloping sandbanks Brahmins
ministered to those who had bathed. Through a haze of
blown sand, yellow and sinister as a London fog, the midday sun, invisible, thrust its battery of heat and light.
Odours and cries, the soft tramp of innumerable bare feet,
the insistence of hurrying bodies, broke upon my dazed
consciousness. Humanity was pervaded by an intense emo-
tion, nebulous and universal as the sand in the air, as
though the nerves of the throng, strung tighter than violin
strings, were emitting sound in a key beyond the human
ear.[31]

Hinduism remains all pervasive as a religion and as a cultural
heritage. Even self-proclaimed agnostics, such as Jawaharlal
Nehru, had no objection to being cremated and having their
ashes spread on the Ganges. Nirad C. Chaudhuri is one of many
Indians who concede that, despite their secular stance, Hinduism remains of paramount importance in shaping their view
of life and of the world.

Even to this day I have not been able to shake off this feeling, this conviction of the material world around me being
insubstantial, although I have completely lost religious

conviction and also faith in the other world. Therefore I find myself at times in the curious position of being a denier of this world without having anything to put in its place. Though I have not the assurance of that duration which makes pyramids pillars of snow and all that's past a moment; though I have not the hope which makes one ready to be anything in the ecstasy of being ever, and as content with six foot as the moles of Adrianus; yet the earth seems to lie in ashes for me. And this happens to me not only in regard to the world which is of the world worldly, the world of far-stretched ambitions and maddening vices, but even with the world which is made up of the wild loveliness of the face of the earth; of the grace of animal forms; of light raining down from the heavens – the light of the milky spray of the stars which illuminates only when the universe is composed to rest by a vast darkness. The feeling seems to cut the ground from under my feet and throw me down from the only country I know into a dark abyss.[32]

6

TRAVEL AND TRANSPORT

'And now we come to the broad road,' said he, after receiving the compliments of Kim; for the lama was markedly silent. 'It is long since I have ridden this way, but thy boy's talk stirred me. See, Holy One – the great road which is the backbone of all Hind. For the most part, it is shaded, as here, with four lines of trees; the middle road – all hard – takes the quick traffic. In the days before rail-carriages the Sahibs travelled up and down here in hundreds. Now there are only country-carts and such like. Left and right is the rougher road for the heavy carts – grain and cotton and timber, bhoosa, lime and hides . . . All castes and kinds of men move here. Look! Brahmins and chumris, bankers and tinkers, barbers and bunnias, pilgrims and potters – all the world going and coming. It is to me as a river from which I am withdrawn like a log after a flood.'

And truly the Grand Trunk Road is a wonderful spectacle. It runs straight, bearing without crowding India's traffic for fifteen hundred miles – such a river of life as exists nowhere else in the world.

Rudyard Kipling, *Kim*[1]

There is still something Biblical about travel in the Subcontinent, a feeling which is enhanced by the appearance of huge numbers of the more penurious travellers in their robes with staves and bullock carts. Pilgrims add to the effect, often walking hundreds of miles to attend a festival before dispersing silently back along the roads at all hours of day and night. The bullock cart has not altered its purpose or appearance much in 2,000 years and still far outnumbers the fledgling car population of several million. And the movement of people is quite staggering. Chandni Chowk, Old Delhi's main thoroughfare, which is less than two miles long, is said to be host to nearly a million people on a busy day. Even if the actual figure is not half that, it is still an awesome spectacle, with all stages of road transport jostling and shoving for space already occupied by crowds of pedestrians, hawkers, mendicants and even the odd elephant. This kaleidoscope of vehicles and conveyances continues on the roads leading out of all the major cities, with the lethal addition of buses which lurch and honk their way through most obstacles. And then there is Indian Railways, endlessly carrying millions of passengers on thousands of routes every day in a profusion of categories ranging from the lofty 'First class AC' to the stifling 'Third class unreserved'.

Roads and railways may be the main means of transport in twentieth-century India but it was not always so. The most important mode of travel for many centuries was by river, not just in this existence but in the journey after death to the next cycle of life. The River Ganges, or Ganga, has been at the heart of Indian consciousness for 3,500 years. As Jawaharlal Nehru writes,

> the Ganges [is] above all the river of India, which has held India's heart captive and drawn uncounted millions to her banks since the dawn of history. The story of the Ganges, from her source to the sea, from old times to new, is the story of India's civilization and culture, of the rise and fall of empires, of great and proud cities, of the adventure of man and the quest of the mind which has so occupied India's thinkers, of the richness and fulfilment of life as well as its denial and renunciation, of ups and downs, of growth and decay, of life and death.[2]

The travel writer Eric Newby made an intrepid journey down the Ganges in the 1960s, usually by hiring whatever local transportation was available. After getting as far as Patna in Bihar, he and his wife were finally offered the chance of travelling on a motorboat which for some unexplained reason was owned by Indian Railways.

> It was a strange sensation being in a boat with a Captain, a Pilot and a real crew. For the first time since leaving Hardwar, we were in a boat with nothing to do. It was

the forty-third day of our journey and sitting on the deck, looking across the water, was like many other days we had spent on the Ganges but all run into one reel and speeded up. Women in mustard-coloured saris were bathing in the river and we passed villages of houses built of bricks and mud with red-tiled roofs and with cows and water-buffaloes huddled under the walls and others roofless and deserted. We passed dead palm trees which looked like old bent candles standing alone or in pairs in the flat country-side, groves of mangoes and willows with their branches streaming in the wind, and banyans balanced precariously on eroded earthless roots. We swept down past small white-spired temples, old men sitting in niches carved in the banks and places where little fleets of fishing-boats were moored under steep banks which had been worn as smooth and shiny as leather by the stream.

The navigation was difficult but the pilot never spoke. He leaned over the bows sniffing the river through his ragged moustache like a clever old hound on a scent. Sometimes he raised his hand and one of the deck-hands put a sounding pole over the side; sometimes he pointed to the left or the right and the boat crawled off across the stream at right angles to it; sometimes he waggled his hand and the helmsman reversed until he could nose it into another channel.

The boat only drew two and a half feet; but the river was a maze of shoals, and it was full of culs-de-sac with corpses floating in them on which big grey gulls paced up and down. In the narrows the water seethed like a pot of brown soup on the boil and in the long, wider reaches, where the silt had a chance to settle, it was a brilliant shade of turquoise. In these deep places dolphins came to the surface and nuzzled the bows of the boat.

Sitting on the roof of the engine-room, looking down into this great and noble river, the face of which was capable of such extraordinary changes of expression all in the space of a few moments, we both experienced that feeling which comes so rarely to human beings of wishing that the moment in which we were living, might be infinitely prolonged.[3]

By the time the Newbys made their journey, there was virtually no long-haul transportation left on the river. It was still crucial, but only for local transportation. However, river trade remained important around the mouth of the Hooghly, as Geoffrey Moorhouse observed in *Calcutta*.

There are flat boats moving round here with cargoes of hay so huge and overwhelming that the boat itself is invisible and all you can see is a floating haystack on the water; they are often moored in their dozens just above Howrah bridge, like an aquatic farmyard, and their crews have created a tunnel inside each stack, which makes a sort of home. There are tipsy little boats, long, slim, with low pointed prows, canting over at speed as the wind leans into their lateens. Outriggers flick by, bearing fishermen off to look for bhekti and hilsa. Sharp-stemmed and narrow lighters, with a canvas shelter stretched tight in a hump over the sterns, are parked in rows where they toss and bump each other like flotsam. And down the middle of the Hooghly there is always a procession of vessels moving rather grandly under square sails cocked at a jaunty angle, known as junks to the European and noayka to the Bengali. They are to be seen at their best when the wind has dropped, however, or when they are trying to make their way against it. For on the high curved poop, the serang leans against his tiller above the great triangular sweep of a rudder plunged vertically into the water, while in front of him four or six men stand up and work oars the size of saplings in one of the most graceful movements imaginable. In perfect time together they take three measured and swinging paces along the deck, dip in the blades and then lean back from the shafts while the boat slides forward under their pull. Rhythmically, almost studiously, they and their craft get the better of this turbulent river, which flows so fast that any boat trying to move straight across it rocks and rocks like a mad thing.[4]

Before the Europeans, who preferred the sea, both traders and conquerors usually came by land. There is a vast network of roads and tracks running the entire length of Asia that formed part of the Silk Road, and many of the offshoots of this network still function today. In 1333, when the Moroccan traveller Ibn Battuta first arrived in Sind on the border of India, he was deeply impressed by the quality of the road network created by Muhammad Tughluq, Sultan of Delhi from 1324 to 1351. The roads may not have been paved as in ancient Rome, but they were serviceable for most of the year, except during the monsoon. Providing there were enough runners available, the roads provided an efficient communications network between the Sultan's capital in Delhi and the furthest reaches of his territory.

From Sind to the city of Delhi, the sultan's capital, it is fifty days' march, but when the intelligence officers write to the sultan from Sind the letter reaches him in five days by the postal service. In India the postal service is of two kinds. The mounted couriers travel on horses belonging to the sultan with relays every four miles. The service of couriers on foot is organized in the following manner. At every third of a mile there is an inhabited village, outside which there are three pavilions. In these sit men girded up ready to move off, each of whom has a rod a yard and a half long with brass bells at the top. When a courier leaves the town he takes the letter in the fingers of one hand and the rod with the bells in the other, and runs with all his might. The men in the pavilions, on hearing the sound of the bells, prepare to meet him, and when he reaches them one of them takes the letter in his hand and passes on, running with all his might and shaking his rod until he reaches the next station, and so the letter is passed on till it reaches its destination. This post is quicker than the mounted post. It is sometimes used to transport fruits from Khurasan which are highly valued in India; they are put on plates and carried with great speed to the sultan. In the same way they transport the principal criminals; they are each placed on a stretcher and the couriers run carrying the stretcher on their heads. The sultan's drinking water is brought to him by the same means, when he resides at Dalwat Abad, from the river Kank [Ganges], to which the Hindus go on pilgrimage and which is at a distance of forty days journey from here.[5]

The Delhi Sultanate was ultimately supplanted by Babur, the first of the Mogul emperors. One of the independent warlords who briefly wrested power from Humayun, Babur's son and successor, was Sher Khan Suri, who ruled from 1540 until his accidental death in 1545. He was particularly renowned for establishing a strong government bureacracy and for developing the road network of northern India.

[Sher Khan Suri] on his side neglected no means for reconciling the spirits of the people, and rending himself worthy of the Throne he had seized. There was wanting at that time in the Indies one main conveniency for carrying on commerce. There were no settled stages on the roads, nor Inns for the entertainment of travellers. The Usurper therefore judged it necessary in order to invite dealers into a country abounding with all kinds of riches, to erect after the manner of the Persian Caravanseries or public houses of entertainment. Accordingly, he caused such to be built at convenient distances in the open country and in the villages.

Certainly did the invasion of Sher Sha produce no other advantage to the Indies than this alone, his reign could not be adjudged unprofitable. He did something more in favour of travellers. He settled in every inn a certain number of servants, who were to wait upon passengers *gratis*. Some had the charge of making the beds, and others that of looking after the furniture, and keeping them clean and in good order. He set a reasonable price upon all sorts of provisions for man and beast. He ordered baths and stoves to be built in most of those caravanseries, and rows of trees to be planted about them for the passengers to walk in. *In fine*, he ordered all poor travellers to be lodged and entertained at his own expense.[6]

Thomas Coryate, the eccentric English traveller, walked down what was later to become known as the Grand Trunk Road in the early seventeenth century and his speed suggests that it was well-maintained by the Mogul emperors. Coryate was a renowned joker and hanger-on in the court of King James I, where he was considered to be a 'privileged buffoon', although historians later admitted he was 'no contemptible scholar'. After writing *Coryates Crudities* about his wanderings around Europe in 1616, he set off on foot for 'the Court of the Great Moghull', spending a total of £2 10s during the ten-month trip from Aleppo to Agra.

> From the famous citie of Lahore I had twentie daies journey to another goodly citie, called Agra, through such a delicate and even tract of ground as I never saw before, and doubt whether the like bee to be found within the whole circumference of the habitable world. Another thing also in this way beeing no lesse memorable then the plainenesse of the ground; a row of trees on each side of this way where people doe travell, extending itselfe from the townes end of Lahore to the townes end of Agra; the most incomparable shew of that kinde that ever my eies survaied.[7]

The most detailed accounts of Indian travel in the seventeenth century were made by Jean Baptiste Tavernier, a French jeweller and trader with the rulers of central and southern Asia. He made six journeys to the East and, while he borrowed freely from other traveller's tales, there is an enormous amount of first-hand information in his accounts. Tavernier remarked that travel in India 'in my opinion, is not less convenient than all the arrangements for marching in comfort either in France or in Italy'. He described the virtues of the palanquin for 'those who can afford to take their ease'. For those who wished to make a proper impression, Tavernier had some useful advice.

> He who desires to travel with honour in India, whether by carriage or palankeen, ought to take with him 20 or 30 armed men, some with bows and arrows and others with muskets, and you pay them as much per month as those who carry the palankeen. Sometimes, for greater show, you carry a flag. This is always done by the English and the Dutch, for the honour of their Companies. These attendants not only conduce to your honour, but they watch also for your protection, and act as sentinels at night, relieving one another, and striving to give you no cause of complaint against them. For it should be mentioned that in the towns where you hire them they have

a head man who answers for their honesty, and when you employ them, each one gives him a rupee.[8]

More than a century later, the French botanist Victor Jacquemont confirmed the passable standards of comfort on the road when he set off for the Himalayas with a personal retinue of servants.

From Rogonatpore although the engineers have displayed but little ability, the road is nevertheless always good for a horseman; and my oxen and cars, tried as they have been, rolled on gloriously. Relays of porters are stationed along this line, to carry travellers who go past in palanquins; I have met two within the last sixteen days. There are also bungalows to receive them, as well as those who travel, like me, by marches. They are about the distance from each other that the oxen, camels, elephants, or servants on foot, can go in a day: five, six, seven, and eight leagues, according to the difficulties of the road. In these bungalows there are two very neat apartments, two bedsteads, two tables, and six chairs: in fact, two families might, at a push, find accommodation in them. Three servants attached by the administration of the post-office to each, are particularly useful to those who travel by palanquin alone. I found that at Rogonatpore occupied by a collector, on a journey with his wife and young child. He has an elephant, eight cars like mine, two cabriolets, and a particular car for his child, two palanquins, six saddle and carriage-horses; sixty or eighty porters to carry him from one bungalow to another, independently of at least sixty household servants. He dresses, changes his dress, and dresses again, breakfast, *tiffs*, dines, and in the evening takes tea exactly as at Calcutta, without abating an atom; glass and china are packed and unpacked from morning till night; glittering plate, clean linen four times a day, &.&.[9]

In 1842, Richard Burton, the Orientalist and translator of the *Kama Sutra*, set sail for Bombay with his bull terrier. He spent seven years in central India and in Sind ostensibly as a military officer, but really as a travelling linguist and scholar, or 'white nigger' as his contemporaries crudely put it. In Northern India the traveller risked being waylaid by groups of dacoits (bandits) or thuggees, the quasi-religious gangs who terrorized unsuspecting travellers until the middle of the nineteenth century. But in the south, the hazards, as described by Burton during a period of convalescence in the Nilgiri Hills, were of a different nature.

For the conveyance of your person, India supplies you with three contrivances. You may, if an invalid, or if you wish to be expeditious, engage a palanquin, station bearers on the road, and travel either with or without halt, at the rate of three or four miles an hour: we cannot promise you much pleasure in the enjoyment of this celebrated Oriental luxury. Between your head and the glowing sun, there is scarcely half an inch of plank, covered with a thin mat, which ought to be, but never is, watered. After a day or two you will hesitate which to hate the most, your bearers' monotonous, melancholy, grunting, groaning chaunt, when fresh, or their jolting, jerking, shambling, staggering gait, when tired. In a perpetual state of low fever you cannot eat, drink, or sleep; your mouth burns, your head throbs, your back aches, and your temper borders on the ferocious. At night, when sinking into a temporary oblivion of your ills, the wretches are sure to awaken you for the purpose of begging a few pice [the smallest Indian monetary unit], to swear that they dare not proceed because there is no oil for the torch, or to let you and your vehicle fall heavily upon the ground, because the foremost bearer very nearly trod upon a snake. Of course you scramble as well as you can out of your cage, and administer discipline to the offenders. And what the result? They all run away and leave you to pass the night, not in solitude, for probably a hungry tiger circumambulates your box, and is only prevented by a somewhat superstitious awe of its general appearance, from pulling you out of it with claw and jaw, and all the action of a cat preparing to break her fast upon some trapped mouse.

Burton considered that his comments on the palanquin were generous compared with those he reserved for its humble cousin, the mancheel. This simple device consisted of a pole with a canvas sheet suspended beneath it and a simple curtain which provided some respite from both wind and sun.

> In this conveyance you will progress somewhat more rapidly than you did in the heavy wooden chest, but your miseries will be augmented in undue proportion. As it requires a little practice to balance oneself in these machines, you will infallibly be precipitated to the ground when you venture upon your maiden attempt. After that a sense of security, acquired by dint of many falls, leaves your mind free to exercise its powers of observation [and] you will remark how admirably you are situated for combining the enjoyments of ophthalmic glare, febrile reflected Heat, a wind like a Sirocco, and dews chilling as the hand of the Destroyer. You feel that your back is bent at the most inconvenient angle, and that the pillows which should support your head invariably find their way down between your shoulders, that you have no spare place, as in the palanquin, for carrying about a variety of small comforts, no, not even the room to shift your position – in a word, that you are a miserable being.
>
> If in good health, your best plan of all is to mount one of your horses, and to canter him from stage to stage, that is to say, between twelve and fifteen miles a day. In the core of the nineteenth century you may think this style of locomotion resembles a trifle too closely that of the ninth, but, trust to our experience, you have no better.[10]

The Post Office was responsible for arranging much of the transport system in the Victorian era and usually had dak bungalows situated every fifteen to fifty miles on major roads which were available for individuals as well as officials. The postmaster was also responsible for arranging transport by palanquin, conveyed by a group of twelve men, which consisted of eight *palkee-burdars* (palanquin-bearers), two *mussalchees* (torchbearers) and two *bhangy-burdars* (luggage porters). The cost of this team was not cheap – the rate was usually one shilling per mile.

One of the more romantic aspects of the Post Office was its use of *hikaras*, or mail-runners, in the foothills of the Himalayas.

The runners were often of tribal origin and were renowned for their willingness to take on wild beasts and wandering criminals in order to get their mail bag through to its destination, although they sometimes detoured for miles to avoid the ill-effects of straying too close to a tree which possessed an evil spirit. One of the most celebrated routes of the runners was that between Kalka and Simla, before the advent of the glorious mountain train which still makes the spectacular journey today. Rudyard Kipling gave full vent to his nostalgia for the Raj in his poem 'The Overland Mail'.

In the name of the Empress of India, make way,
    O Lords of the Jungle, wherever you roam,
The Woods are astir at the close of the day –
    We exiles are waiting for letters from Home.
Let the robber retreat – let the tiger turn tail –
In the Name of the Empress, the Overland Mail!

With a jingle of bells as the dusk gathers in,
    He turns to the footpath that heads up the hill –
The bags on his back and a cloth round his chin,
    And, tucked in his waistbelt, the Post Office bill: –
'Despatched on this date, as received by the rail,
Per runner, two bags of the Overland Mail.'

Is the torrent in spate? He must ford it or swim.
    Has the rain wrecked the road? He must climb by
                                        the cliff.
Does the tempest cry halt? What are tempests to him?
    The service admits not a 'but' or an 'if.'
While the breath's in his mouth, he must bear
                                        without fail,
In the Name of the Empress, the Overland Mail.

From aloe to rose-oak, from rose-oak to fir.
    From level to upland, from upland to crest,
From rice-field to rock-ridge, from rock-ridge to spur,
    Fly the soft-sandalled feet, strains the brawny,
                                        brown chest.
From rail to ravine – to the peak from the vale –
Up, up through the night goes the Overland Mail.

There's a speck on the hillside, a dot on the road –
  A jingle of bells on the footpath below –
There's a scuffle above in the monkey's abode –
  The world is awake and the clouds are aglow.
For the great Sun himself must attend to the hail:
'In the Name of the Empress, the Overland Mail!'

Sir Geoffrey Clarke, who was Director-General of the Department of Indian Post and Telegraphs during the 1920s, recounted in his history of the Post Office of India a poignant tale of heroism and bureaucratic idiocy which came to his attention.

The Audit Office, that soulless machine which drives executive officers out of their minds, sent in an objection to a gratuity being given to the family of a runner who, when carrying the mails, had been eaten by a tiger. The objection was that gratuities were only given for death in special circumstances, for instance, when death occurred in the performance of some specially courageous action, and that, since carrying the mails was part of the man's ordinary duty, his family were not entitled to any consideration. The actual story of the runner's death, as told by the villagers and the village watchman, is this: The runner's beat had been recently frequented by a man-eating tiger, and several of the country people had been carried off by him during the previous few days. On the afternoon in question the tiger was known to be in the neighbourhood, and when the mails arrived the villagers warned the runner not to go then, but to wait until morning. Since the man-eater was an early feeder – that is to say, he killed his prey early in the afternoon, the runner waited until five o'clock and then persuaded the village watchman to accompany him. He hadn't got more than two miles when out came the tiger and seized him. The watchman escaped and took the mails to the next stage, and the family of the man who nobly faced death in the execution of his duty was deprived of its wage earner. This is a very bald account of a very heroic deed, and it is pleasing to learn that Mr Levett Yeats, the Accountant-General of the Post Office at the time, who was the very soul of romance and chivalry, dealt with his objecting subordinate in a manner worthy of the heinous nature of his offence.[12]

With the advent of the motor car there has arisen a pleasant myth that drivers on Indian roads are unconcerned about their meanderings because of an ingrained faith in their karma or fate. While this may be an appropriate explanation for the habits of the odd cyclist at a New Delhi traffic circus, it is totally inadequate when it comes to the vast majority of travellers. The determining rule is, to put it in a nutshell, *force majeure*. The driver of the rust-infested lorry that lurches straight at you on a narrow highway is safe in the conviction that, no matter the justice of the situation, if you are in a fragile Japanese car, you are going to head for the gravel. It is a minor miracle how Indian taxi-drivers keep their vehicles on the road. If a doorlock finally gives out, a stout piece of rope suffices to moor the door permanently to the chassis. The writer and journalist James Cameron provides an excellent first-hand account of the perils of riding in an Indian taxi in a modern city.

The rush-hour traffic of Bombay is a nightmare – not from dementia, as in Tokyo, nor from exuberance, as in Rome; not from malice, as in Paris; it is a chaos rooted in years of practised confusion, absent-mindedness, selfishness, inertia, and an incomplete understanding of mechanics. There are no discernible rules. The little Fiat cabs are old, but not as old as they appear; a few years of the Bombay free-for-all have aged them beyond their years. Our taxi's bumpers were tied on with wire; the steering-wheel had a play of about fifty degrees. It also appeared to be firing on about one and a half cylinders, and the driver had difficulty maintaining any revolutions. In consequence when he achieved any momentum he was reluctant to lose it, so that we would always swerve rather than brake, with a steady obligato on the horn.

Everything went too fast for safety, too slow for speed. The pedestrians abounded, swarming like white butterflies in vague, suicidal trances, either in violent conversation or in a mindless reverie.[13]

The weight of numbers has a profound impact on Indian travel as was eloquently described by Trevor Fishlock, the distinguished Delhi correspondent of *The Times*, in the early 1980s.

There is no Plimsoll line in India and House Full is a negotiable and elastic term carrying no idea of finality. Safety laws and ideas of danger are bulldozed by the weight of people. Two-wheeled tonga carts, drawn by desperate horses with toast-rack ribs, are piled high with swaying people and lolling babies. Bicycles often carry three. Motor scooters are often seen captained by father, with the eldest son standing in front of him, mother elegantly sidesaddled behind, a daughter clinging to her waist and a baby on her knee. Three pot-bellied men, comical in their gravity, ride by astride a motorcycle. Lorry drivers have three or four companions in the cab and knots of labourers on the back. Cage-carts, drawn by bicycles, are stuffed with little school-children on their way to lessons. If mother, uncle and brother-in-law are not too fat, a car may be able to carry seven or ten. In the cities pedestrians walk in the roads because they are often forced off the pavements by the communities living, sleeping and trading on them. The popular letter-drafting books, which contain specimen letters covering myriad circumstances and predicaments, have letters you can copy to complain of overcrowding on the pavements and in offices.

Buses are jammed, their proprietors packing them like the ruthless masters of slaving ships. At bus stops young men are disgorged from the windows of these ramshackle stinking monsters like weevils abandoning a tapped biscuit. Others scramble in to replace them. Women and children get little quarter. People wait in a mob on the road, eyeing the middle distance like anxious rugby fullbacks awaiting kick-off. Those who cannot get in cling to the outside and perhaps fall off, or are wiped off by other buses. When buses fall into rivers or canals, as they frequently do, the squirming passengers are too tightly jammed to extricate themselves, and the papers publish pictures showing corpses among the melting ice blocks of the morgue, cheek by jowl in death as they were in life.[14]

There were three great pillars of the British presence in India which still remain crucial for the country's unity – the English language, the Army and, last and probably most important of all, the railways. Despite all the obvious limitations of the railway service, tens of millions of passengers continue to rely on it for their daily needs. From a faltering start in 1845, the railway network gradually expanded. A direct rail link between Bombay and Calcutta was completed by 1870 and by the turn of the century railway lines crossed the entire Subcontinent. George Steevens, an ambitious young foreign correspondent for the *Daily Mail* who was later to die at Ladysmith during the Boer War, summed up the perils and virtues of the rail system at the very beginning of Lord Curzon's term as Viceroy.

Your own Indian carriage is not unlike the Indian house. It has space and all indispensables for existing in a bad climate, but little of finish or embellishment. In Europe, the sleeping-car mimics the drawing-room; in India, where often the very drawing-room is but a halting-place in a perpetual journey, a sleeping-car is merely a car you can very well sleep in. To it, as everywhere in India, you bring your own bedding and your own servant to lay it out. You take your meals at stations by the way; if there is no refreshment room at the right time and place, you bring your food with you. The European train is like a hotel; the Indian like a camp. Your servant piles in your canvas bundle of bedding, your battered dressing-case, your hat-box, your despatch-box, your topi, your stick, your flask, your tiffin-basket, your over-coat, your cricket-bat, your racquet, your hunting-crop, your gun, and your dog; you insert yourself among them and away you go.[15]

The most moving description of railways from an Indian writer is contained in a novel by Bibhutibhusan Banerji, published in the 1920s – *Pather Panchali*, which roughly translates as *Song of the Road*. This Bengali novel was the inspiration for Satyajit Ray's first and perhaps greatest film of the same name. The novel revolves around the lives of two Brahmin village children – Opu and his elder sister Durga. The author writes from a child's perspective, as shown by this description of the first time Opu sees a railway line.

A little way on Opu noticed with surprise that there was a road ahead of them. It stood high above the fields and looked like the metalled road to Nawabganj. It cut right through the countryside from far on the left to far on the right. Red-coloured stones were piled up in tiny heaps alongside it and there were pillars of white metal joined one to another by long lines of string. And the pillars went on and on; indeed as far as his eye could see there were white pillars and strings stretched between them.

'Look, child!' said Horihor. 'That's the railway line.'

Opu bounded through the gate on to the line. He looked up and down the track, his eyes wide open with surprise as he took in every detail. Why do those two iron rails run side by side like that? Are they what the train goes on? Why should it? Why should it go along them instead of across the fields? Doesn't it ever come off? What are those things? Are they what are called wires? What is that whispering noise that they are making? Is it a message going along them? Whose message can it be and why is he sending it? Where is the station? Is it this way or that?

'I want to see the train, Daddy. What time will it come?'

'How can you see a train now? There isn't one till midday; and that's two hours off.'

'It doesn't matter, Daddy. I want to wait and see it. I've never seen a train. So please let me stay, Daddy, please!'

'Don't make a fuss now. That's why I don't like taking you out with me. How can you see a train now? We should have to stand about in this sun until twelve or one o'clock. Run along now. I'll let you see a train on the way back.'

There were tears on Opu's eyes, but he had to go on after his father.[16]

The extent of the rail network in the Subcontinent is vast – one of the favourite statistics of Indian bureaucrats is that fifteen million people travel by train every day, which may be true though it cannot be proved with any certainty because of massive over-crowding. The following letter was reportedly written by a professional letter-writer to the Indian Railways just before Independence, asking for the guard and train driver concerned to be sacked because of an alleged incident.

Honoured Sir.
I was travelling on night train from Calcutta to Bombay side on first July. When the train stopped at Nagpur I got down from train with belly too much full with Jack fruit to do nuisance. Honoured Sir, whilst I was emptying bowels, bloody guard blew whistle. What could I do but run down platform holding my lotah [brass container holding water, used instead of lavatory paper] in one hand and my dhoti in the other exposing my shockling. Many people laughed. Honoured Sir, it is too much bad when passenger cannot get down from train to do dung in peace.[17]

English writers rarely mention such incidents when describing the railways, focusing instead on the exotic and humorous aspects of rail travel. Thus Rumer and Jon Godden on travelling on the railways in the 1920s:

Not only humans used the stations: there was always a sacred bull, wandering from camp to camp and calmly helping itself to the food; there were goats, chickens, pigeons and pie dogs which were well-fed compared to street ones – people threw scraps from the trains. The beggar children knew this; people even threw money, perhaps because travelling was so spendthrift anyway that a pice or two more or less did not matter. Beggars were not allowed on the platform – the railways had some rules – but the children bobbed up on the other side of the train and stood between the tracks rubbing their stomachs and wailing, 'No Mummy. No Daddy. No foo-oo-d,' but as they wailed they laughed and pulled faces at us. All along the platform were booths, kiosks and barrow stalls that sold inviting things, especially hot good-smelling Indian food but, 'Not safe,' said Mam and Aunt Mary. In those days there were no ice-cream barrows but sherbet was sold, and brass trays held sticky Indian sweets. Mam bought oranges and bananas, but not the open figs or dates. There were sellers of green coconuts who would obligingly hack off the top of the nut so that the customer could drink the cool juice, and sellers of soda water, lemonade and the virulently red raspberryade we always longed to try.[18]

Not so Denis Kincaid, who wrote in a far more realistic manner about the atmosphere of rail travel in the second and third classes in the 1930s, with no trace of the romanticism which usually plagues such descriptions.

In the carriage it grew hot. Turbans were pushed back from foreheads, saris slipped from shoulders, bodices were loosened. A party of mendicants began to sing their *kirtans*, strumming on single-stringed guitars, clacking castanets. A gramophone wheezed, wearily, over an incessantly repeated record, 'My lover is late. I can wait no longer. The autumn moon sinks among the palms and high overhead the wild geese are stirring at the rumour of dawn.'

People spat everywhere, urinated on the floor, waited in a queue for the single lavatory, which had never been cleaned, whose pipe had long ago been blocked and whose floor was ankle-deep in filth. An old *bania* seemed to be occupying the lavatory for an unconscionable time. They hammered on the door and, receiving no reply, burst the rusty lock to find the old man dead, having fallen in a fit and suffocated, his face among the excrement.

Hotter and hotter. Flies buzzed about the windows, sand streamed in at every crevice, hung in a grey cloud and settled heavily, inescapably, upon everything. Sweating faces were masked with a film of dust. At each station everyone left the carriage for a drink at the single tap fixed to the outer wall of the waiting-room. It was strangely silent at those little remote stations, to ears now attuned to the rattle and clamour of the train. The passengers walked up and down the platform, their sandals scrunching on the hot gravel. The bare and ochre landscapes shimmered in the noon heat. Vultures and Brahminy kites wheeled slowly in the sky. The air was full of the metallic clicking and murmuring of countless insects. Perched on a telegraph pole a crow cawed monotonously, meaninglessly. Then the engine whistled, everyone turned excitedly and scampered back to the carriages, laughing, pushing, shouting.[19]

There is certainly no danger of railways being supplanted by air transport in India, at least not until well into the next century, if my experience and those of numerous other travellers is anything to go by. On his epic journey recreating the original air voyage of Imperial Airways from London to Brisbane, it was only in India that the author Alexander Frater came close to defeat. It was nothing to do with routing, or inclement weather; the obstacle was a more tenacious one familiar to all who have attempted to make a reservation on Indian Airlines. The fun began when Frater attempted to reconfirm his booking. He vainly journeyed to the dank Indian Airlines office near Connaught Place in Delhi.

Dingy concrete steps led up to a dark landing posted with signs advertising the building's tenants. Indian Airlines was there among the lawyers, loss adjusters, astrologers and accountants, a large, low-ceilinged room with a man sitting at a curious little desk near the entrance. He wore loud checks and a flash tie and, peering through heavy spectacles, cocked a forefinger and beckoned, as though hoping to sell me a lottery ticket. I told him I'd come to confirm some flights.

'You mean reconfirm.'

'Yes,' I said. 'Actually, I was looking for Endorsements and Reconfirmations and Adjustments. It's the same thing, I suppose?'

'Reconfirmation is reconfirmation but adjustment is not endorsement.' His voice was hectoring, his manner combative. 'So what is it you are wanting? To adjust, endorse or reconfirm?'

'Reconfirm. Some flights for tomorrow.'

'How many flights?'

'Five. And one for the day after that. That's six.'

'How can you be taking so many flights?'

I showed him the tickets and, with a sigh, he drew a chitty pad towards him, wrote '6' on the top one and drew a careful circle around it. 'They will never reconfirm 6,' he said with absolute certainty, and handed me the chitty which had the number 145 stamped in a corner. 'Counter 24,' he said. The room was lined with counters, most manned by solitary clerks who, with nothing to do, dozed or gazed vacantly into space. Only counter 24, surrounded by a jostling scrum of men clutching tickets, was trading today. Above it a device showed an illuminated red number. It said 122. When it changed to 123 a magnified gong went 'boing!' and one of the three clerks in attendance shouted 'One two three!' It was going to be a long wait so I leant against a neighbouring counter and watched the clerk painstakingly mending a bicycle bell with his nailfile. When, eventually, my number was called I pushed through and handed my chitty to a plump lady in an orange sari.

'*Six*?' she exclaimed. Her lipstick was smudged and perspiration beaded her chin. 'Golly, I cannot reconfirm all this.'

'But I'm making five of them tomorrow. Delhi to Kanpur, Kanpur back to Delhi, Delhi to Allahabad, Allahabad to Varanasi then Varanasi to Calcutta. Calcutta is the day after. I *have* to reconfirm them now.'

'I can reconfirm Delhi – Kanpur only,' she said.

'What about Kanpur back to Delhi?'

'Kanpur – Delhi you must reconfirm in Kanpur.'

'But I'm returning on the same plane. It's only there for half an hour.'

'Then you will have to reconfirm double quick. Look, in Kanpur you must confirm for Delhi, in Delhi for Allahabad, in Allahabad for Varanasi, in Varanasi for Calcutta. And so on. Each flight must be reconfirm before each flight.'

I stared at her. 'Can't you just do it all on the computer?'

That got a loud laugh. Everyone joined in, including the customers. '*What computer*?' she said. 'There is no computer. All this reconfirmation business must be done manually by telephone and written chitties.'

Then she picked up my tickets, walked into an inner office and returned five minutes later to tell me that Flight 415 to Kanpur in the morning was full. 'But you are wait-listed. Be at Palam by 0700 and maybe you will get on. Also, your flight Delhi – Allahabad – Varanasi is cancel. It does not go tomorrow. It goes on Monday, but Monday flight is full. You wish to be wait-listed for that?'[20]

Indian Airlines may have a computer now, but the rigmarole involved in purchasing and confirming a ticket is no less nightmarish for the contemporary traveller who, to add further insult to injury, is obliged to pay a premium if he or she is a foreigner. V.S. Naipaul brings the experience up to date with his time in Bombay Airport.

Crowd and noise and threat and urgency outside, taxis coming and going in the mid-afternoon sun. Crowd inside as well, and noise, but it was a different kind of noise: it was more stable: it was noise of people going nowhere. There was only one internal airline in India; it was a state airline, and it was in a mess. It was said by various spokesmen that the flights of this airline had to be late because many of them originated in Delhi and there was fog in Delhi on many mornings. There were other pro-blems. The airline had never had enough aircraft, and in the last few weeks a number of aircraft had been with-drawn for one reason and another. Services were now in chaos. But air travel remained a necessary badge and privilege for important people, scientists and adminis-trators and business executives; and for weeks a fair por-tion of the country's most eminent men and women was, at any given moment, becalmed in the country's airports, as if by an act of enchantment.[21]

7

THE GREAT CITIES

The city fascinated me and repelled me, like Yoga,
like India. It was no good pretending the repulsion
did not exist: Benares is an incarnation of the Hindu
mind, full of shocks and surprises. You cannot view
her through the eyes of the flesh, or if you do you
will want to shut them. Her real life burns in the
Unconscious . . . Three miles of crumbling palaces
that lie in tumbled heaps with other palaces growing out of their ruins; and a confusion of richly-
carved cupolas pushing their way between tamarind
trees and tall flag-poles; and a fluttering of endless
companies of pigeon among a forest of straw
umbrellas; and below them a multitude of people
who worship by the glittering water–peasants and
priests, beggars and monstrosities and dwarfs,
sacred bulls that have been married to four holy
cows, cows with five legs, sleek girls with a skin
of ivory and very poor and parched old women, fat
merchants and thin fakirs, wise men and madmen,
old and young, birds and beasts, all mingling on the
bank and washing in the sacrosanct waters of the
Mother – that is the river-front at Benares.

Francis Yeats-Brown, *Bengal Lancer*[1]

Age in India is a deceptive thing. Benares, or Varanasi as it is
now known, has been an important city for nearly 3,000 years;
indeed it may be the oldest continually inhabited city in the
world. Despite its antiquity, however, there are no buildings
there that are even 500 years old because of a combination of
river erosion, invasions and constant rebuilding. The buildings
in India's four largest cities (Bombay, Calcutta, Madras and
New Delhi) are also all relatively new for the simple reason that
these cities were all founded by Europeans. As a consequence,

they are markedly different from earlier Indian cities. Delhi is a good example. Old Delhi, which sprang up nearly 1,000 years ago, is a maze of narrow lanes leading into courtyards crammed with traders and plastered with garish signs, whereas New Delhi, which was only completed in the 1930s, is centred on a grid of avenues and classical bungalows.

Life for the vast majority of urban dwellers in India is anything but idyllic. In some high-rise districts of Bombay and Calcutta, the population density reaches 400,000 per square mile. Despite the rigours of urban life in the Subcontinent, thousands of people continue to move to the cities every day out of economic necessity. The range of employment to be found in an Indian city is staggeringly diverse, and even without any prospect of employment there is always the possibility of begging to survive.

Factors other than that of economic necessity come to the fore in the growth of cities like Benares. For nearly 3,000 years, pilgrims have been flocking to the sandbanks of the Ganges at Benares to worship Shiva, the Lord of All, who is said to have made the city his permanent residence since the beginning of creation. It is also the place where Buddha preached his first sermon six centuries before Christ. The chief fascination of Benares for contemporary travellers lies in the city's vast profusion of temples and idols, which provide intercession for a multitude of problems, ranging from smallpox and death to marriage and food. Yet while one may marvel at Benares' divine inhabitants, its human ones provoke mixed reactions.

There is a strong streak of chauvinism amongst Benares' Brahmin élite. Ravi Shankar, India's best-known sitar player, invariably receives a frosty reception when he returns to play, usually for no better reason than that the residents feel he does not spend enough time with them. And then there is the behaviour of the middle classes. It is not unusual to hear of cycle-rickshaws being halted by residents or even policemen who throw out the fare-paying passenger in order to take it for themselves or a friend. Contemporary Indian travellers also complain that they have to negotiate a barrage of pandits, or Brahmins, who attempt to latch on to them upon arrival.

Ralph Fitch, the Elizabethan merchant, was the first Englishman to visit Benares, in 1584. Travelling down the

Ganges from Allahabad with a group of merchants, Fitch described the Hindu priests he encountered at Benares as beggars. 'They be a kind of crafty people, worse than the Jews.' However, he thought that Benares was an impressive city with 'many faire houses . . . a great place made of stone, like to a well with steps to go down, wherein the water standeth very foul and stinketh.' He provided a portrayal of Hindu worshippers in the Ganges which would be recognizable to any modern observer.

And by breake of day and before, there are men and women which come out of the towne and wash themselves in Ganges. And there are divers old men which upon places of earth made for the purpose, sit praying, and they give the people three or foure strawes, which they take and hold them betweene their fingers when they wash themselves; and some sit to marke them in the foreheads, and they have in a cloth a little rice, barlie, or money, which, when they have washed themselves, they give to the old men which sit there praying. Afterwards they go to divers of their images, and give them of their sacrifices. And when they give, the old men say certaine prayers, and then all is holy.[2]

Reginald Heber, the Anglican Bishop of Calcutta in the 1820s, also spent some time in Benares. From his perspective of living in Calcutta, it seemed an alien place.

[It] is a very remarkable city, more entirely and characteristically Eastern than any which I have yet seen, and at the same time altogether different from anything in Bengal. No Europeans live in the town, nor are the streets wide enough for a wheel-carriage. Mr Frazer's gig was stopped short almost in its entrance, and the rest of the way was passed in tonjons [sedan-chairs carried by four bearers], through alleys so crowded, so narrow, and so winding, that even a tonjon sometimes passed with difficulty. The houses are mostly lofty, none I think less than two stories, most of three, and several of five or six, a sight which I now for the first time saw in India. The streets, like those of Chester, are considerably lower than the ground-floors of the houses, which have mostly arched rows in front, with little shops behind them. Above these, the houses are richly embellished with verandahs, galleries, projecting oriel windows, and very broad and overhanging eaves, supported by carved brackets. The number of temples is very great, mostly small and stuck like shrines in the angles of the streets, and under the shadow of the lofty houses. Their forms, however, are not ungraceful, and they are many of them entirely covered over with beautiful and elaborate carvings of flowers, animals, and palm-branches, equalling in minuteness and richness the best specimens that I have seen of Gothic or Grecian architecture.[3]

Edward Lear's experience of Benares was surprisingly positive, given that he had feared he would have nothing to do during his brief stay there in 1873. He concluded that 'I am half wild when I think of my folly in coming to India at all. The only thing now is to make the best of a miserable mistake, even if I stay here for a week.' On his way to the centre of Benares, Lear gradually modified his opinion, although he did find the 'ape-temple, highly pagan and queer. Didn't like the fanaticals at all, at all', and the narrow lanes reminded him of Cairo, although the inhabitants were 'far more various in costume and manners'. Two days later, when he went to the Ganges to sketch the river ghats (flights of steps) and temples, he changed his mind entirely.

December 14, 1873

Got a boat, a large one, for no one can have the least idea of this Indian city's splendour without this arrangement. Utterly wonderful is the rainbow-like edging of the water with thousands of bathers reflected in the river. Then, the colour of the temples! and the strangeness of the huge umbrellas!! and the inexpressibly multitudinous detail of architecture, costume, &c &c &c &c !!!!Drew, more or less, as I was slowly row'd up and down the river, yet doubt if I can ever work out any satisfactory result after all. How well I remember the views of Benares by Daniell, R. A.! - pallid, - gray, - sad, - solemn, - I had always supposed this place a melancholy, - or at least a 'staid' and soberly-coloured spot, – a gray record of bygone days! Instead, I find it one of the most abundantly *bruyant*, and startlingly radiant of places full of bustle and movement!!! – Constantinople, or Naples, – are simply dull and quiet by comparison!!! Drew till 11.30, and then had the boat moored, and came below, where I and Giorgio had a bad lunch, with sherry and water *qua* consolation. It seems queer that people who charge five rupees a day, should send out uneatable mutton and fowl for breakfast! Happily, there are also eggs and bread. About 1.30 or 2, after having sate in the boat doubled up to avoid the hot sun, and gazing at the wondrous world of bathers, huddled close together, or shewing themselves singly to the devout multitudes of Benares, I began a drawing of the temples which I had vainly tried yesterday, and managed to get what, should photographs be unobtainable, may one day prove more or less useful. The mealy man of meditation came to the surface, and stood for a time wildly acting, and apparently intending a header, but he subsided into squatting and lute-playing; today he sports a feeble bit of string as dress. Many corpses are carried to burn at these steps. Some buffali and human corpses are thrown into the water; big black vultures congregate thereon, with no end of black crows. The pretty myna birds are numerous everywhere; pigeons by the 10,000,000. At 3, finished my last Benares drawing, and am truly glad to have seen this wonderful place.[4]

Raghubir Singh, India's greatest photographer, has a love-hate relationship with the city, which he has visited on numerous occasions while producing his photographic book on the city. He describes a typical day of a wealthy Brahmin.

He begins the day with a glass of *thundai* [milk-based aromatic drink] which is often laced with cannabis. Sometimes fine deposits of Ganges silt are also added to it. The morning ablutions are then performed across the river, on the sandbank facing the city. There the sick and the dying do not venture, because it is believed that those who die there will be reborn as asses. The healthy Baranasi washes and dries his clothes on the sandbank, exercises,

prays to the seven sacred rivers, anoints himself with san-
dalwood paste and pats himself with perfumed cotton
wisps. These rituals are performed in a leisurely manner,
interrupted only by exchanges of views with friends. It
is traditional for Baranasis to row out in groups to the
sandbank. On the way home, after praying at a temple,
they buy curds, sweets and snacks. The midday meal is
preceded and followed by a rest. After the afternoon siesta
the Baranasi attends to business. If he earns enough to
cover that day's expenses he is satisfied. He will close his
shop or office and resume his *masti* [reverie]. He is back
on the riverbank late in the afternoon and the morning
activities are more or less repeated. At dusk prayers are performed in a temple. He then slowly wanders through the
bazaar. A connoisseur of *paan*, he must stop at his chosen
shop for a chew of betel leaf and betel nut. The preparation
of paan is a delicate and subtle art in Banaras. Thousands
of paan makers vie with each other for the artful and taste-
ful assemblage of the Baranasi paan – famous throughout India. Chatting, exchanging greetings and gossip, the
Baranasi will then amble towards his favourite *kotha*
[room] to be entertained by dancing girls.[5]

Benares may be India's holiest city but for sheer influence on
the inhabitants of the country, Bombay is a strong rival. It is
the oldest of the 'new' major Indian cities and was first occupied
by the Portuguese in 1534 when it was little more than seven
islands surrounded by tidal mud flats. The Portuguese had
landed there in 1509, but the only comment the captain of the
expedition made then was 'Our men captured many cows and
some blacks who were hiding among the bushes, and of whom
the good were kept and the rest were killed'. Although the
Dutch also had designs on Bombay it was eventually ceded to
England by the Portuguese in 1665 as part of Catherine de
Braganza's dowry when she married Charles II. It was thought
a great prize at the time, but later Pepys called it '. . . a poor
little Island; whereas they made the King and Lord Chancellor
and the other learned men about the King believe that that
and other Islands which are near it were all one piece; and
so the draught was drawn and presented to the King and

expected to prove so when our men came thither; but it is quite otherwise'.[6]

The East India Company, then based at Surat to the north, formally annexed Bombay in 1668 from Charles II in return for a loan of £50,000 at 6 per cent interest and an annual rent of £10. Originally a small settlement created by a Muslim prince, it was known as 'Maha-Amba-Aiee' or 'Mumba Devi', after a local deity. The early British residents assumed its name came from '*Buan Bahai*', which means the good bay in Portuguese, but even before it was created, the Portuguese called it Bombaim. After less than a decade of British rule, its population had increased sixfold to 60,000, thanks to the vision of Gerald Aungier, the first Governor, who always had his meals announced by trumpets and usually served to the accompaniment of music. John Fryer, an East India Company surgeon, described the transformation of Bombay in 1675.

> At a distance enough from the Fort lies the town, in which confusedly live the English, Portuguese, Topazes [Indo-Portuguese], Gentoos [Hindus], Moors [Muslims], Coolies and Christians – mostly fishermen. It is a full mile in length; the houses are low and thatched with oleas of the coconut tree; all but a few the Portuguese left and some few the Company have built. The customhouse and warehouses are tiled and plastered and instead of glass use panes of oyster-shell for their windows. There is a reasonably handsome bazaar at the end of the town looking onto a field where cows and bufalloes graze [the east end of what was to become the Esplanade, which is approximately the site of the Bombay Gymkhana] . . . The Portuguese have a pretty house and church [on what became the site of the Victoria Terminus, next to the original Mumba Devi temple], with orchards of Indian fruit adjoining. The English have only a burying ground called Mendham's Point from the first man's name therein enterred, where are some few tombs that make a pretty show at entering the haven; but neither church nor hospital, both of which are mightily desired.[7]

Aungier himself also wrote to the East India Company at the same time, proudly announcing that before the arrival of the

English, the trade had merely been in coconuts and coir whereas now 'the country merchants derive a great trade with Surat, Broach, Cambay and Gogo, and also to Dabull, Kelsey, Rajapore and Goa, to Mocha, Persia, Scindia, Bussora, in salt, coconuts, cairo [coir], betel-nut, rice, elephants teeth, broadcloth, lead, sword blades and some other European goods'.[8]

Bombay flourished but it was to be overshadowed by events on the other side of the Subcontinent after Calcutta was founded thirty years later. For the next two centuries, Calcutta was the capital of India and also the most influential centre of economic activity. Bombay came back into its own after the opening of the Suez Canal in 1869. The time taken to ship Indian cotton and other products to London was slashed by weeks and local merchants became powerful members of the business community. With growing prosperity came the trappings of a great city. In the late nineteenth century, according to legend, Jamshetji Nusserwanji Tata, a prominent Parsee merchant, was ejected from Watson's, which was then Bombay's grandest hotel. In revenge, in 1903, he created the Taj, sparing no expense in installing Turkish baths, an electric laundry, a post office, resident medical staff and a chemist. The Taj is still the pre-eminent grand hotel between Rome and Bangkok, although in the 1930s the American writer Louis Bromfield was clearly less than enamoured with it.

In those days the Taj Mahal Hotel had the air of a vast and dreary county jail. Built around two or three great wells which ran the full height of the building, the stairs were of stone and the railings of iron, and around the great wells ran galleries, likewise with stone floors and iron railings. Off these the rooms opened, each one more like a cell than a hotel room, each specially furnished with an iron bed covered with netting and with a single hard mattress, a wash stand, and a couple of stiff, uncomfortable chairs. Overhead there was a large old-fashioned *punkah*, and outside on the cool slate floors slept the bearers. They slept there not only at night, but all through the hot days, when they were not gossiping with other bearers. The jail-like corridors were as much an exchange place of gossip as any market place. The bearers from one end to the other of the vast hotel knew everything about every guest of the hotel, his vices, his peculiarities, his meannesses or generosities. It was as if each room were walled with glass for all the world to look inside.

And downstairs on the ground floor there was a vast hall and a huge stairway which led up and up into the heights of the big hotel. Through the hall and the bazaar which occupied half its area, came and went a procession of Arab horsedealers, British Governors and Civil Servants, Russian and German trollops, Indian princes, jewel merchants, Parsee millionaires, comic middle-aged tourists, gamblers, oil prospectors. The procession went on day and night, for in the heat of the city and with the fantastic character of many of the guests, the place was as alive at four in the morning as at midday.

Above the vast hall there was another great room for dancing and drinking – a room with vast windows opening opposite the Readymoney Building against the heat, with a huge bar which ran across all one end of it where a score of bartenders, working on shifts, mixed gimlets and gin slings and *chota pegs* and served gin and tonic in quantities vast enough to float a ship. Around the edges of the dance floor, inside the tables, 'advanced' Indian girls and Russian and German tarts danced odd versions of what they believed to be the latest American dances. In those days, Bombay was a wide open town. The Taj Mahal, like the Raffles Hotel in Singapore and the Hôtel des Indes in Batavia, was a famous rendezvous for men and women from all over the East. They came from Sumatra and Macassar and the Malay States, from Medan Deli and Semarang and Borneo and Ceylon and Sourabaya. There is a legend that the hotel was designed to face the bay but that the Indian contractors who built it put it up the wrong way round, and that the English architect who designed it took one look at it on his arrival in Bombay and, seeing what they had done, hanged himself. Like the designer of Cologne Cathedral, rumoured to have been the devil, his name has been lost.[9]

Although this is an amusing tale, there is no truth in it – the reason the hotel's gardens are located at the back is so that they could offer guests a safe haven from the noise and filth of Bombay. Shiva Naipaul thought that Bombay was a particularly fragmented sort of place with no coherence.

> Much of the life of the city is invisible. It runs underground, rarely surfacing, conducted through the parallel but non-communicating channels of the various communalisms. Parsi politics (for example) touches only parsis and is, in fact, known to few outsiders. It is entirely self-contained. One of the first things that strikes one about the city – and Bombay, it should be noted, crawls with journalists – is the absence of any overall community of news and intellectual exchange. 'Bombay', as such, is an administrative abstraction. A strike of thousands of government workers passes almost unnoticed: no one discusses the issues involved. Who, you ask, are those people marching down the street waving banners? What are they protesting about? Nobody is certain. Every event is isolated, as significant or insignificant as any other, appearing out of the blue and disappearing into the blue. Nothing joins up to make a coherent picture. In countries where journalism is a developed art, the newspapers tell a continuing story. The stranger finds himself, as it were, plunged into the middle of a long-running serial. After a while, however, he begins to pick up the strands of the plot. He becomes familiar with the issues and the main characters of the drama. This does not happen in Bombay. The city is permanently out of focus.[10]

With a population density of 100,000 per square mile – more than four times that of Manhattan – people can hardly be blamed for averting their gaze from their neighbours and concentrating on those with whom they have something in common. Yet Shiva Naipaul does acknowledge the main appeal of Bombay – its unlimited prospects, if you happen to be highly energetic and have a huge amount of luck.

> Bombay gives everyone a chance. A walk along any stretch of pavement will reveal a hundred minute specialisations

of function, a hundred strategies for survival. You can hawk anything; water, nuts, cheap pens, toys, peacock feathers, religious bric-a-brac, plastic flowers, aphrodisiacs, quack medicines, lottery tickets, hard-luck stories – 'Ladies and Gentlemen,' says the handwritten appeal thrust into my hand by the teary-eyed, demurely dressed young girl, 'We are unfortunate people, we have been driven from our land by poverty. We ask donations from charitable and human people . . .'; you can grind lenses, repair broken locks, stitch leather, sell cage-birds, charm snakes, read palms, interpret dreams, clean out the ears of passers-by; you can parade your dancing monkey, display your acrobatic skills, pick pockets. The will to live is capable of infinite articulation. When life is hard, a man will do anything.[11]

Today, Bombay is unquestionably the premier city of India. New Delhi may have more politicians and influence-pedlars but the real financial muscle resides in Bombay. Property prices in Malabar Hill rival those in fashionable parts of London. Bombay is also the centre of the Hindi film industry, which still attracts huge investors desperate either for a quick buck or for intimate encounters with the latest starlets. Shoba De, for a long time the queen of the local gossip columnists, recently wrote a novel which captures the essential fickleness and ostentatious display of Bombay society.

> Anjali's wedding made it to the pages of a city glossy as the 'Event of the Fortnight'. It was quite spectacular. Mr Mercedes Benz had obviously gone to town on the production. The entire street leading up to his palatial marble palace on the beach was strung with tiny lights. The marble chips in the driveway had been shampooed for the occasion and were gleaming white. There were 'instant palm trees' in the garden – hauled in a couple of days earlier by his company's heavy-duty cranes and a special police *band-bast* had been organized with extra traffic police on duty for almost a mile down the road. The enormous swimming pool had been emptied out and resembled a brightly lit womb. This was supposed to be the discotheque for the night. All in all, pretty weird. While Cyndi Lauper wailed

in the blue-tiled pool disco, live *shehnai* players greeted guests at the entrance with wails of a different sort. Traditional marigold garlands were strung up over all the doors, while enormous western-style flower arrangements wilted in strategic places under strong spotlights.[12]

While Bombay has always been a melting-pot, Madras, which was founded by the East India Company in 1639, half a century earlier than Calcutta, was and remains a bastion of Tamil culture. It is now the rival film centre in India, although as its output is usually in Tamil, it does not have the same national attraction. The early settlers in Madras made a rather grander start than was thought prudent by the Company's directors who rapped them over the knuckles for their extravagance. They stated that it was 'A very indiscreete action to goe about the building of such a Fort when the Companies stocke was soe small', though they admitted that 'if ever the Companie have a plentifull stocke it may bee very comodious and advantagious for them . . .'

In 1780, Eliza Fay stopped off at Madras *en route* to Calcutta with her lawyer husband. Unlike later travellers, who often found the city dull, she was suitably impressed with the place.

Madras 13th April 1780

There is something uncommonly striking and grand in this town, and its whole appearance charms you from novelty, as well as beauty. Many of the houses and public buildings are very extensive and elegant – they are covered with a sort of shell-lime which takes a polish like marble, and produces a wonderful effect. I could have fancied myself transported into Italy, so magnificently are they decorated, yet with the utmost taste . . .[13]

In February 1810, Mrs Maria Graham (later Lady Callcott), who was living with her husband Captain Thomas Graham in Bombay, travelled to Ceylon to improve her health. Stopping off at Madras on her return, the 23-year-old visitor waxed lyrical, saying 'I do not know anything more striking than the first approach to Madras.'

The low flat sandy shore extending for miles to the north and south, for the few hills there are appear far inland, seems to promise nothing but barren nakedness, when, on arriving in the Roads, the town and Fort are like a vision of enchantment. The beach is crowded with people of all colours, whose busy notions at that distance make the earth itself seem alive. The public offices and store-houses which line the beach are fine buildings, with colonnades to the upper storeys, supported by rustic bases arched, all of the fine Madras chunam, smooth, hard and polished as marble. At the short distance Fort George, with its lines and bastions, the Government House and gardens, backed by St Thomas' Mount, form an interesting part of the picture, while here and there in the distance minarets and pagodas are seen rising from among the gardens.

Observing the fashionable meeting places for Europeans in Madras, she noted that the modish thing for the English community to do was

to repair in their gayest equipages to the Mount Road, and after driving furiously along, they loiter round and round the Cenotaph [in memory of Lord Cornwallis] for an hour, partly for exercise, and partly for the opportunity of flirting and displaying their fine clothes, after which they go home, to meet again every day in the year . . .

But the greatest lounge at Madras is during the visiting hours, from 9 o'clock till 11, when the young men go from house to house to retail the news, ask commissions to town for the ladies, bring a bauble that has been newly seyt, or one which the lady has obliquely hinted, at a shopping party the day before, she would willingly purchase but that her husband does not like her to spend so much, and which she thus obtains from some young man, a quarter of whose monthly salary is probably sacrificed to his gallantry. When all the visitors who have any business are gone to their offices, another troop of idlers appears, still more frivolous than the former, and remains till tiffin, at 2 o'clock, when the real dinner is eaten, and wines and strong beer from England are freely drunk. The ladies then retire, and for the most part undress and lay down with a novel in their hands, over which they generally sleep. About 5 o'clock the master of the family returns from his office; the lady dresses herself for the Mount Road, returns, dresses, dines, and goes from table to bed, unless there be a Ball, when she dresses again, and dances all night; and this, I assure you, is a fair, very fair, account of the usual life of a Madras lady.[14]

Twentieth-century travellers often find Madras dull and the surviving colonial architecture 'debased Victorian'. Madras is still the most important Tamil city in India and has been the power base for several political movements which have in the past advocated secession because of perceived northern Indian domination over Tamil Nadu. The city has a very different atmosphere from the rest of India and is certainly unique in the Subcontinent in possessing well-mannered porters at the airport. A local guide-book published in 1979 is delightfully honest about the charms of the city. 'The hurry scurry of a Metropolitan City is totally missing here. People of Madras believe in the maxim "early to bed and early to rise". As a result there is no night-life worth talking about.'

The attractions of Calcutta are somewhat different. In 1775, Robert Clive described Calcutta as 'one of the most wicked Places in the Universe'. A century later, Rudyard Kipling captured the essence of the place.

There is only one city in India. Bombay is too green, too pretty, and too strugglesome; and Madras died ever so long ago. Let us take our hats off to Calcutta, the many-sided, the smoky, the magnificent, as we drive in over the Hughli Bridge in the dawn of a still February morning. We have left India behind us at Howrah Station, and we now enter foreign parts. No, not wholly foreign. Say rather too familiar . . . 'Why, this is London! This is the docks. This is imperial. This is worth coming across India to see!'

Then a distinctly wicked idea takes possession of the mind: 'What a dive – what a heavenly place to *loot*!' . . . adorned, docked, wharfed, fronted, and reclaimed by Englishmen, existing only because England lives, and dependent for its life on England. All India knows of the Calcutta Municipality; but has anyone thoroughly investigated the Big Calcutta Stink? There is only one.

Benares is fouler in point of concentrated, pent-up muck,
and there are local stenches in Peshawar which are stronger
than the B.C.S.; but for diffused soul-sickening expan-
siveness, the reek of Bombay beats both Benares and
Peshawar. Bombay cloaks her stenches with a veneer of
assafoetida and tobacco; Calcutta is above pretence. There
is no tracing back the Calcutta plague to any one source.
It is faint, it is sickly and it is indescribable; . . . it is certainly not an Indian smell. It resembles the essence of corruption that has rotted for the second time – the clammy
odour of blue slime. And there is no escape from it . . .
The thing is intermittent. Six moderately pure mouthfuls
of air may be drawn without offence. Then comes the
seventh wave and the queasiness of an uncultivated
stomach. If you live long enough in Calcutta you grow
used to it. The regular residents admit the disgrace, but
their answer is: 'Wait till the wind blows off the Salt Lake
where the sewage goes, and *then* you'll smell something.'
That is their defence![15]

Calcutta was founded in 1690 by Job Charnock, an East India
Company official who was granted a tract of land eighty miles
up the Hooghly river by the Nawab of Bengal. He had earned
the respect of Emperor Aurangzeb by sending him a physician
to cure him of a carbuncle. Charnock had reputedly met his
Indian bride as she was about to be immolated on the funeral
pyre of her late husband. Charnock was a pretty rough diamond; he allegedly liked to have erring servants beaten near his
dining-room window so he could personally hear their moans.
There were good strategic reasons for founding Calcutta on its
present site – it was the farthest navigable point on the
Hooghly river and was protected from attack by the river to
its west. The other major advantage of the Hooghly was that
it tapped the vast riches of the Ganges river basin so that the
wealth of the hinterland of Bengal had to pass through
Calcutta.

By the end of the eighteenth century, Calcutta was a formidable economic powerhouse as well as the capital of the East
India Company's government. Many impoverished Englishmen
made their fortunes there as traders before returning to

England to flaunt their new-gotten gains. William Hickey, for many years a Calcutta lawyer and one of the most lively diarists of the period, described the revelry of these nabobs in the 1780s.

A *fête-champêtre* announced as to be given by Mr Edward Fenwick, a gentleman high in the Civil Service, entirely engaged the public attention and conversation during the greater part of the month of May. It was intended to be celebrated at his country house, situated upon the banks of the river, in Garden Reach, about five miles from Calcutta, which thentofore had been the property and place of residence of my esteemed friends Mr and Mrs Lacam. The gardens were to be brilliantly illuminated with many thousands of coloured lamps; an eminent operator in fireworks had been brought down from Lucknow to display his talents; the company to appear in fancy dresses, those that chose it wear masks. Ranges of tents were fixed in different parts of the garden, wherein tables were laid covered with all the dainties the best French cooks could produce, for the accommodation of three hundred persons, besides which every room in the house was stored with refreshments of every sort and kind; different bands of martial music were stationed in several parts of the gardens, and also in the house, with appropriate and distinct performers for the dancers. The last two miles of the road were lighted up with a double row of lamps on each side, making every object as clear as day. In short, nothing could exceed the splendour of the preparations of this rural entertainment.

Hickey, who confessed to having become 'sadly intoxicated' at a get-together he gave before the party, fell off his phaeton and scraped half the skin off his face 'although the quantity of claret I had swallowed rendered this a matter of indifference . . . My dress was a light blue silk domino which from my tumble into a deep brick dust, added to the blood streaming from my lacerated face, was in a sorry condition.'[16] However, he continued to entertain everyone until the celebrations broke up at seven in the morning.

In marked contrast to this high living, Calcutta's general

corruption and degradation were a constant theme of travellers such as William MacIntosh, writing at the same period.

It is a truth that, from the western extremity of California to the eastern coast of Japan, there is not a spot where judgement, taste, decency and convenience are so grossly insulted as in that scattered and confused chaos of houses, huts, sheds, streets, lanes, alleys, windings, gullies, sinks and tanks, which, jumbled into an undistinguished mass of filth and corruption, equally offensive to human sense and health, compose the capital of the English Company's Government in India. The very small portion of cleanliness which it enjoys is owing to the familiar intercourse of hungry jackals by night, and ravenous vultures, kites, and crows by day. In like manner it is indebted to the smoke raised in public streets, in temporary huts and sheds, for any respite it enjoys from mosquitos, the natural productions of stagnant and putrid waters.[17]

The current population of Calcutta is somewhere around twelve million, but such a figure is at best an educated guess. The crowded conditions may seem to be the result of overpopulation but in fact Calcutta was always straining to contain its inhabitants. In a letter written in 1901, Sir Rabindranath Tagore, the celebrated Bengali poet, explained to a friend that he could not return to live in the city because 'for me life is fruitless, somehow, in Calcutta's crowds: they put me in such a bad mood that every trivial thing annoys me. I can't preserve my peace of mind there, forgiving people and avoiding conflict.'

The entire population of India increases by approximately 40,000 a day and no small proportion of them are either born in or head for the big cities in the vain hope of bettering their prospects. The number of beggars in Calcutta, too, is a matter of conjecture. Geoffrey Moorhouse described the situation twenty years ago – since then, conditions have deteriorated.

No one knows how many beggars there are in the city; the only clue is the estimate that there are 400,000 men in town without a job. There is beggary all over India, but nowhere is there beggary on the scale of Calcutta's. There are not many places where a European can move a hundred yards in the certainty that his charity will not be invoked. An old man with one leg, using a quarter staff in place of the other like a figure from Bruegel, stumps up and mutters subservience with downcast eyes and outstretched tin bowl. A woman rushes to your side and almost thrusts her sleeping child into your face, supplicating mournfully. These are commonplace figures of the landscape. So are the children who come at you with terrible histrionics in which tears begin to stream and sobs become uncontrolled and hands are held upstretched below chins to the cry of 'No Mamma, no Papa, paise, paise'; and round the corner there is a dwarf woman with the same cry on her lips, though her bandy little legs must have been carrying her around for the best part of fifty years. There are beggars who are horribly mutilated; a small boy without feet or hands, who clumps along an arcade upon wooden blocks which have been strapped to his knees and elbows, while he holds a bowl between his teeth; a man who lies on his back outside the Grand Hotel, his limbs at grotesque angles, squirming violently while he bangs his tin on the ground for attention; and twenty-five yards away, another fellow who uses one arm as a crutch to lever the rest of an apparently lifeless and rigid body along, while tendons stand out on his neck like ropework and his mouth bares its teeth in a werewolf grin.[18]

Despite the frequently repeated horror stories of life in Calcutta, it is a stimulating experience to visit the city because of the intellectual exuberance of the Bengalis. There is no city in the Subcontinent which possesses more publications on, and interest in, the arts of all kinds. It is as if life takes on a greater degree of urgency when death is such a near neighbour. In recent years, west Bengal has been ruled by the Communist Party and the municipal authorities have a good reputation for coping as best they can with the day-to-day running of the city. In the 1970s, Calcutta was finally eclipsed by Bombay as the economic capital of India but the scale of the buildings remains as strong evidence of its imperial past.

A casual visit to Old Delhi leaves no one in any doubt that

this too was an imperial capital. Any visitor to the Red Fort will be struck by the scale of it – the vast red stone walls which appear to go on for miles, the huge entrance over the dry moat, and the remnants of grandeur inside the fort itself. This, and the numerous other more ruinous high walls which suddenly emerge next to a bustling road, all reinforce the notion of Delhi's past greatness as the nexus of the Mogul Empire. And then, of course, there are the spectacular tombs which are spread about Delhi. The Lodi tombs are the focus of the Lodi Gardens, while Humayun's tomb dominates Nizamuddin; elsewhere there are innumerable other mausoleums which now stand cheek by jowl with modern structures. Some scholars say that there were at least seven cities on the sites of Old and New Delhi, while others place the figure at twice that. It is hardly surprising that at the turn of the century Lord Curzon should have defined Delhi as little more than 'the deserted cities of dreary and disconsolate tombs'. In 1921, the French politician Georges Clemenceau was shown over the work in progress on New Delhi, prompting him to remark to the Viceroy, Lord Chelmsford, 'Magnificent! It will certainly make the finest ruin of the lot.'

It was not a new observation. When Leopold von Orlich was visiting Delhi in the 1840s, his reverie over the view of ruined fortresses, mosques, minarets and memorials from the top of the Qutub-Minar was rudely interrupted by his guide, 'a handsome Hindoo', who reputedly remarked: 'Sahib, here nothing is durable; much tribulation and little joy: the living thought only of reposing after death in splendid sepulchres, and their descendants have thought only of destroying what was intended for eternity.'[19]

The Italian traveller Niccolao Manucci gave a detailed description of seventeenth-century Delhi, when it was reconstructed by Shah Jehan, the builder of the Taj Mahal. Like all past and future rulers of Delhi, he incorporated the existing walls and structures in his own grand plan.

> The walls of the city are built one half of brick and the rest of stone. At every hundred paces is [a] strengthening bastion, but on these there is no artillery. The chief gates are the one leading to Agra and the one leading to Lahore.

Within the city are large and well built bazars, where are sold things of every kind. The chief bazars are those that correspond with the streets leading to the fortress, and end with the two above-named gates. There are also in Delhi fine palaces for the nobles; a great number of the other houses have thatched roofs, but are highly decorated and commodious inside. The city on the eastern side along which the river Jamnah flows, has no wall. In one corner of the city, on the northern side, is the royal fortress, facing to the east. In front of it, between it and the river, is left a sufficient space for the elephant fights. The king sits at a window to look on, as likewise the women, but they are behind gratings. Thence also the king beholds the parades held on the same space, of the omaraos [umara, grandees], rajahs, and nobles. Beneath the royal balconies there is, night and day, a mad elephant kept out of ostentation.[20]

The concomitant of this extraordinarily lavish display was that it acted as a magnet to every central Asian warlord or looter, and consequently Delhi was sacked with sickening regularity over the centuries. The last major sacking, if we exclude British vengeance after the Mutiny, occurred in 1739, when the Persian ruler Nadir Shah succeeded in looting a considerable amount of treasure, including the Peacock Throne which contained the Koh-i-noor diamond. The destruction of Delhi continued unabated during the next two decades, as rivals for the throne fought it out, joined at a later stage by Maharattan armies which further terrified the remaining residents, some of whom reportedly resorted to cannibalism to survive. Even allowing for the exaggerated style of the following account by a Mogul poet, the city was not a pretty sight.

How can I describe the desolation of Delhi? There is no house from where the jackal's cry cannot be heard. The mosques at evening are unlit and deserted, and only in one house in a hundred will you see a light burning. Its citizens do not possess even the essential cooking pots, and vermin crawl in the places where in former days men used to welcome the coming of spring with music and rejoicing. The lovely buildings which once made the famished man forget his hunger are in ruins now. In the once-beautiful gardens where the nightingale sang his love songs to the rose, the grass grows waist-high around the fallen pillars and ruined arches. In the villages round about, the young women no longer come to draw water at the wells and stand talking in the leafy shade of the trees. The villages are deserted, the trees themselves are gone, and the wells are full of corpses. Delhi, you never deserved this terrible fate, you who were once vibrant with life and love and hope, like the heart of a young lover, for whom men afloat upon the ocean of the world once set their course as to the promised shore, you from whose dust men came to gather pearls. Not even a lamp of clay now burns where once the chandelier blazed with light. Those who once lived in great mansions now eke out their lives among the ruins. Thousands of hearts once full of hope are sunk in despair. Women of noble birth, veiled from head to foot, stand in the streets carrying in the arms their little children, lovely as fresh flowers; they are ashamed to beg outright, and offer for sale rosaries made from the holy clay of Karbala.

But Sauda, still your voice, for your strength fails you now. Every heart is aflame with grief, every eye brimming with tears. There is nothing to be said but this: We are living in a special kind of age. So say no more.[21]

Within thirty years, the British had managed to set themselves up in Delhi, while still maintaining the Mogul emperor as a figurehead. Real power resided with David Ochterloney, the first British Resident of Delhi and one of the most colourful of the early British adventurers. His large classical Delhi residence still stands off Chandni Chowk, although it is now owned by the Delhi Technological Institute. By the time Victor Jacquemont, the French botanist, arrived in Delhi in 1830, Ochterloney was long gone, but the enfeebled Emperor remained.

Delhi! Delhi is the most hospitable part of India. Do you know what had well nigh happened to me this morning? I was near being made *the light of the world*, or *the wisdom of the state*, or *the ornament of the country*, &.; but fortunately I got off with the fear only. The explanation is as follows: you will laugh. The Great Mogul, Shah Mohammed Acbar Rhize Badshah, to whom the political resident had addressed a petition to present me to his majesty, very graciously held a *durbar* [public levee] in order to receive me. Being conducted to the audience by the resident, with tolerable pomp, a regiment of infantry, a strong escort of cavalry, an army of domestics and ushers, the whole completed by a troop of richly caparisoned elephants, I presented my respects to the emperor, who was pleased to confer on me a *khelat* or dress of honour, which was put on with great ceremony, under the inspection of the prime minister; and, accoutred like Taddeo in Kaimakan (if you recollect the Italiana in Algieri) I re-appeared at court. The emperor then (mark, if you please, that he is descended in a direct line from Timour or Tamerlane) with his imperial hands fastened a couple of jewelled ornaments to my hat (a white one), previously disguised into a turban by his vizier; I kept my countenance excellently well during this imperial farce, seeing there are no looking-glasses in the throne room, and that I could only see in my masquerade my long legs in black pantaloons appearing from under my Turkish dressing gown. The emperor inquired if there was a king in France, and if English was spoken there.[22]

In 1911, residents of Calcutta were horrified when what was then termed the world's best-kept secret – the plan to move the capital from there to Delhi – was announced by King George V. There was a certain logic to the move from the British point of view, as explained by Lord Hardinge in his dispatch to the Secretary of State for India of 25 August 1911. He claimed that 'the change would strike the imagination of the people of India as nothing else could do, would send a wave of enthusiasm throughout the country and would be accepted by all as the assertion of an unfaltering determination to maintain British rule in India.' The following year, the English architect Edwin Lutyens was appointed to supervise the planning of the new city, which is located to the south of Old Delhi amongst the tombs and mausoleums of past empires. He crowned the new city with the magnificent Viceroy's Residence, now the home of the President of India. The traveller Robert Byron spent some time in Delhi in the late 1920s *en route* to Tibet. A passionate student of architecture, he was deeply impressed with the work in progress. Byron was highly critical of the Mogul buildings in Old Delhi – they filled him 'with horror', even the Red Fort, which he conceded had 'moments of beauty but it is all so *bad* fundamentally'. No such complaints were voiced about New Delhi.

Hotel Cecil, Delhi
December 30, 1929

I can't *describe* to you how beautiful it is – nothing but the Piazza of St Peter's can compare with it. The work of an Artist triumphing after 17 years' struggle over every stone, bush and drop of water with official India. The Viceroy's House is the first real vindication of modern architecture, it *succeeds*, where all the others have only been attempts. It is *really* modern, not quite cubist, or skyscrapery. My admiration for Lutyens is unbounded. His versatility is so astounding – every niche and ornament of the inside is his, every flower in the garden. It is so fantastic too, a lot of it – fountains all over the roof – gold dome – glass star 15 ft high on a column (this isn't up) – pillar of smoke from the top of the War Memorial Arch. And the *size*, miles of waterways all coped in the local deep red sandstone, a delicious deep red with a cream in it. While above the foundations the buildings are of cream stone from the same quarries. I could go on for ever about it. People don't *realise* what has been done, how stupendous it is, and such a work of beauty, so unlike the English – one would never have thought of them – it will be a mystery to historians. Such a triumph, to have created this to leave behind us, when no one talks of anything but 'welfare' and 'our Mission' and the King Emperor and all the whole damned rot. Not content with not realising what has been done, people of all kinds and opinions set out to crab for all they're worth – what a waste of money when there aren't enough midwives – 'Modern' too, why weren't the arches pointed? Why have anything Indian about it? Why move the capital from Calcutta at all? It makes one sick, and what Lutyens must have endured to get it done at all passes belief.[23]

After New Delhi was completed in 1931, there were many critics who found it arid and formal, rather like a grander version of a military cantonment. Alan Moorehead, the brilliant Australian war correspondent, passed through Delhi during the Second World War and was one of those who was highly critical of the entire operation.

The British wanted an Imperial City, a place of spreading avenues and fountains, of massive administrative blocks and ponderous monuments. They got it. Lutyens spared nothing. The central post office went *here*, the commander-in-chief's house went *there*, the imperial arch at this end of the park and the Viceroy's house at the other . . . New Delhi, as a result, looks exactly like it was in the beginning – a set of architect's drawings . . . It is a mistake, however, to imagine that New Delhi has anything to do with India. It still is an enormous English club, the finest in the world.[24]

After Independence, the overall layout of Lutyens' New Delhi remained until well into the 1970s, with the central area relatively intact and satellite suburbs and slums absorbing most of the growing population. Since Independence, Delhi has gained the reputation of being ill-mannered and crude, as described by Khushwant Singh in his eponymous novel.

To the stranger Delhi may appear like a gangrenous accretion of noisy bazaars and mean-looking hovels growing round a few tumbledown forts and mosques along a dead river. If he ventures into its narrow, winding lanes, the stench of raw sewage may bring vomit to his throat. The citizens of Delhi do little to endear themselves to anyone. They spit phlegm and bloody betel-juice everywhere; they urinate and defecate whenever and wherever the urge overtakes them; they are loud-mouthed, express familiarity with incestuous abuse and scratch their privates while they talk.[25]

In the past two decades opportunistic development has taken its toll and ruined some of the more elegant areas of New Delhi. Enormous profits have been made by demolishing many of the fine bungalows and erecting ugly, often poorly built sky-scrapers in their place. Just after the wholesale vandalism began, Jan Morris wrote that Delhi was 'the capital of the losing streak. It is the metropolis of the crossed wire, the missed appointment, the puncture, the wrong number.'

Delhi is not just a national capital, it is one of the political ultimates, one of the prime movers. It was born to power, war and glory. It rose to greatness not because holy men saw visions there but because it commanded the strategic routes from the Northwest, where the con-querors came from, into the rich flatlands of the Ganges delta. Delhi is a soldier's town, a politicians' town, a journalists', diplomats' town. It is Asia's Washington, though not so picturesque, and lives by ambition, rivalry and opportunism.[26]

Because of the growing power of the central government, Delhi is now far more influential than it was only two decades ago. Although Bombay remains the economic and financial cen-tre of India, Delhi is where all influence-seekers end up at some point, so that those who imagine that New Delhi may become the grandest ruin of them all may have some time to wait.

8

VILLAGE INDIA

Unfortunately, India has few important towns.
India is the country, fields, fields, then hills, jungle, hills, and more fields. The branch line stops,
the road is only practicable for cars to a point, the
bullock-carts lumber down the side tracks, paths
fray out into the cultivation, and disappear near a
splash of red paint. How can the mind take hold of
such a country? Generations of invaders have tried,
but they remain in exile.

E. M. Forster, *A Passage to India*[1]

About 80 per cent of India's population live in villages, of which
there are perhaps 700,000. Nearly half of all villages have no
electricity and in most of them life is prescribed by the boun-
daries of the neighbouring settlement except in times of pilgrimage or migration for work. A contemporary historian has
estimated that one-third of all Indian villages lie more than five
miles from the nearest road and that most villagers live virtually
cut off from the remainder of the population. The villages, too,
are bastions of traditional social beliefs. In some of the remoter
villages in Rajasthan, the primary schools will have only a handful of girls to twenty or more boys, which leads to suspicions
of female infanticide.

Within the village itself, there are still clear divisions along
caste lines which determine where most families can live. In
villages in western Rajasthan, Brahmins actually paint their
houses sky blue to denote their caste and in some remote
villages there is little prospect of a member of the harijan or
untouchable caste being allowed to draw water from the communal well because of Brahmin prejudice that such an act would
pollute the well.

James Forbes, an early East India Company administrator
who spent nineteen years in India, returned to Britain in 1784

with 52,000 pages of manuscripts and sketches. During the next thirty years he worked this material into his masterly four-volume *Oriental Memoirs* which provide a detailed account of all aspects of Indian flora and fauna, archaeology and village life. In the following description, Forbes depicts an orderly society in which each villager knows his place.

> Thus it is in Hindostan: the lands appropriated to each village belong to the government; the ryots or peasants, who cultivate the fields, under the orders and inspection of the patell, or superior of the village, are in a manner attached to the spot. The cattle for the plough, and other services of husbandry, are sometimes the common stock of the village, oftener the property of individuals. The patell provides seed and implements of agriculture, takes care that such as are able cultivate the land, and at the time of settling the jummabunda, or harvest-agreement, with the collector of the revenue, allots to each family their portion of grain, or a share of the money for which it has been sold; according to the number of the family, the quantity of their cattle, and the extent of the land they have cultivated. Some particular fields, called pysita and vajeessa lands, are set apart in each village for public purposes; varying, perhaps, as to the mode of application, in different districts; but in most the produce of these lands is appropriated to the maintenance of the brahmins, the cazee [native judge], washerman, smith, barber, and the lame, blind, and helpless; as also to the support of a few vertunnees, or armed men, who are kept for the defence of the village, and to conduct travellers in safety from one village to another.[2]

Indian villages present an exotic picture to the newcomer, especially in Bengal with its lush tropical foliage. The paintings of eighteenth- and nineteenth-century European artists bear this out. Bishop Reginald Heber sailed out to Bengal in the 1820s. As the boat sailed up the Hooghly river towards Calcutta, he reported that 'nothing met the eye but a dismal and unbroken line of thick, black, wood and thicket, apparently impenetrable and interminable, which one might easily imagine to be the habitation of everything monstrous, disgusting, and danger-

ous, from the tyger and the cobra di capello down to the scor-
pion and mosquito, – from the thunderstorm to the fever.'
Soon afterwards he put down near a village south of Calcutta.

> I never recollect having more powerfully felt the beauty
> of similar objects. The greenhouse-like smell and tempera-
> ture of the atmosphere which surrounded us, the exotic
> appearance of the plants and of the people, the verdure of
> the fields, the dark shadows of the trees, and the exuberant
> and neglected vigour of the soil, teeming with life and
> food, neglected as it were, out of pure abundance, would
> have been striking under any circumstances; they were still
> more so to persons just landed from a three months'
> voyage; and to me, when associated with the recollection
> of the objects which have brought me out to India, the
> amiable manners and countenances of the people, contrast
> with the symbols of their foolish and polluted idolatry
> now first before me, impressed me with a very solemn
> and earnest wish that I might in some degree, however
> small, be enabled to conduce to the spiritual advantage
> of creatures so goodly, so gentle, and now so misled
> and blinded. 'Angeli forent, si essent Christiani!' As
> the sun went down, many monstrous bats, bigger than
> the largest crows I have seen, and chiefly to be distin-
> guished from them by their indented wings, unloosed
> their hold from the palm-trees, and sailed slowly around
> us. They might have been supposed the guardian genii of
> the pagoda.[3]

Major-General Sir William Sleeman, one of the Raj's most
effective senior officers and civil servants, wrote of the relatively
democratic nature of village rule in the eighteenth and nineteenth century. There were good reasons for this highly evolved
system – in a country as vast and yet fragmented as India, there
was precious little that any invader, whether Islamic or Christian, could do beyond the city walls. Sir William was Resident
at Lucknow in the 1840s when it was ruled by the feckless and
sybaritic Nawab of Oudh. This state of affairs led Sir William
to draw the conclusions he did regarding the lack of reciprocal
rights flowing from the ruler to the ruled.

There is perhaps no part of the world where the communities of which the society is composed have been left
so much to self-government as in India. There has seldom
been any idea of a reciprocity of duties and rights between
the governing and the governed; the sovereign who has
possession feels that he has a right to levy certain taxes
from the land for the maintenance of the public establish-
ments, which he requires to keep down rebellion against
his rule, and to defend his dominions against all who may
wish to intrude and seize upon them; and to assist him in
acquiring the dominions of other princes when favourable
opportunities offer; but he has no idea of a reciprocal duty
towards those from whom he draws his revenues. The
peasantry from whom the prince draws his revenues feel
that they are bound to pay that revenue; that, if they do
not pay it, he will, with his strong arm, turn them out
and give to others their possessions – but they have no idea
of any right on their part to any return from him. The
village communities were everywhere left almost entirely
to self-government; and the virtues of truth and honesty,
in all their relations with each other, were indispensibly
necessary to enable them to govern themselves.[4]

Sir William was not partial to local officials in Oudh who
preyed on villagers. He reserved his most intense contempt for
revenue collectors, whom he accused of being 'thorough-bred
ruffians'. Indeed, he compiled painstaking reports of the perfidy
of the tallookdars, or revenue officials.

Now the tallookdars keep the country in a perpetual state
of disturbance, and render life, property, and industry
everywhere insecure. Whenever they quarrel with each
other, or with the local authorities of the Government,
from whatever cause, they take to indiscriminate plunder
and murder over all lands not held by men of the same
class; no road, town, village, or hamlet is secure from their
merciless attacks; robbery and murder become their
diversion – their sport; and they think no more of taking
the lives of men, women, and children who never offended
them, than those of deer or wild hogs. They not only rob
and murder, but seize, confine and torture all whom they

seize, and suppose to have money or credit, till they ransom themselves with all they have, or can beg or borrow.[5]

Whereas English accounts in the nineteenth century emphasized the lawlessness of village life, Indian writers often spoke of the countryside in a religious, almost mystical tone. Sir Rabindranath Tagore, the Nobel Prize-winning Bengali poet, wrote a letter to a friend in 1891 about the inner meaning of the countryside in Bengal.

I was thinking, why is there such a deep note of mourning in the fields, *ghats*, and sunshine of our country? I think perhaps the reason is that Nature is constantly before our eyes: the wide, open sky, flat and endless land, shimmering sunshine – and in the midst of this men come and go, crossing to and fro like a ferry-boat. The little noises that they make, the ups and downs of their happy or sad efforts in the market of the world, seem in the context of this endlessly reaching, huge, aloof Nature so small, so fleeting, so futile and full of suffering! We feel in Nature's effortless, unambitious stillness and serenity such vast, beautiful, undistorted, generous Peace; and compared to that such an effortful, agonized, tormented, petty, perpetually unstable *lack* of peace inside ourselves, that when we look at the distant blue line of the shady woods on the river-bank we are strangely unsettled.[6]

The most exquisite description of an Indian village was written by another Bengali, Nirad C. Chaudhuri, in his masterly *Autobiography of an Unknown Indian*, published when he was in his fifties and before he had ever left the Subcontinent. His birthplace, Kishorganj in east Bengal, was a subdivisional headquarters, which merely meant that it was an administrative unit adjacent to a principal town where an English Collector (senior district official) lived. Chaudhuri's father was the vice chairman of the municipality.

The town had grown around and along a visible thread, a three-stranded thread, which was formed by a little river with two roads running along its two banks. We inherited the tradition that the river once had its day, but what we saw was only its impoverished old age. Except during the rains, when it was full to the brim and shining across its whole breadth of some two hundred yards between one road-bound bank and another, it was an emaciated channel where the water never was more than waist-deep and in most places only knee-deep. But we loved the stream. To compare small things with great, it was our Nile. Our town was the gift of the river. We drank its water, although this water was never allowed to see the sides or the bottom of the tumbler unless fetched very early in the morning. We bathed in the river, paddled in it, and when we got dry after our bath we looked fairer than we really were with a coat of fine white sand. Sometimes we even glinted in the sun, thanks to the presence in the sand of minute flecks of mica. The cows and elephants of the town also bathed in the river but, as a rule, only after we had had our turn and never alongside us. Often we ran after our cow when the servant took her down for a wash. We took up the water in our folded hands and, sniffing it, found it charged with the acrid smell of cattle. We also looked on with delight when the elephant of Joyka, a near neighbour of ours, waded majestically into the river and disported herself in it. She had a young companion, not her own calf though, who also came with her on occasion and had his bathe in the river.[7]

Village life was not simply an aquatic paradise. When Chaudhuri was five years old, one of his neighbours just two doors away was decapitated by an unknown assailant. Yet despite the proximity of lawlessness and violence, Chaudhuri still felt that there was a benign spirit protecting the village.

The many-sided world which lay around us was, in one of its aspects, a world of murder, assault, robbery, arson, rape, abduction; and, in another, a world of disputed inheritance, contested possession, misappropriation of money, betrayal of widows and minors, forged wills and purloined title-deeds. But there was consolation and security in the clear feeling which all of us had that these terrifying aspects of the world constituted only a thin layer between the more solid ones. The layer of simmering greed and violence which preyed on our peace of mind seemed to rest on a rock-like foundation of quite different composition never permeated or corrupted by it. We called this lower stratum religion and morality, things in which everybody believed and things to which in the last resort everybody returned. Overhead there appeared to be, coinciding with the sky, an immutable sphere of justice and order, brooding sleeplessly over what was happening below and swooping down on it when certain limits were passed. Its arm seemed to be long and all-powerful, and it passed by different names among us. The common people still called it the Company, others Queen Victoria, and the educated, the Government. The feeling, thus ever present, of there being a watchdog and protecting Government above us vanished at one stroke with the coming of the nationalist agitation in 1905. After that we thought of the Government, in so far as we thought of it in the abstract, as an agency of oppression and usurpation. None the less, although deprived of its subjective halo, the protective power survived for many decades. Today everything is giving way. The thing overhead, once believed to be immutable, has blown up, and the primordial foundation of rock below, on which we thought we had our feet firmly planted, is rotting in the dust.[8]

Village life in the early twentieth century was also described in *Pather Panchali*, the classic novel about a Bengali village by Bibhutibhusan Banerji, a school-teacher. He portrays the village through the eyes of Opu and his elder sister Durga.

Opu strode along happily. From time to time as he walked he knelt down, rummaged among the bushes for bitter berries and stuffed them into the pockets of the new red satin shirt his mother had made for him. He could not have described his happiness in words, but the further he went the more thrilled he became with the beauty all around him, the bitter tang from the earth, the way the shadows fell across the *dub* grass, the wide sweep of the open country burning white in the heat of the sun, the path itself, the trees, the birds, the thickets, the swinging clusters of

flowers and fruit, the *alkushi* plants, the thorn bushes, and
the blue creeper which bore the name of the goddess
Durga. How could his mother have wanted him to stay
indoors when there was a world like this outside? And
what fun it would be if his father said to him, 'There's
no need for you to stay in any more and do lessons, my
lad. The out-of-doors is yours. Go and walk in it.' Yes,
what fun it would be! He would walk through shady
copses like these, with fruit swinging overhead, his eye
fixed on the distance where a dove was calling from a tree.
That was all he asked for, to walk and walk. He would
listen to the rustle and creak of the bamboos; and in the
warmth of evening, when the light was gold and red,
many birds of many colours would sing to him.

Day by day, as the years of his childhood passed, Opu
had walked with Nature. When one season went and
another came, the trees, the sky, the wind, the singing of
the birds told him about it . . . He knew so well what
changes of the maturing year would spell out in the trees,
on land and water, in the sky, and in the fruit and flowers.
He loved them all as if they were his brothers and sisters,
and he could not imagine a life without them. Ever since
he was born Nature's vast and lovely canvas had been
spread before his eyes. The sombre magnificence of the
thick black robes which enshrouded the sky as the fierce
and airless summer burned to its end; the play of colour
in the clouds of the sky as the sun set across the
Shonadanga plain; the wide sand-bank of Madhobpur at
the end of the rains, with its deep carpet of flowering
herbs; the enchanting criss-cross of light and shade in the
bamboo grove on a moonlit night: the incomparable and
inexhaustible loveliness of all these had stamped itself
indelibly on his keen, ardent, and innocent mind as he
journeyed on towards manhood; they had opened his eyes
to the quintessence of beauty, and murmured in his ears
the words which open the gates to the palace of the
gods.[9]

English writers active at this time were still expressing a sense
of wonder at the exotic landscape and people. Robert Byron,

in the 1920s, was particularly struck by the beauty and poise of village women in Sind.

Standing beneath the shiny dark-green leaves of a spreading tree late one afternoon in Sind, I gazed in fascination upon the ingenious mechanism of a Persian wheel: the bullocks, coupled and blindfolded, treading out their antique circle; the tortured interaction of the wooden cogs, each carved from a whole tree stump; the long iron band with its burden of pots falling for ever and ever into the black orifice, and for ever rising out of it a-drip with cold silver water; each pot, before following the heels of its predecessor into the depths again, emptying its water into a narrow groove of clay; the groove giving on to an embankment stream; then finally the stream, running swiftly down an incline, branching out into a myriad capillaries over the surrounding fields. The shadows were lengthening. A chestnut pony fidgeted on its tether. As I stood, engrossed with the perfect beauty of the scene, a line of women defiled through an opening in a high bank and made towards the stream. Poor women they were, cultivators since childhood; some old, some young; their hands, had I shaken them, would have felt horny and calloused. Yet as they walked, walking as all Indian women do, it was with such aristocracy of movement, such evidence of measureless tradition, such absolute control of every muscle, yet with such absolute flexibility, that I might have watched with less profit a passage of Louis XIV through his court, or a performance of the Imperial *Corps de Ballet* before the Tsar. From the head of each flowed a *sari* of dull crimson dotted with black circles, beneath which was revealed a black bodice, short-sleeved, tight-fitting, and powdered with small pieces of mirror that glinted gently against the falling sun. On the head of each reposed a jar of Rhodian shape decorated in Rhodian fashion. Arms hung bare, save for a casing of bangles above the wrist. Round their ankles, hoops of massive silver drew the eye to the source of poise, the slow-moving, flat-spread feet.

The silence remained unbroken. One by one each came

to the stream, took her jar from her head, bent down, and moved noiselessly away. The impression of them will never fade. Just a year later I attended a charity ball in a London hotel, at which the beauties of contemporary England consented to exhibit themselves in procession upon a raised platform. One by one they too came forward, but staggering and strutting like marionettes on a string, their arms and legs flying this way and that, their bodies propelled with jerks and starts, their eyes goggling and their lips wriggling. I remembered the women of Sind, and I asked myself, as I shall always ask myself, why and how the cultivation of an Indian field should produce such taste and beauty, and what effect that beauty must exercise on those perpetually in contact with it.[10]

This tendency to romanticize the beauty and purity of village life was not so common amongst residents of India. Robert Byron's lyrical description bears no relation to Denis Kincaid's portrayal of a village. Kincaid, the son of a distinguished Indian Civil Service (ICS) officer and grandson of the Resident of Bhopal, came to India in 1928 with the judicial arm of the ICS and wrote two novels, – *Cactus Land* and *Durbar*, and a *Social History of the British in India* which was published shortly after his death at the age of 32 in 1937. The following extract appears in *Durbar*, published in 1933.

In the bazaar a profound torpor had succeeded the febrile trafficking of the noon market. Even the policeman stationed at the cross-roads had retired into the shadow of a vegetable shop and slumbered heavily, his head resting on a pillow of cabbages. But now as the sunlight declined and the fresher breeze of evening blew down the street he awoke, yawned, blew his nose on the fringe of his turban, coughed, cursed and stretched cramped limbs. He trundled an empty whisky-case to the middle of the cross-roads, spread a red umbrella, and sat there blinking and rubbing bloodshot eyes.

An obsequious hotel-keeper hurried across the road with a cup of hot tea, salaamed, grinned, carefully proffered his offering with both hands as though it were a gift of incalculable value. The policeman nodded, adding gruffly:

'And some cigarettes?'

Shopkeepers sprinkle rose-water in the dust before their houses. Slops are emptied from windows. Urine and human excrement trickle thinly from under wooden doorways. Piles of paper and rotting straw and stinking linen and fly-spotted faeces clutter every angle of the streets. Pink-manged mongrels nuzzle and roll and lift boil-scarred hind-legs above these reeking dumps. Green slime and trickling filth rope verminous clay walls.

In the houses women begin their preparation for the evening meal. Dry branches crackle in cavernous ovens; green twigs hiss, brown-bubbling, oozing gummy sap. Rose-water is sprinkled over stone-flagged courtyards, wet linen hung to dry. The acrid haze of burning cowdung mingles with the heavy perfume of synthetic roses. Window shutters clatter open; and the breeze billows pink curtains, bellying them round and back into frowsy rooms smelling of old meals.[11]

A number of ICS officers devoted their lives to improving Indian villages through a combination of sound advice and example in order to overcome superstition and the innate lethargy of the village environment. F. L. Brayne, the former deputy commissioner of Gurgaon District, which is only thirty miles south of Delhi, wrote a number of books in the 1920s with such rousing titles as *Village Uplift in India* and *Socrates in an Indian Village*. The latter was a catalogue of conversations the author had had during his time in Gurgaon, describing his trials and tribulations in his attempts to educate the villagers in basic hygiene and decent living. The chapter entitled 'Honour your Women' provides an example of his philosophical style and robust common sense.

Socrates came into the chaupal [common meeting place in a village] in a very cheerful mood, chuckling to himself, and the village elders were so surprised to see him in such an unusual vein that they hardly knew how to address him.

VILLAGERS: Good morning, Socrates. What has happened, old worthy? Have you found a clean village or a child without dirt and ornaments, or an educated village woman, or what?

SOCRATES: No, brother, far from it; I have got into awful trouble this morning (*and he chuckled again*).

VILLAGERS: Do let us share your mirth, old man. We suffer from your wrath so often, it is but fair we should share your very occasional laughter.

SOCRATES: Very well (*laughing out loud*) I will tell you all about it, but promise you won't be angry when you hear.

VILLAGERS: No, Socrates; we will not spoil your pleasure by getting angry, whatever you may say this time.

SOCRATES: Well, it was like this: I met a political gentleman and we fell to discussing things, and went well till he said, with rising indignation and repeated expressions of wrath and bitterness, that 'our India, with its ancient civilization and culture, is not respected as she should be in the world.' I foolishly burst out laughing, and this made memberji still more angry, and he turned on me and abused me too, as well as the rest of the world.

'Sorry,' I said, 'memberji, but I can't help laughing at such an astounding statement.'

'Why?' he said.

'Why, how can you expect the rest of the world to respect you when you don't respect yourselves?' and I laughed again. 'Oh, you refer to the untouchables,' he said with sarcasm; 'that's an old story and half as important as you make out.' 'No, I don't refer to the untouchables,' I said, 'though they are bad enough and quite sufficient to make us all hang our heads in shame.' 'Then what do you refer to?' he said. 'Well,' I said, 'half the population is female isn't it?' 'Yes,' he said, 'of course it is.' 'And all the men are born of women?' 'Yes,' he said, 'why ask such foolish questions?' 'Well, then,' I said, 'until you treat women with respect, and while you pay more respect to cattle than to women, how can you be said to be respecting yourselves, and how can you expect other people to respect you?' Memberji got so angry and abusive then, and started talking so loudly about ancient civilizations and so on, that I hurried away.[12]

Mr Brayne then catalogued the various oversights of the male village population, which have changed hardly at all in sixty years, such as no latrine facilities for women, purdah, the overwhelmingly larger number of village girls who die in infancy than boys, child marriages and feelings of sorrow if a daughter rather than a son is born.

Another English scholar on village life was Verrier Elwin, who lived in the Subcontinent for four decades, initially as a social activist and later in Independent India as a senior civil servant in charge of tribal policy. He married twice – in both cases to tribal women from north-east India. His first contact with village poverty was in the United Provinces in the 1930s.

> It is utterly heart-breaking to see these wretched tumble-down villages, with their pools of filth, their cheerlessness, the thin scarcely-clad bodies of their inhabitants, with a hunger and despair in their eyes. Near Meerut, a villager was crippled in an accident. All day he had to lie on his rough bed. No one could be spared to nurse him. As the time for paying the rent drew near, the family began to wonder how he was to be fed. They carried him tenderly to the doctor. I saw the poor man with his body covered with ghastly bed-sores. And his friends who loved him said to the doctor, 'We cannot feed him. There is no one to care for him. Can't you give him something to take him to another world?'[13]

Mahatma Gandhi was the most passionate advocate of the virtues of village life because he saw the villages as representing the essence of India and as least affected by the inroads of Western colonialism. His campaign in the 1920s to encourage people to spin their own cloth was both a way of boycotting imported goods and also of sustaining his campaign to encourage people to look to their roots for their growth. He saw villages as a logical building block in the quest for Independence.

> Independence must begin at the bottom. Thus, every village will be a republic, or panchayat having full powers. It follows, therefore, that every village has to be self-sustained and capable of managing its affairs even to the

extent of defending itself against the whole world . . . In this structure, composed of innumerable villages, there will be ever widening, never ascending circles. Life will not be a pyramid with the apex sustained by the bottom. But it will be an oceanic circle whose centre will be the individual always ready to perish for the village, the latter ready to perish for the circle of villages, till at last the whole becomes one life composed of individuals, never aggressive in their arrogance but ever humble, sharing the majesty of the oceanic circle of which they are integral units. There, the outermost circumference [the national government] will not yield power to crush the inner circle but will give strength to all within and derive its own strength from it . . .

The end to be sought is human happiness combined with full mental and moral development. I use the adjective moral as synonymous with spiritual. This end can be achieved under decentralisation. Centralisation as a system is inconsistent with [the] non-violent structure of society.[14]

Despite Gandhi's campaign, many of the more adventurous and energetic villagers spent much of their time devising schemes to escape from the narrow life led there. The huge shift of the rural population to urban centres began in the last century but has been particularly marked in the Subcontinent since Independence. Premchand, in his famous novel *Gift of a Cow*, written in the 1950s, describes the future plans of Gobar, the son of a farming couple.

He had heard that labourers in the city were earning five or six annas a day. If he could make six annas a day and live on one anna, he'd be saving five, which would add up to ten rupees a month, or a hundred and a quarter in a year. If he came back with a purseful like that, no one would dare say anything against him. Those Datadins and Pateshwaris would fawn over him, and Jhuniya would burst with pride. If he kept earning that kind of money for three or four years, the family poverty could be wiped out entirely. Right now the entire family was not making a hundred and a quarter, and here he would earn that much all by himself. Of course people in the village would sneer. That kind of work was no sin. And it wasn't as though he'd always be earning only six annas a day. As he got more skilled, his wages would go up too. Then he could tell his father to sit at home and relax and spend his time singing praises to God. This farming was nothing but a waste of a man's life. First of all he'd buy a good western cow, one that gave four or five quarters of milk a day; and then he'd tell his father to look after her, bringing the old man happiness both in this world and the next.

He could easily live on one anna a day. He wouldn't need a house – he could sleep on someone's porch, or there were those hundreds of temples with free rest-houses for pilgrims. And after all, wouldn't his employer give him a place to live? Of course a rupee would buy only twenty pounds of wheat flour. That meant an anna would buy only a little more than a pound, and in a day he'd eat that much flour alone. Where would he get wood, dal, salt, greens and all that? Two meals a day would require a good two pounds of flour. But why all this worry about food? People can make do with just a handful of gram [pulses] or they can live on sweets and delicacies, depending on what they're able to afford. He could manage perfectly well on a single pound of flour. Dung cakes picked up here and there would do just as well as firewood. Once in a while he could spend a pice [one quarter of an anna] on dal or potatoes . . . baked potatoes were easy to prepare. After all, it was a question of getting by, not of living in luxury. Knead the dough on a leaf, bake it over a dung fire, cook a potato, eat your fill and then go to sleep content. Even at home they didn't have chapatis for both meals – at one there was only gram. He could do the same in the city.

He hesitated . . . What would he do if he didn't get work? But why wouldn't he? If he put his whole heart into it, a hundred employers would ask for his services. What they really wanted was work, not good looks. Besides, here in the village people had to face droughts and frost, termites in the sugar cane, and blight on the barley and mustard seeds. If he got night work too, he'd accept

that also. He could do manual labour all day and then serve
as a watchman at night. If the night job brought in two
annas more, he'd really be in luck. He'd come back with
saries for all of them, along with a bracelet made especially
for Jhuniya and a turban for his father.[15]

Very little has been written by villagers themselves about
their existence. Amazingly, the first such book was Prafulla
Mohanti's *My Village, My Life*, which was only published in
the early 1970s. Mohanti provides an eloquent description of
an ordinary village in Orissa, 200 miles south-west of Calcutta.
The inhabitants were all strict Hindus who adhered strongly
to the caste system, their main diversion being frequent
religious festivals. Mohanti trained as an architect in Bombay
and later studied town planning in London and Leeds. After
developing an interest in painting he returned to India to live.

My childhood was very happy and secure. I felt I belonged
to the village and the village belonged to me. My father
worked as a forester, away from home, and I was looked
after by my mother, grandmother and many uncles and
aunts, who treated me as their own child.

I played with my friends in the dust of the village
streets. We improvised games. We did not have many
toys to play with. Nobody disturbed us, even the cows
walked carefully by. In the monsoon, the village streets
became small rivers on which we sailed small paper boats.
I danced happily in the rain . . . I looked forward to the
festivals and ceremonies. They were full of colour and
movement. The characters in the all-night plays intrigued
me. The music and dancing inspired me to participate. I
instinctively started to draw and paint on the walls and
floors at religious festivals. I spent long hours reading
religious epics, short stories and novels. Life was full and
exciting.

But there were darker sides of village life which worried
me. I was aware of the poverty. Many of us could not
afford to buy a slate and we wrote directly on the mud
floor with a piece of clay chalk. My cousins did not have
enough to eat and without telling my mother I gave them
some of my food. Many of my school friends died suddenly

from cholera, typhoid, diphtheria and other diseases. Some were disfigured by smallpox. I accepted this as inevitable . . .

Storms, floods and cyclones happened regularly. They frightened me when I was a child, but as I grew older I got used to them. I even began to enjoy the floods, when we made rafts from banana trunks and visited our friends in the next settlement.

That was my world. It was completely isolated. There were no proper roads, no radio or newspaper. People had no need for them. Occasionally an aeroplane flew overhead to remind us that there was somewhere outside.[16]

On his return to the village some years later, he was shocked to discover that a large and ugly concrete bridge had been erected over the river, obscuring the view of the hills, and that the new road was a virtual race-track for lorries at all times of day and night. There was also a steady depletion of local skills in the arts and crafts as more young men joined the mass migration to the cities to work in factories doing menial tasks. He feared the end of village life as he knew it, replaced by a bland, featureless cluster of houses and shops around a highway.

R. K. Narayan, the south Indian writer who still lives in Mysore, writes about village life in the south, which is not dramatically different from that in the north, except there are fewer Muslims.

Of the seven hundred thousand villages dotting the map of India, in which the majority of India's five hundred million live, flourish, and die, Kritam was probably the tiniest, indicated on the district survey map by a microscopic dot, the map being meant more for the revenue official out to collect tax than for the guidance of the motorist, who in any case could not hope to reach it since it sprawled far from the highway at the end of a rough track furrowed up by the iron-hooped wheels of bullock carts. But its size did not prevent its giving itself the grandiose name Kritam, which meant in Tamil 'coronet' or 'crown' on the brow of this subcontinent. The village consisted of fewer than thirty houses, only one of them built with brick and cement. Painted a brilliant yellow and blue all over with gorgeous carvings of gods and gargoyles on its balustrade, it was known as the Big House. The other houses, distributed in four streets, were generally of bamboo thatch, straw, mud, and other unspecified material. Muni's was the last house in the fourth street, beyond which stretched the fields. In his prosperous days Muni had owned a flock of forty sheep and goats and sallied forth every morning driving the flock to the highway a couple of miles away. There he would sit on the pedestal of a clay statue of a horse while his cattle grazed around. He carried a crook at the end of a bamboo pole and snapped foliage from the avenue trees to feed his flock; he also gathered faggots and dry sticks, bundled them, and carried them home for fuel at sunset.

His wife lit the domestic fire at dawn, boiled water in a mud pot, threw into it a handful of millet flour, added salt, and gave him his first nourishment for the day. When he started out, she would put in his hand a packed lunch, once again the same millet cooked into a little ball, which he could swallow with a raw onion at midday. She was old, but he was older and needed all the attention she could give him in order to be kept alive.

His fortunes had declined gradually, unnoticed. From a flock of forty which he drove into a pen at night, his stock had now come down to two goats, which were not worth the rent of a half rupee a month the Big House charged for the use of the pen in their backyard. And so the two goats were tethered to the trunk of a drumstick tree [also known as the Horse-radish tree] which grew in front of his hut and from which occasionally Muni could shake down drumsticks. This morning he got six. He carried them in with a sense of triumph. Although no one could say precisely who owned the tree, it was his because he lived in its shadow.[17]

In the early 1960s, on his first journey to India, V. S. Naipaul returned to his ancestral village in Uttar Pradesh, a century after his ancestors had left to become indentured labourers in the West Indies.

When you drive through parts of western and central India you wonder about the teeming millions; settlements are so few, and the brown land looks so unfruitful and abandoned. Here wonder was of another sort. The land was flat. The sky was high, blue and utterly without drama; below it everything was diminished. Wherever you looked there was a village, low, dust-blurred, part of the earth and barely rising out of it. Every tiny turbulence of dust betrayed a peasant; and land was nowhere still.

At a junction we took on a volunteer guide and turned off on to an embankment of pure dust. It was lined with tall old trees. Below them my grandfather had doubtless walked at the start of his journey. In spite of myself I was held. For us this land had ceased to exist. Now it was so ordinary. I did not really want to see more. I was afraid of what I might find, and I had witnesses. Not that one, not that, cried the guide, excited both by my mission and the unexpected jeep ride, as village after village died in our dust. Presently he pointed: there, on our right, was the village of the Dubes.

It was set far back from the embankment. It exceeded anything I had expected. A large mango grove gave it a pastoral aspect, and two spires showed white and clean against the dark green foliage. I knew about those spires and was glad to see them. My grandfather had sought to re-establish the family he had left behind in India. He had recovered their land; he had given money for the building of a temple. No temple had been built, only three shrines. Poverty, fecklessness, we had thought in Trinidad. But now, from the road, how reassuring those spires were!

We got out of the jeep and made our way over the crumbling earth. The tall, branching mango trees shaded an artificial pond, and the floor of the grove was spotted with blurred sunshine. A boy came out. His thin body was naked save for his dhoti and sacred thread. He looked at me suspiciously – our party was large and ferociously official – but when the IAS [Indian Administrative Service] officer who was with me explained who I was, the boy attempted first to embrace me and then to touch my feet. I disengaged myself and he led us through the village, talking of the complicated relationship that bound him to my grandfather and to me. He knew all about my grandfather. To this village that old adventure remained important: my grandfather had gone far beyond the sea and had made *barra paisa*, much money.

A year before I might have been appalled by what I was seeing. But my eye had changed. This village looked unusually prosperous; it was even picturesque. Many of the houses were of brick, some raised off the earth, some with carved wooden doors and tiled roofs. The lanes were paved and clean; there was a concrete cattle-trough. 'Brahmin village, brahmin village,' the IAS man whispered. The women were unveiled and attractive, their saris white and plain. They regarded us frankly, and in their features I could recognize those of the women of my family. 'Brahmin women,' the IAS man whispered. 'Very fearless.'

It was a village of Dubes and Tiwaris, all brahmins, all more or less related. A man, clad in loincloth and sacred thread, was bathing, standing and pouring water over himself with a brass jar. How elegant his posture, how fine his slender body! How, in the midst of populousness and dereliction, had such beauty been preserved? They were brahmins; they rented land for less than those who could afford less. But the region, as the *Gazetteer* said, 'abounds in brahmins'; they formed twelve to fifteen per cent of the Hindu population. Perhaps this was why, though they were all related in the village, there appeared to be no communal living.[18]

In 1967, the writer Paul Scott described in a lecture the impact of his return visit to India in the 1960s. Scott had been briefly based in the Subcontinent during the Second World War and returned fifteen years later to gather material for his series of novels, *The Raj Quartet*.

I stayed for ten days in somewhat primitive conditions in a village. By primitive, I mean there was no formal arrangement for what polite people call one's morning duties, but I call going to the loo. It was a comic, fascinating, highly emotional experience, and taught me a lot about the European's fear of black countries. It was a severe strain on my civilized liberal instincts. Towards the end of my stay I found myself shouting. Lizards popped out of my dressing-gown pocket. The daughter of the house washed my feet every time I entered the compound of the hut. The smell of breakfast cooked in clarified butter turned my stomach. Three or four times a day I was forced to walk, water-jug in hand because toilet paper would have offended the sensibilities of my hosts, to that distant bourne of an open field from which I felt this traveller one day would certainly not return. I accompanied my host in the dark to a village where illicit liquor was distilled, because my gin had run out. I attended a cock-fight. I did puja [worship] to the Lord Venkateswara – a manifestation of Vishnu the preserver – in the local temple, and drank during the course of it what, from its bitter taste, I suspected to be cow's urine. I was made to eat alone. I was watched everywhere. I slept under the stars, nudged awake by restless warm-breathed cattle. I was shaving each morning without soap – my soap might have been made, they thought, from the fat of a dead animal. The barber shaved my face with a cut throat and water – forehead, cheeks, chin, eyelids. I smiled and was in terror of being blinded by a slip of his hand. While I was shaved a group of men sat and watched the extraordinary sight of a white man getting rid of his bristles. One felt like a cross between Sanders of the River and the King of Siam. Sometimes a bus passed through that village and sometimes my host took me for a ride in it. A chair would be brought out of the house, placed by the roadside and I would be made to sit on it. To wait at a bus-stop on a kitchen chair gives you a curious sense of your own unlikelihood . . .

What had happened really was that I had added to my knowledge – not just of the customs, the manners and the artefacts of an alien culture – *but of the terrible dependence we have on our own familiar way of doing things if we are to spare thought and expend kindness on people apparently different from ourselves*. I understand better therefore the physical and emotional impulses that had always prompted the British in India to sequester themselves in clubs and messes and forts, to preserve, sometimes to the point of absurdity, their own English middle-class way of life. It was a simple enough lesson. One could learn it from books. It is better for a writer to learn lessons from life.[19]

Sarah Lloyd, a young Englishwoman, had a somewhat different experience in the Punjab, where she lived with a young Sikh villager while she wrote notes about her experiences, which were eventually published as *An Indian Attachment*.

If the landscape gave the villagers pleasure, they didn't express it. Their appreciation would be in the wonder of God manifested through His creation of the land's capacity to fill their stomachs rather than a curiosity about the life it supported or a recognition of its beauty. Nature was just there, it was nothing, it was too familiar, it was a clock: the sun to get up by and the rain to stay in by.[20]

She also observed the impact of the changing seasons on village life in the Punjab.

Crops rose – some to ten feet and more – turned dry and were gone in what seemed like contracted time. One volume would heighten while another was razed: the interaction of man and nature inadvertently created a dynamic Ben Nicholson landscape expressed in oscillating rectangular planes of green and gold.

It was this constant metamorphosis, the fourth dimension, time, and the little unplanned delights that materialized along its seams and hems that made the Punjabi plain interesting. In itself it wasn't an endearing landscape, composed as it was of imported vegetation and smudged with alien artefacts. With minor variations it stretched monotonously up to the Himalayan foothills, across central Pakistan and southeastwards over Uttar Pradesh and Bihar. But it had its moments, and one of them coincided with my arrival, in the short apple-green spring, when the wheat was high and the clover lush and the trees clad in crisp new leaves. It was mid-March, one of the two short periods in the year when it was not too hot, too cold or too wet.

During the next few weeks the flowers disappeared; the trees remained green but the wheat turned the yellow-buff of the mud walls in the village. Mid-April heralded the harvest, and the village turned out and the fields were briefly as animated as English ones must have been in the days of poppies and cornflowers (which had gone, if ever they were there, from Punjab too). By mid-May the fields lay dry and brown: only the straw stacks with their pointed caps – like primitive tribesmen's huts in an African desert – in any way compensated for the sense of desecration. The earth baked under a vast, featureless sky.

With the rains in July came an intense greening, of ground that had seemed barren, of trees that had shed their leaves in the long white heat and of crops that burst upwards in triumphant growth. With the rains in July the land that in March had resembled southern England grew lush and tropical: it was at this time that to me it was most beautiful of all. Vegetation burgeoned, soft, sensuous and full-blooded. Villagers in white squelched in the mud beneath black umbrellas, and giant storks and crested cranes fed in the wet earth. Water filled the pits on the barren land and pathways turned to mud.

By the end of September the rains were over and the sorghum was house-high. Weeks of rain had bleached the straw stacks and made them saggy and shapeless like the breasts of old women. Along the roads plumes of thatch grass soared majestically in the whitewashed sky and silver in the moonlight. Those few weeks between the rains and cold weather were a period of heady scent and rapid change: crops crumpled, turned chrome, turned crimson, turned khaki and crackled in the dry air. Then they were gone, and once more the landscape was devastated and once more ploughed in preparation for the winter wheat.

Having left Punjab for Uttar Pradesh at the end of the rains, I returned briefly at the end of November, by bus. Dawn melted into rows of white eucalyptus trunks receding into a thick white mist. As the sun rose the mist went pink and gradually cleared. A wispy carpet of wheat seedlings veiled the pale earth, interrupted here and there by small rugs of lush young clover. In mid-January I again returned, at the coldest time of year when ice thin as a brandy glass lay over dawn puddles and early annuals had greened in the fields and verges. In two months the wheat would be knee high and pea green, and it would be spring.[21]

Upamanyu Chatterjee's novel *English, August* published in the 1980s, offers a new perspective on the Indian Administrative Service officer posted to a remote district to preside over law and order. When not actually on duty, the narrator appears to spend most of his free time reading the meditations of Marcus Aurelius, smoking marijuana and fantasizing about sexual conquests. One day a tribal woman comes to see him to plead for help with the village well, which has unaccountably dried up. He drives to the remote village to inspect the well.

> He was relieved to see more people around the well, who turned at their approach. But something was odd, and he realised in a moment that it was the muteness of the village, there seemed to be no laughter and no conversation. The village did have children, but they were all busy. Women were tying them to ropes and letting them into the well.
>
> After a while, the ropes were bringing up buckets. He went closer. The buckets were half-full of some thin mud. The only sounds were the echoing clang of the buckets against the walls of the well, and the tired snivelling of a few children on the side. He looked at them. Gashed elbows and knees from the well walls, one child had a wound like a flower on his forehead. The woman who had come to the office was looking at him in a kind of triumph. He looked into the well. He couldn't see any water, but the children were blurred wraiths forty feet below, scouring the mud of the well floor for water, like sinners serving some mythic punishment.[22]

A retired English ICS officer has a similarly emotional experience in a village where he had once wielded authority. Philip Mason was surprised at what he found when he returned to the Subcontinent a decade after Independence and visited a village near the foothills of the Himalayas, where he had held his first real post as a sub-divisional officer.

I walked across a few fields to a large village, where I saw a man of about sixty sitting by the door of his cottage. After a few preliminary politenesses, I said:

'I see you have electric light in this village now. That is something you never used to have. You must be pleased at that?'

Yes, he agreed. He was pleased at that.

'And the road has been improved,' I said. It used to be full of pot holes. And there used to be a bridge of boats which was closed in the rains, instead of which there's an iron bridge now which is open all year round.'

He agreed that this was a good thing too and we went on for some time like this, I pointing out advantages and benefits that had happened recently and he agreeing. At last I said: 'But what about taxes? And prices? Aren't they rather higher than they used to be?'

He was very philosophic about it. Yes, taxes were high and prices were high, but wasn't that the same all the world over? You can't have everything just as you want it. 'Well,' I went on, 'there must be something you want. Isn't there any way your life can be changed for the better?'

'Yes,' he said, suddenly alert, 'there is one thing you could do for me. Down there, where the track turns a corner, there's a hole that fills with water in the rains. My bullock sticks there. Can you get that filled up for me?'

'Who do you think I am?' I asked.

'I don't know who you are, but you must be some commissioner or collector or something to do with the Government – or you wouldn't be asking these questions.'

'Nothing of the kind,' I told him. 'Twenty-five years ago I was the sub-divisional officer here – but now, I'm nothing. I'm just a man who wanders about the world, writing books.'

'Oh, in that case,' he said – scrambling to his feet and

becoming much more animated – 'things are frightful! Taxes are terribly high and so are prices! And what good are all these improvements to me? I don't want electricity. I go to bed when it's dark. I haven't got a motor car. I don't want to drive along a smooth road. I don't want an iron bridge.'[23]

9

MAHARAJAS

Amid the levelling tendencies of the age and the inevitable monotony of government conducted upon scientific lines, they keep alive the traditions and customs, they sustain the virility, and they save from extinction the picturesqueness of ancient and noble races. They have that indefinable quality, endearing them to the people, that arises from their being born of the soil. They provide scope for the activities of the hereditary aristocracy of the country, and employment for native intellect and ambition. Above all, I realise, more perhaps in Rajputana than anywhere else, that they constitute a school of manners, valuable to the Indian, and not less valuable to the European, showing in the person of their chiefs that illustrious lineage has not ceased to implant noble and chivalrous ideas, and maintaining those old-fashioned and punctilious standards of public spirit and private courtesy which have always been instinctive in the Indian aristocracy, and with the loss of which, if ever they be allowed to disappear, Indian society will go to pieces like a dismantled vessel in a storm.

Lord Curzon discussing Indian princes in Jaipur, 1902[1]

Just before Independence was granted, there were 565 princely states in the Subcontinent. Some were little more than feudal backwaters of no consequence that consisted of a few square miles of barren land, but others were greater in area than Britain and possessed comparable populations. In all, one-third of the Subcontinent's area and a quarter of its population were nominally under the control of the princely states, though in reality a British Resident acted as suzerain for most of them.

Some of the princes could trace their ancestry back to medieval times. Others were mere figments of the British imagination and were unceremoniously dumped or ousted once they failed to fulfil their purpose, which was to keep the local population quiet and add a semblance of legitimacy to the alien rule of the British.

Rajasthan, which incorporated the twenty princely states known under the Raj as Rajputana, is still the best place in the Subcontinent to gather an impression of what princely India was really like. Princely forts, palaces and *havelis* (town houses) survive in the majority of the cities and towns, and most continue to be occupied by the direct descendants of the original princes. James Tod, British Resident at Udaipur in the early nineteenth century, is still an invaluable guide to princely affairs. One of Tod's more memorable comments, just as relevant today as then, was that 'half the political and moral evils which have vexed the royal houses of Rajpootana, take their rise from polygamy'.

Tod was appointed Political Agent of western Rajasthan in 1818. His task was to restore peace amongst the feuding princely states of Rajasthan – a task which he undertook with such skill that within twelve months of his appointment, 300 deserted towns and villages were repopulated and trade resumed on a much grander scale than ever previously seen. In his superb two-volume work, *The Annals and Antiquities of Rajasthan*, which remains the classic account of the region's history, Tod relates his success in gaining control of the fortress of Kumulghar, on the edge of the Aravalli Range north-west of Udaipur. Kumulghar is one of the most starkly romantic forts anywhere in the world. Its exterior still survives intact today and radiates romance and grandeur on an extraordinary scale – assisted by its possession of a twenty-five-mile-long surrounding wall.

The garrison at Kumulghar had revolted because they had not received their pay but Tod managed to appease the troops and restore control to a ruler sympathetic to the British.

The Mahraja Dowlut Sing, a near relative of the Rana, and governor of Komulmer [Kumulghar], attended by a numerous suite, the crimson standard, trumpets, kettle-

drums, seneschal, and bard, advanced several miles to meet
and conduct me to the castle. According to etiquette, we
both dismounted and embraced, and afterwards rode
together conversing on the affairs of the province, and the
generally altered condition of the country. Dowlut Sing,
being of the immediate kin of his sovereign, is one of the
babas or infants of Mewar, enumerated in the tribe called
Ranawut, with the title of Mahraja. Setting aside the
family of Sheodan Sing, he is the next in succession to
the reigning family. He is one of the few over whom the
general demoralisation has had no power, and remains
a simple-minded straight-forward honest man; blunt,
unassuming, and courteous. His rank and character particularly qualify him for the post he holds on this western
frontier, which is the key to Marwar. It was in February
1818 that I obtained possession of this place (Komulmer),
by negotiating the arrears of the garrison. Gold is the
cheapest, surest and most expeditious of all generals in the
East, amongst such mercenaries as we had to deal with,
who change masters with the same facility they would
their turban. In twenty-four hours we were put in possession of the fort, and as we had not above one-third of the
stipulated sum in ready cash, they without hesitation took
a bill of exchange, *written on the drum-head*, on the mercan-
tile town of Palli in Marwar: in such estimation is British
faith held, even by the most lawless tribes of India! Next
morning we saw them winding down the western
declivity, while we quietly took our breakfast in an old
ruined temple. During this agreeable employment, we
were joined by Major Macleod, of the artillery, sent by
General Donkin, to report on the facilities of reducing the
place by siege, and his opinion being, that a gun could not
be placed in position in less than six weeks, the grilling spared the European force in such a region was well
worth the £4,000 of arrears. My own escort and party
remained in possession for a week, until the Rana sent his
garrison. During these eight days our time was amply
occupied in sketching and decyphering the monumental
records of this singularly diversified spot. It would be vain
to attempt describing the intricacies of approach to this

far-famed abode. A massive wall, with numerous towers
and pierced battlements, having a strong resemblance to
the Etruscan, encloses a space of some miles extent below,
while the pinnacle or *sikra* rises, like the crown of the
Hindu Cybele, tier above tier of battlements, to the summit, which is crowned with the *Badul Mahl*, or 'cloud
palace' of the Ranas. Thence the eye ranges over the sandy
deserts and the chaotic mass of mountains, which are on
all sides covered with the *cactus*, which luxuriates amidst
the rocks of the Aravulli.[2]

At the time of the Mogul invasions in the 1520s, this area
was of great strategic importance for it controlled the entrance
to south-western Rajasthan. The rulers of Rajasthan remained
autonomous during the Mogul Empire though they often came
to an arrangement with the emperors in Delhi or Agra. The
British maintained this policy with the larger princely states.
By the nineteenth century, the only maharaja in northern India
who was powerful enough to cause the British real concern was
Ranjit Singh, otherwise known as the Lion of Punjab. He succeeded his father as ruler of Lahore in 1892 at the age of twelve
and later controlled a vast area from the borders of Nepal to
those of Kabul, making him the most powerful ruler in India.
Although a devout Sikh, he managed to maintain an almost
secular approach to government and was scrupulous in his
respect for all religious faiths. For defence, he relied on an army
trained by a handful of French and Italian mercenary officers
whom he based at Lahore. His court included a troupe of 150
female 'Amazons' carefully selected from the most beautiful
women in Kashmir, the Punjab and Persia. According to one
observer, these spectacularly dressed female warriors were
armed with bows and arrows and made quite an impact as they
strutted on horseback through Lahore on ceremonial occasions.

Several European travellers have left vivid portraits of Ranjit
who was short, pockmarked and blind in one eye. Emily Eden,
the sister of Lord Auckland, who succeeded Lord William
Cavendish-Bentinck as Governor-General, spent some time
with Ranjit in the 1830s.

The instant Runjeet sat down, three or four of his attendants came and knelt down before him – one, the Fakeer

Uzeez-ood-deen, who is his interpreter and adviser and the comfort of his life. We all ought to have Uzeez-ood-deens of our own, if we wish to be really comfortable. The other arranged his gold bottle and glass, and plates of fruit, and he began drinking that horrible spirit, which he pours down like water. He insisted on my just touching it, as I had not been at his party on Saturday, and one drop actually burnt the outside of my lips. I could not possibly swallow it.

Those two little brats [Ranjit's adopted children], in new dresses, were crawling about the floor, and he poured some of this fire down their throats. We had two bands to play; and when the fireworks were over, a large collection of nautch-girls came in front of Runjeet, and danced and sang apparently much to his satisfaction. They were a very ugly set from Loodheana. I could not help thinking how eastern we had become, everybody declaring it was one of the best-managed and pleasantest parties they had seen. All these satraps in a row, and those screaming girls and crowds of long-bearded attendants, and the old tyrant drinking in the middle – but still we all said: 'What a charming party!' just as we should have formerly at Lady C.'s or Lady J.'s. I could not talk with any great ease, being on the blind side of Runjeet, who converses chiefly with his one eye and a few signs which his fakeer makes up into a long speech; and Kurruck Singh was apparently an idiot. Luckily, beyond him was Heera Singh, who had learnt a little English, and has a good idea of making topics, and when C. came and established himself behind the sofa I got on very well with Runjeet . . . He is a very drunken old profligate, neither more nor less. Still he has made himself a great king; he has conquered a great many powerful enemies; he is remarkably just in his government; he has disciplined a large army; he hardly ever takes away life, which is wonderful in a despot; and he is excessively beloved by his people. I certainly should not guess any part of this from looking at him . . . There is something rather touching in the affection his people have for him. The other day, in going through the city, it struck us all, the eagerness with which they called out

'Maharajah!' and tried to touch him, which is easy enough in these narrow streets, and the elephants reaching to the roofs of the houses.[3]

Another traveller to Ranjit's kingdom was Victor Jacquemont, the peripatetic French botanist. His journey was eased by the presence of the French mercenaries who trained Ranjit's army.

Lahore, March 16

I have several times spent a couple of hours in conversing with Runjeet '*de omni re scribili et quibusdam aliis*, (about everything, and something more besides). His conversation is like a nightmare. He is almost the first *inquisitive* Indian I have seen; and his curiosity balances the apathy of the whole of his nation. He has asked a hundred thousand questions to me, about India, the British, Europe, Bonaparte, this world in general and the next, hell, paradise, the soul, God, the devil, and a myriad of others of the same kind. He is like all people of rank in the East, an imaginary invalid; and as he has a numerous collection of the greatest collection of beauties of Cashmere, and the means of paying for a better dinner than anyone else in this country, he is generally annoyed that he cannot drink like a fish without being drunk, or eat like an elephant and escape a surfeit. Women now please him no more than the flowers of his parterre, and for a good reason – and this is the cruellest of his afflictions. He had the decency to call the function which he complains of being weak, a digestive one. But I knew what *stomach* meant at Lahore, when in the king's mouth; and we conversed minutely about his complaint, but the words were well wrapped up on either side. To prove how much reason he had to complain, the old *roué*, the day before yesterday, in full court, that is in the open field, on a fine Persian carpet on which we were seated, surrounded by some thousands of soldiers, sent for five young girls of his seraglio, whom he made to sit down before me, and concerning whom he smilingly asked my opinion. I had the candour to say that I thought them very pretty, which was not a tenth part of what I thought of them. He made them sing, *mezza voce*, a little Seikh air, which their pretty faces made me think agreeable; and told me that he had a whole regiment of them, whom sometimes he ordered to mount on horseback for his amusement; and he promised to afford me an opportunity to see them . . . Runjeet has often exhibited himself to the good people of Lahore, mounted on an elephant, with a Mussulman courtesan, amusing himself with her in the least innocent manner. Although he is only fifty-one, he is now reduced to the scandalous resource of old debauchees, and complains of it without shame.[4]

After Ranjit's death in 1839, his Punjab empire slowly disintegrated, and within a decade precious little remained. In 1849, the British finally took over his kingdom and looted the Koh-i-noor diamond, which was then presented to Queen Victoria. In many of the smaller princely states, as their thrones fell vacant, Britain selected and installed successors, allowing them merely the semblance of power. Real power lay with the British Resident who, tactfully or otherwise, managed to ensure that the state remained solvent. This policy suited the East India Company, as they were loath to burden themselves with the problems of direct rule when others could be called upon to do so – as long as trade expanded and profits rose, why bother about such minutiae? On many occasions, though, such a simple formula was found wanting.

The kingdom of Oudh was one such example where, try as they might not to meddle in the internal affairs of the Nawab at Lucknow, it became increasingly difficult to refrain from participation, given the extent of the Nawab's corruption and incompetence. Sir William Sleeman was appointed Resident at Lucknow in 1849. His tour through the surrounding kingdom of Oudh revealed a catalogue of outrages being committed by crooked rulers or their satraps, who relied on the Nawab's indifference in order to pursue whatever profit they could find at the district level.

In the Gungwal district similar atrocities were committed by Rugbur Sing's agents and their soldiers. These agents were Gouree Shunkur and Seorutun Sing. The district formed the estate of Rajah Sreeput Sing, who resided with his family in the fort of Gungwal. The former Nazim, Suraj-od Dowlah, had attacked this fort on some frivolous pretence; and, having taken it by surprise, sacked the place and plundered the Rajah and his family of all they had. The Rajah died soon after of mortification, at the dishonour he and his family had suffered, and was succeeded by his son, Seetul Persaud Sing, the present Rajah, who was now plundered again, and driven to an exile in the Nepaul hills. The estate was now taken possession of by the agents, Goureeshunker and Seorutun Sing. Seorutun Sing seized a Brahmin who was travelling with his wife and brother, and, on the pretence that he must be a relation of the fugitive Rajah, had him murdered, and his head struck off on the spot. The wife took the head of her murdered husband in her arms, wrapped up in cloth, and, attended by her brother, walked with it a distance of fifty miles to Ajoodheea, where Rugbur Sing was then engaged in religious ceremonies. The poor woman placed the head before him, and demanded justice on her husband's murderers. He coolly ordered the head to be thrown into the river, and the woman and her brother-in-law to be driven from his presence. Many other respectable persons were seized and tortured on a similar pretext of being related to, or having served or assisted, the fugitive Rajah. Moistened gunpowder was smeared thickly over the beards of the men, and when dry set fire to; and any friend or relative who presumed to show signs of pity was seized and tortured, till he or she paid a ransom. All the people in the country around, who had moveable property of any kind, were plundered by these two atrocious agents, and tortured till they paid all that they could beg and borrow. Many respectable families were dishonoured in the persons of wives, sisters, or daughters, and almost all the towns and villages around became deserted.[5]

Although Sir William thought the Nawab of Oudh 'a crazy imbecile', he did not advocate direct annexation of the kingdom, which occurred just before the Mutiny in 1857. Elsewhere, many princely states were so obscure that they were of no interest except for their picturesque nature. One was the state of Swat, which Edward Lear immortalized in his poem, 'The Akond of Swat'. The inspiration for Lear's nonsense was an item which appeared in *The Times of India* on 18 July 1873 about the native ruler of Swat. 'It is reported from Swat that Akhoond's son had quarrelled with his father, and left the parental presence with a following of 500 sowars [horsemen], refusing to listen to the Akhoond's orders to come back.'

Lear enclosed the following in a letter to Lady Waldegrave a month before he actually went to India.

The Akond of Swat

Who or why, or which or – what – ,
　　　　　　　　　Is the Akond of SWAT?
If he catches them then, either old or young,
Does he have them chopped in pieces or hung,
　　　　　　　　　　or – SHOT –
　　　　　　　The Akond of Swat?
Is he wise or foolish, young or old?
Does he drink his soup and his coffee cold,　　or HOT,
　　　　　　　The Akond of Swat?
Does he sing or whistle, jabber or talk,
And when riding abroad does he gallop or walk,
　　　　　　　　　or TROT,
　　　　　　　The Akond of Swat?
Does he wear a turban, a fez, or a hat?
Does he sleep on a mattress, a bed or a mat,
　　　　　　　　　or a COT,
　　　　　　　The Akond of Swat?
When he writes a copy in round-hand size,
Does he cross his T's and finish his I's　　with a DOT,
　　　　　　　The Akond of Swat?
Can he write a letter concisely clear
Without a speck or a smudge or smear　　or BLOT,
　　　　　　　The Akond of Swat?
Do his people like him extremely well?
Or do they, whenever they can, rebel,　　or PLOT,
　　　　　　　At the Akond of Swat?[6]

The danger confronting native rulers during the Raj was often of a more subtle and insidious nature, as outlined in the following extract from a turn-of-the-century novel, *The Broken Road*, by A.E.W. Mason, one of the most popular and celebrated novelists of his time. Mason had just been elected to Parliament as a Liberal and was anxious to make use of his journey to India in order to bolster his credentials as an authority on the Subcontinent. The novel seems to have had the desired effect, for Lord Curzon wrote Mason a nine-page letter praising *The Broken Road* for its accurate portrayal of Indian life. The theme of the book is the wrongheadedness of sending Indian rulers to be educated in the West. The ageing Khan wishes to send his heir Shere Khan to Eton and Oxford, a policy which is vigorously opposed by Luffe, the British Political Agent. In his last dying breath on the frontier, Luffe speaks of his dread for the future of the empire should this policy continue.

'What danger do you foresee?' asked Dewes. 'I will remember what you say.'

'Yes, remember it: write it out, so that you may remember it, and din it into their ears at Government House,' said Luffe. 'You take these boys, you give them Oxford, a season in London – did you ever have a season in London when you were twenty-one, Dewes? You show them Paris. You give them opportunities of enjoyment, such as no other age, no other place affords – has ever afforded. You give them, for a short while, a life of colour, of swift crowding hours of pleasure, and then you send them back – to settle down in their native States, and obey the orders of the Resident. Do you think they will be content? Do you think they will have their hearts in their work, in their humdrum life, in their elaborate ceremonies? Oh, there are instances enough to convince if only people would listen. There's a youth now in the South, the heir of an Indian throne – he has six weeks' holiday. How does he use it, do you think? He travels hard to England, spends a week there, and travels back again. In England he is treated as an *equal*; here, in spite of his ceremonies, he is an *inferior*, and will and must be so. The best you can hope is that he will be merely unhappy. You pray that he won't take to drink and make his friends among the jockeys and the trainers. He has lost the taste for the native life, and nevertheless he has got to live it. Besides – besides – I haven't told you the worst of it.'

Dewes leaned forward. The sincerity of Luffe had gained upon him. 'Let me hear all,' he said.

'There is the white woman,' continued Luffe. 'The English woman, the English girl, with her daintiness, her pretty frocks, her good looks, her delicate charm. Very likely she only thinks of him as a picturesque figure; she dances with him, but she doesn't take him seriously. Yes, but he may take her seriously, and often does. What then? When he is told to go back to his State and settle down. What then? Will he be content of a wife of his own people? He is already a stranger among his own folk. He will eat out his heart with bitterness and jealousy. And, mind you, I am speaking of the best – the best of the Princes and the best of the English women. What of the others – the English women who take his pearls, and the Princes who come back and boast of their success? Do you think that is good for British rule in India? Give me something to drink!'[7]

In 1905, when Lord Curzon was still Viceroy, the Prince and Princess of Wales visited Agra, where Private Frank Richards of the Royal Welch Fusiliers was one of the signallers responsible for passing on messages as to who was about to arrive at a procession in their honour. His straightforward approach to life made him an interesting observer, especially of the amount of finery and display indulged in by the various Indian princes who turned up for a grand procession which was headed by the Royal couple.

All the native princes who had arrived at Agra to pay homage to the Prince turned out in their pomp and splendour. For over a week we had signallers at the railway station to semaphore the names of the Princes, as soon as they arrived, to the gunners at the Fort; so that they could give them the salute of guns to which each was entitled. Some were entitled to larger salutes than others. Those who

were only entitled to a small salute would have willingly
paid lakhs of rupees for another few rounds to be added.
Each prince had done his best to display in this procession
as much wealth as he possibly could. The diamonds and
precious stones that some of them were wearing dazzled
my eyes as they drove slowly by in their open carriages.
Their horses were magnificent and many of the carriages
had gold and silver mountings. But the turnout that I
admired most was a conveyance drawn by four of the
cleanest racing-camels I have ever seen. Standing up in it
was a Prince simply dressed in white silk with a drawn
sword in one hand and a shield in the other. I do not know
who he was, but he was the only one who looked a real
native prince: the others looked like stuffed and gilded
peacocks. From the surrounding villages many thousands
of natives had turned out to watch the procession. They
were in ecstasies of delight at this display of wealth and
pomp, yet they themselves were only living by the skin
of their teeth in dirt and extreme poverty. A few months
later thousands of them died from plague, which was
raging in the neighbourhood, and the survivors died in
further thousands from the great famine that followed in
the wake of the plague.[8]

Amar Singh, a Rajput from a medium estate in Jaipur
state with the relatively minor rank of Thakur of Kanota –
something akin to a Baron or Baronet – was an extraordinary
observer of life in Rajasthan. A cadet in the Imperial Cadet
Corps, he became a major in the British Indian Army and served
in China after the Boxer Rebellion. He was later commander
of the Jaipur State Forces but is better known today for having
kept perhaps the longest diary of the twentieth century – 90
volumes of 800 pages each – which he wrote up every day from
1898 until the day of his death in November 1942. It was
kept primarily for his own amusement but contains fascinating
insights on the aspirations of seemingly loyal British subjects,
such as in this extract from December 1903.

Even in our own homes we Indians are excluded from
European society. Here at Alwar the Englishmen used to
sit on the best of chairs and sofas in the middle while the

Indians used to stand most of the time, or if they sat, it was outside the pavilion and on the rude common chairs. Even the ruling chiefs were not at home amongst these European swells. God only knows what is going to be our dignity in a few years' time. Ruling chiefs are considered nothing more than puppets in the hands of the political people. I wish God would show a day to me when we Indians would be a free nation moving about at our own free will and ranked as a nationality on the same footing as England, France or Russia. I fear I shall never see it . . . [9]

Certainly, if the likes of Lord Reading had had any say in the matter, Amar Singh's fears would have been justified. In a letter to the Nizam of Hyderabad in 1926, Lord Reading, then Viceroy, left no room for doubting the permanency of British rule in the Subcontinent, adding that 'no ruler of an Indian state can justifiably claim to negotiate with the British Government on an equal footing.'

The popular and even the literary perception is that the maharajas were endearing scalliwags, acting as if they were naughty children with too much latitude for their own good, surrounded by retinues and jewels, Rolls Royces and ciné cameras. There is a modicum of truth in this assessment when it comes to some of the obscure states which were of little consequence to either the British or Indian nationalists. But it is a serious mistake to imagine that the larger princely states were all farcical and run merely on the whim of the princely court. Louis Bromfield touched on this in his masterly novel *The Rains Came*, published in 1937. Major-General Agate, a bluff old soldier, visits the fictional state of Ranchipur to see his old friends, the ruling family, some of whom had been educated at Cambridge.

These Indians were important because they were rich, they were powerful, and they knew the game of politics in Europe as well as they knew it in India. This was no obscure state ruled by a doddering depraved prince. Ranchipur, even the General was able to understand, was important – and not only important but dangerous – because it had exploded the whole theory of the White

Man's burden. In the fifty years that the old gentleman, asleep a good quarter mile away in another part of the palace, had been reigning, it had lifted itself out of the malarial apathy and superstition of ancient India into the position of a modern state, admirably staffed and administered. It had proved that Indians could be good administrators, that they could be good economists, that they could solve such complicated problems as that of the Depressed Classes. It was a state more civilized and more advanced than many parts of England and America – the Midlands or Pittsburgh (although to the General nothing in America mattered or even existed).

He would have preferred entering Ranchipur on an elephant at the head of a column of troops, with the populace flat on their faces lining both sides of the avenue from the old palace to the race-course. That was how a British general should make an entrance, not like any bloody civil servant in a railway coach, to be met with condescension (of this he could never quite be sure and it troubled him) by a Rolls-Royce and a nephew of the Maharajah who explained that uncle sent profound regrets but was kept at home by gout. (Why should a Maharajah have gout, which was a disease of retired generals?) If he had had the say he would have treated all India differently. If he had had the say there would be no Indian problem. He'd soon fix that. But the India Office was always getting in his way. Those civilian louts back in Whitehall thought they knew more of the situation than he himself, Major-General Agate, who had spent half his life on the North-West Frontier.

He even fancied himself as a diplomat, convinced that the handsome black-eyed old lady opposite him believed him to be as gentle as a lamb and the most devoted of her friends. He had no suspicion that behind her poker hand she knew exactly what he was thinking and exactly how much he was her friend. To her he was simply a rather tiresome old boaster whom she on her account must entertain because it was all a game anyway, an interminable game of waiting which must be played with a poker face until Europe destroyed itself or fell into decay. It was easier to entertain him by playing poker than by listening to him talk about the necessity of enclosing British wives and mothers on the North-West Frontier behind defences of barbed wire in order to save them from rape at the hands of those wild handsome Muslim tribesmen (an experience, the old Maharani thought, which might have its own richness).[10]

The absurd nature of many of the minor maharajas was depicted brilliantly by J.R. Ackerley in his semi-fictional account of his time as private secretary to the Maharaja of Chhatarpur – an obscure state in central India. Ackerley had gained the position in the early 1920s through the assistance of his friend E.M. Forster, who had earlier served the Maharaja of Dewas Senior in a similar role. Ackerley was an enthusiastic homosexual, as was the Maharaja, who kept several favourites amongst his servants as well as regularly holding plays in which the female parts were invariably played by attractive youths.

> I told His Highness that I had mistaken the tomb of his grandfather for a palace.
> 'He was poisoned,' he remarked.
> 'Indeed?' I said. 'How did that happen?'
> 'My great-grandmother. They quarrelled, and she poisoned him.'
> He added that a King could never trust his relatives, they were always scheming and giving trouble of some sort; in fact, he said gravely, he had just received a report that some of his own kinsmen were plotting together in a neighbouring State to destroy his son with black magic.[11]

The Maharaja also dreamt of Hellenizing his state, something which outraged the British Political Agent, who advised the Maharaja to put the money into road-building schemes.

> During our drive today His Highness returned to the subject of ancient Greeks.
> 'Would you call me an imaginary man?' he asked.
> I said I thought it suited him very well.

'There was an English lady staying with me once,' he continued, 'who said to me, "Maharajah, you soar like a skylark and then fall on the ground." '

He was overcome with merriment, and hid his face in his sleeve.

'What did she mean?' he asked, when he had recovered himself.

'She meant,' I said, 'that although they sometimes come down to earth, your thoughts are usually on higher things.'

'Yes, yes; that I am an imaginary and not a practical man?'

'Quite so, Maharajah Sahib.'

'You know, Mr Ackerley, I like the old times. I like the Greeks and the Romans. I think of them always, always. I would like to have all my people dressed like Greeks and Romans. In my palace, I keep a Greek toga, and when my friends in England used to come and stay with me and talk about those times, I would put on my toga and recline on my couch like this.' He laid the palm of one hand against his cheek, setting the other on his hip, and sank sideways into the corner of the car, which pushed his hat rather tipsily to one side. 'And my friends would clap their hands and say "The Greeks have been born again in Chhokrapur." '

He sat up. 'Ah, I like those old times. And Charles the First and all the Stuarts. I like them very much.'

'Why Charles the First?' I asked, very bewildered.

'I find many things in him like myself. And the Tsar. Don't they say "Like likes like"?'   Some monkeys fled into the bushes before the car's approach, and their antics were so absurd that I burst out laughing.[12]

Both in the smaller and larger states much time was spent on social trivia. It was not just the tiny states that indulged in such bizarre activities. T.E. Bronsdon was appointed personal assistant to the British Resident of Hyderabad after his predecessor had disgraced himself when his bull terrier relieved himself against the sofa in the drawing-room. Hyderabad was the greatest princely state in the Subcontinent, with an area only

slightly smaller than Britain and vast revenues. Bronsdon relates
how

> The Resident would give me an idea of whom to invite
> and of the menu. It was then my duty, when the accep-
> tances were in, to arrange the seating plan. This was a
> tricky job in India where everyone had, and knew they
> had, a specific place in the order of priority, and woe betide
> the Personal Assistant who got it wrong. It was by no
> means unusual to receive a phone call or a letter after a
> function asking 'Why Mrs So-and-So was sitting above
> me'. Our bible was the Warrant of Precedence for India,
> an enormous document which laid down the exact order
> of precedence for every imaginable official in the country.
> We spent hours ascertaining that the Superintendent for
> the Opium Factory at Ghazipur was junior to the General
> Manager of the Rajputana Salt Resources.
>
> Once the seating plan was approved and the menu
> translated into French (we had a special little book for this)
> the details were sent to our own printing press in the
> Residency Office and they were printed in beautiful gold
> lettering. The dining table was laid with official china and
> cutlery, every piece embossed with the rather smug motto
> of the East India Company, *Heaven's Light our Guide*. We
> had a most efficient butler, a Tamil, a spy in the Nizam's
> pay, and everything that happened in the residency was
> immediately reported. But we took no action against him
> because it was better to know who was the spy than to
> sack him and then not know who was planted in the
> place.[13]

Sometimes, etiquette could be thoroughly misleading.
Several years later Philip Mason was asked by the Nizam of
Hyderabad to visit him to discuss the possibility of his taking
charge of the education of the Nizam's children.

> The palace was on top of a steep conical hill; we drove up
> a spiral approach and stopped at the foot of a lofty flight
> of steps. On either side of the steps were rank on rank of
> courtiers; they wore silk *sherwanis* in cream, dove-grey,
> palest blue, belts of gold and silver brocade, tall hats

shaped like tulips and of all the colours of all the tulips in
Holland – crimson and gold, russet, pink and lilac. They
made two pillars of tulips, stretching away, up and up in
a narrowing perspective to the great doors at the head of
the steps. It was an impressive scene, but in India there
is often some discordant note in a carefully arranged occasion; sure enough, there was such a note here – an ill-
dressed man in an old nondescript *sherwani*, rather dirty,
not buttoned up to the neck, with a dingy cap, hanging
about at the foot of the steps. He seemed uncertain of his
role and indeed [seemed] to have no place in the proceedings; we thought it tactful to ignore him and addressed
ourselves to the stairs. But elegant, agonized ADCs
appeared at our elbows, hissing like geese or samovars:
'His Exalted Highness!' So we turned and presented our
humble duty.[14]

The British were less concerned about showing respect for
the minor rulers who demonstrated eccentricity or indifference to the mores of British civil servants. Charles Chenevix
Trench describes several fine examples of this genus in *Viceroy's
Agent*, his descriptive history of the Indian Political Service –
the institution which acted as a buffer between the princely
states and the British government. According to Chenevix
Trench, eastern Rajasthan had more than its fair shair of
'bad and eccentric rulers'. In this category few were able to
compete with the ruling family of Bharatpur, now the site
of a famous game reserve. The Maharaja Kishan Singh succeeded his insane father in 1900 after he was deposed for
murder. The newly installed Maharaja, who was invested in
1918, insisted on his guard wearing leather uniforms and that
all vehicles – from lorries to limousines – be Rolls Royces.
African lions and South American jaguars were also purchased
and released into the jungle, although the chief engineer was
sacked as an economy measure which resulted in the breakdown of the state's irrigation system and then disastrous
floods. His scandalous behaviour became so flagrant, following the misappropriation of flood relief monies, that the Viceroy, Lord Irwin, wrote to his superiors in London about his
difficulties.

I have been much concerned with the affairs of Bharatpur. I told the Maharajah that I was gravely disturbed at the accounts which were reaching me of his financial state and I most earnestly wished he would put all his cards on the table and allow us to help him get straight. He evinced the utmost willingness to do whatever I told him. He always has a great polo gymkhana tea in each Simla season and he asked me which date would suit me to be his guest. I told him that until his finances were cleared up, I did not think I could properly encourage him to spend his money on my entertainment, and I advised him to abandon it for this year. This he did with good grace but I suspect a heavy heart . . . The tragedy is that he has the best duck-shooting in India![15]

In despair, the Viceroy finally conceded that 'the young man is really off his head as a result of some hereditary disease . . . The other princes regard him as a very dangerous black sheep.' He was finally banished and died in exile, while his venal Maharanee fled with five Rolls Royces.

The other prominent princely ruler who was a thorn in the British side in this period was the Maharaja of Alwar, of whom the Secretary of State for India, Edwin Montagu, said 'There is no Indian as intelligent as he is.' However, he was a fanatical Hindu who loathed physical contact with Britishers, whom he considered to be, in effect, untouchables. He was also renowned for his temper and once poured petrol over a polo pony that had let him down and then incinerated it. A single-minded Scot, Arthur Lothian, was appointed as his Prime Minister by the British but even he found it hard going. He described his exasperation to one of his colleagues.

I close this report with a brief account of His Highness's personal equation, for he is a very extraordinary character. The Maharajah is now about 53 years of age, and has always kept himself very fit physically with the result that he looks younger than his actual age. Perhaps the main defects in his character are his gross extravagance and his overweening arrogance. As regards his extravagance I have made a rough estimate of the expenditure of the ruler which suggests that it amounts to well over half the total income of the state, and would note that nine lakhs of unpaid bills are now pending against the state, mostly for articles ordered by His Highness. If he plays tennis, a table displaying anything from ten to twenty rackets has to be set out in front of him; so with guns when out shooting; his office table is festooned with gold-fountain pens in racks like those one sees in a stationer's shop window.

As regards the Maharajah's arrogance, he cannot bear not being in the centre of every picture. In his own state this is natural enough, but he pursues the same policy elsewhere by staging spectacular late arrivals, the wearing of clothes of the most conspicuous possible hue and headgear of extraordinary shape, and by making speeches on any and every occasion. When to his arrogance there is added a vindictive, capricious and cruel temperament, his officials and attendants never dare put up any proposals which are unpalatable to him. He is currently reported to thrash his A.D.C.'s. Be that as it may, and it is quite in keeping with the cruelty in his character, there is a cringing, frightened atmosphere among the members of the Maharajah's staff such as I have never seen in any other state.

I was not sent to Alwar as Censor Morum so I have hitherto refrained from any reference to this aspect of his life. But to complete the picture of conditions in the state, it is necessary to bear in mind that the moral atmosphere of the place is mephitic. The people around the Maharajah have an evil, brutalised look such as I have seen nowhere else. One incident which happened a couple of years ago will give some idea of what goes on under the veil. The Alwar Darbar pressed for the extradition of a man from a neighbouring Rajpoutana state as a deserter from the Alwar Bodyguard; but the other Darbar flatly refused, because the Alwar Bodyguard was not a military unit at all but was well known to have been recruited for another more personal purpose.

Against all this, however, there is something to put on the credit side. He has probably the acutest brain of all the Indian princes. When he cares, he can make himself the most charming host and companion. To see him at a shooting party beguiling the company with story after story of interesting experiences he has had, makes one regret all the more that there is another altogether different side to his character, the Dr Jekyll to his Mr Hyde.[16]

British officials agonized over what to do with this errant prince, concerned about the political outrage that would occur were it ever publicly revealed how outrageous and corrupt his rule had become. One official feared that such disclosures 'would be such as to provoke the horror of the whole civilised world'. Finally, with his state teetering on the verge of bankruptcy, the Maharaja went into exile, turning up in Italy where he failed to get Mussolini to throw a birthday party for him. He then camped on the steps of the Vatican in a vain attempt to receive an audience with the Pope before arriving at a Buckingham Palace garden party uninvited, much to the fury of King George V. Back in India, at the farewell reception for Lord Willingdon, the Viceroy, he said to him after shaking his hand, 'Your excellency, I am sorry to say farewell, but you can leave India knowing that everything you have done to me was entirely justified.' Shortly afterwards, in 1937, he died.

Although the princes were nominally part of a council which acted as their 'trade union', their future was never of prime concern to the British. Lord Wavell, the penultimate Viceroy, showed considerable decency in his dealings with the princes but never had any illusions about them, as shown in his diary entry for 12 August 1946 – a year before Independence.

The Nawab of Chhatari came to see me about the position of the 'loyalists' who had always helped the British; were we really going so soon and leaving them at the mercy of Congress, who had always been anti-British; and now we had got at odds with the Muslim League too; and what were our friends to do? Did I advise them to surrender their titles, as they were being pressed to do by Jinnah? Couldn't we stop another 10 years or so anyway, the Labour Government was surely going much too fast in handing over India. These interviews, of which I had already had a number and shall doubtless have many more, are rather trying and very painful. Some of the so-called

'friends' of the British have done nothing more really than
support us because we kept order and enabled them to
draw their rents from the land in ease and safety; few of
them have been good land-lords or looked after their
tenants; and not one of them hardly has had the political
courage to come out into the open and oppose Congress.
I have not a great deal of sympathy for them. But some
like the Nawab are really genuine and are great gentlemen,
and I am sorry for them. I always feel it is better to be
honest and to say that we are going to hand over power;
that it is right that we should do so and leave Indians to
govern themselves; that while the Congress is not a body
one would have chosen as the representatives of the great
mass of the Indian people, it is the body that the Indian
people have chosen for themselves and we have to do
business with the men of their choice. The Nawab agreed
to all this; and I gave him such comfort as I could by saying
that the experience of history was that people became
much more moderate when they got power and became
responsible and did not do nearly all the violent things that
they threatened. I said I saw no reason why they should
give up well-earned honours at Mr Jinnah's bidding but
that was for them to decide.[17]

Wavell failed to prevent the increasing violence between
Hindus and Muslims and then lost the confidence of Clement
Attlee, the newly elected British Prime Minister. There was
something far more honourable about Wavell than his rather
flashy successor Lord Mountbatten who, although he professed
great empathy with the princes because of his own much touted
regal descent, privately referred to them as this 'bunch of nit-
wits'. In his shrewd politicking with the princes, he wrote a
letter to the Maharaj-Rana of Dholpur, a few weeks before
Independence, cajoling him to join forces with an independent
India.

If you accede now you will be joining a Dominion with
the King as head. If they change the Constitution to a
republic and leave the Commonwealth, the Instrument of
Accession does not bind you in any way to remain with
the republic. It would appear to me that that would be

the moment for Your Highness to decide if you wish to remain with India or reclaim full sovereign independence.

I know that His Majesty would personally be grieved if you elected to sever your connection with him whilst he was still the King of India now that it has been made clear that this would not involve you in accepting to remain within a republic if this was unacceptable to you when the time came.

I too will be grieved if I find that Your Highness refuses to accede before the 14th August, since I shall bitterly feel the fatal isolation of an old friend; and it would be sad that you or your illustrious family would travel without any diplomatic privileges unless Your Highness were able to set up legations or consulates in various parts of the world . . .

You asked me what I thought India would do to Dholpur if you did not accede. To the best of my knowledge and belief they will do nothing; that is precisely the trouble – nothing whatever will be done and your State will remain in complete isolation in the centre of an indifferent India.[18]

Slowly but inevitably the princes threw in their lot with Independent India, even though they knew this would result in their eventual powerlessness. Their continued survival was ensured by the retention of privy purses to be paid by Independent India, although the larger states possessed untold private wealth. Years after Independence, the Maharawl of Dungarpur confided to Charles Chenevix Trench that they had entertained hopes of forming a powerful 'non-aligned' bloc, rather than being stampeded into choosing to merge either with India or Pakistan.

Princes were not fools. Had they been left alone by Lord Mountbatten they would have enlisted the support of the landed aristocracy of the United Provinces and Bihar, not to speak of Rajputana, Central India, Kathiawar and Gujerat. The Moslems would have gladly supported them, as well as the Parsees and the Sikhs. Seventy per cent of the capitalists of British India would have done likewise, including Birla and Tata, both of whom were more akin to Patel [Deputy Prime Minister] than to Nehru. The Depressed Classes would have lent support to Patel, and the complexion of the country would have been changed. Princes would have gathered tremendous bargaining power and their position would have been unassailable. Their support would have been sought by most of the stable elements in India. Popularity was not the monopoly of Nehru alone. I have known princes who have held their own (in democratic elections) having lost their states not for a year or two but for twenty years. A bloc of states in the Indian Union comprising 30 million people with an area of 300,000 square miles (bigger than the present Pakistan) was a feasible proposition, and no dream. But it was not to be.

It was an end brought about by one man and his wife. By making them sign the Instrument of Accession the Viceroy perpetrated the rape of the states. Had the princes been left alone, Congress could never have got them to sign away their powers and heritage within a fortnight. *No, never.* Being a member of the Royal Family, many princes took Lord Mountbatten as a friend. Nothing could be further from the truth. No one wanted protection from the Crown if the Crown could not give it; but the princes expected justice and fair play, not lies and half-truths to beguile them into a snare.[19]

Despite this speculation, princely rule was never a viable proposition at Independence. In fact, Sardar Vallabhbhai Javerabhai Patel, Nehru's right-hand man, presided over the integration of the princely states into Independent India and, in the case of Hyderabad, showed he was prepared to use force. In 1971, Mrs Indira Gandhi peremptorily abolished the privy purses of the princes, leaving their descendants to rely on their existing fortunes, open their palaces as hotels or sink back into the obscurity from which many of them had emerged. The degree of intrigue that characterizes court life is no less now than at the time of Independence. Some prominent former maharajas have had problems with murderous bastard brothers while others are still wrangling in the courts for what they see as their just share of the enormous assets still held by a handful of the leading houses. Others maintain an obsession with European dictators, Napoleon and Hitler being firm favourites in that particular pantheon. Several former maharajas have chosen to become elected politicians and have shown considerable talent as cabinet ministers or chief ministers of their former states.

10

DEPARTURE

I have lived in India for most of my adult life. My husband is Indian and so are my children. I am not, and less so every year. India reacts very strongly on people. Some loathe it, some love it, most do both. There is a special problem of adjustment for the sort of people who come today, who tend to be liberal in outlook and have been educated to be sensitive and receptive to other cultures. But it is not always easy to be sensitive and receptive to India: there comes a point where you have to close up in order to protect yourself. The place is very strong and often proves too strong for European nerves. There is a cycle that Europeans – by Europeans I mean all Westerners, including Americans – tend to pass through. It goes like this: first stage, tremendous enthusiasm – everything Indian is marvellous; second stage, everything Indian not so marvellous; third stage, everything Indian abominable. For some people, it ends there, for others the cycle renews itself and goes on. I have seen it so many times that now I think of myself as strapped to a wheel that goes round and round and sometimes I'm up and sometimes I'm down. When I meet other Europeans, I can usually tell after a few moment's conversation at what stage of the cycle they happen to be.

Ruth Prawer Jhabvala, *How I became a Holy Mother*[1]

The question of departure from India did not arise for most of the early settlers, unless you include an ethereal exit as one of the approved methods. Despite the fearsome record of disease as the final arbiter in most people's fate, there were some, like

William Hickey, who made several trips to Calcutta before deciding to leave for good. Hickey had spent nearly half a century arriving in and leaving India before finally retiring to write his memoirs, which are unequalled in their Boswellian frankness and charm. He describes his final departure from Calcutta in 1808.

> The 9th of February being appointed for the dispatch of the Fleet I fixed upon the 5th for the sale of my furniture, plate, carriages, horses, books etc., Mr Robert Ledlie having kindly invited me to reside with him for the last week of my stay. As the day of my departure approached I became more affected than I had any idea I should have been. The thought of leaving a place I had resided in for so many years, the number of persons I was sincerely attached to that were in it, added to the melancholy and desponding countenances of my favourite servants, who now for the first time began seriously to apprehend I should quit Bengal, all contributed to my dejection and gloom.[2]

He paid each of his sixty-three servants three months' wages, and after many false starts the departure date was finally set.

> After breakfast I got everything out of the sloop that I intended taking with me, and desired the mangee [the steersman] to prepare for his return to Calcutta. My servants now began to look very dejected, for until that moment they had flattered themselves I should not proceed on the voyage. They saw how melancholy and out of spirits I had been from the time of leaving Mr Ledlie's; they likewise knew what two miserable nights I had passed in the passage down the river, and heard me remark that I had not closed my eyes until four o'clock in the morning in my first attempt to sleep in the *Castle Eden*, all which circumstances led them to think I never should bring myself to stay on board, and certain it was I felt the strongest inclination that could be to return with them into the river Hoogley.
>
> Captain Colnett, who watched me closely, said and did all in his power to console and encourage me, and as I felt

what a folly it would be not to adhere to my resolution after having incurred an expense of upwards of five thousand pounds, I determined to remain where I was. Solicitous, however, to avoid the lamentations of my domestics, which I knew would be the case if I had another interview with them, I requested Captain Colnett to prevent any of them from again coming into my cabin, and that he would get rid of them in the best manner he could. This he accomplished vastly well, pretending the business of the ship was impeded by their stay; besides which they ran the risk of being carried out to sea. He then with a loud voice and affected anger called the boatswain, whom he ordered instantly to turn every stranger out of the ship as the Company's surveyor was coming to muster the crew previous to departure.

While this matter was going on upon deck, I locked myself in the cabin with my faithful little Munnoo, and a sad miserable pair we were, our sorrow and distress being greatly increased by a sudden and violent burst of grief which met our ears and came from my poor servants as they passed under the ship's stern on their way to the sloop. A hearty fit of tears which I could not restrain relieved me much, while the wretched boy, my companion, fixed himself at the quarter gallery window where he sat looking the very image of despair. I thought it best not to say anything to him, so there he remained as long as the vessel that was rapidly conveying his old friends from him was discernible, leaving the poor little fellow in the midst of strangers and in a scene as uncouth as it was novel to him.[3]

Hickey lived on for another twenty-two years, his servant Munnoo accompanying him to England and on his travels elsewhere. Munnoo finally became a Christian, being baptized in the Parish of Beaconsfield as William Munnew. It is not certain where Hickey was buried, but he is thought to have died in his eighties in 1830.

Emma Roberts, another talented writer, followed her married sister to India in 1827. 'There cannot be' she later confessed, 'a more wretched situation than that of a young woman in India

who has been induced to follow the fortunes of her married
sister under the delusive expectation that she will exchange the
privations attached to limited means in England for the far-
famed luxuries of the East.' After her sister died in India, she
devoted herself to writing, publishing *Oriental Scenes, Tales and
Sketches* in 1830, in which she wrote about the trials of exile.

> Persons who have never quitted their native land, cannot
> imagine the passionate regrets experienced by the exile,
> who in the midst of the most gorgeous scenes pines after
> the humblest objects surrounding that home to which he
> dares not hope to return. The feeling may be perverse and
> wayward, but where all is strange, the very magnificence
> of the landscape is apt to revolt the mind, and many
> persons will, like the author, in a fit of despair, contrast
> the Ganges with some obscure rivulet, the magnolia
> with the daisy, to the disparagement of the mighty river
> and the monarch of flowers. To do justice to the sunny
> land of India, its visitors should have the power to leave
> it for Europe at pleasure; when the lot seems finally cast,
> the spirit becomes too much depressed to enjoy the dazzl-
> ing novelties which give but too forcible an assurance that
> we are far from home.[4]

After suffering from exhaustion and overwork, she returned
to England in 1832, but in 1839 she went back to India via the
strenuous overland route and died the following year in Poona.
Another writer who met a similar fate was the French botanist,
Victor Jacquemont, who dictated a moving farewell letter to
his family before finally expiring.

Sick-officers' Quarters, Bombay, December 1, 1832
Dear Porphyre, – I arrived here two and thirty days ago,
very ill, and have now been thirty-one days confined to
my bed. In the pestilential forests of the island of Salsette,
exposed to the burning sun, during the most unhealthy
season of the year, I caught the germ of my present illness,
of which, indeed, I have several times, since I passed
through Ajmeer in March, felt some slight attacks, but
about the nature of which I deceived myself. It was inflam-
mation of the liver. The pestilential miasms of Salsette

have completed the thing. From the beginning of the disorder I made my will and put my affairs in order. . . .

The cruellest pang, my dear Porphyre, for those we love, is, that when dying in a far distant land, they imagine that in the last hours of our existence we are deserted and unnoticed. My dear friend, you will no doubt reap some consolation from the assurance I give you that I have never ceased being the object of the kindest and most affectionate solicitude of a number of good and amiable men . . . My sufferings were at first very great, but for some time past I have been reduced to a state of weakness that scarcely allows of any. The worst of it is, that for thirty-one days I have not slept a single hour. These sleepless nights are however very calm, and do not appear so desperately long.

Fortunately the illness is drawing to a close, which may not be fatal, although it will probably be so.

The abscess, or abscesses, formed from the beginning of the attack in my liver, and which recently appeared likely to dissolve by absorption, appear now to rise upwards, and will soon open outwardly. It is all I wish for, to get quickly out of the miserable state in which I have been languishing for the last month, between life and death. You see that my ideas are perfectly clear; they have been but very rarely, and very transiently confused, during some violent paroxysms of pain at the commencement of my illness. I have generally reckoned upon the worst, and that has never rendered my thoughts gloomy. My end, if it is now approaching, is mild and tranquil. If you were here, seated at my bed-side with my father and Frederic, my heart would burst with grief, and I should not be able to contemplate my approaching death with the same fortitude and serenity – console yourself, – console my father – console yourselves mutually my dear friends.

I feel quite exhausted by this effort to write, and must bid you adieu! Farewell! Oh how much you are all beloved by your poor Victor! Farewell for the last time!

Stretched out upon my back, I can only write with a pencil. For fear that these lines may be effaced, the excellent Mr Nichol will copy this letter in writing, in order that I may be sure you will read my last thoughts.

VICTOR JACQUEMONT

I have been able to sign what the admirable Mr Nichol has had the kindness to copy. Once more, farewell, my friends! December 2nd.[5]

Five days later, he died in agony.

The departure of Lord Curzon from India in 1905, while not as final as Jacquemont's, was probably the most bitter moment in his life, as it represented his defeat at the hands of Lord Kitchener, the dishonourable and scheming Indian Army Commander-in-Chief. Kitchener had forced Curzon into resignation by demanding full powers over all military matters in the Subcontinent while plotting behind his back to engineer his downfall. Lady Curzon wrote a letter to her American mother about the frosty departure scene between her husband and Kitchener.

25 October 1905   Jammu

Darling Mother;

We left Simla last Monday at 11 o'clock and had a most touching and dramatic departure. Lord Kitchener had been away ever since George resigned as the feeling against him was so intense that he could not stay in Simla. Well everyone in Simla came to say Goodbye, and we solemnly walked out onto the lawn where hundreds of people were standing. First came the Guard of Honour, and next it stood that unscrupulous warrior Lord K. in uniform surrounded by the whole of his staff. George shook his hand in silence. I said one word 'Goodbye' and passed on, & never spoke to him again. His face was twitching and he undoubtedly felt the icy nature of the situation, & the breaking of our friendship forever; he knows too that he has gained nothing by all this and lost not only our regard but his prestige in India & the respect of the whole of India, for his lying and intrigues are now known.

A great many people were weeping and it was a trying ordeal. When we had made the round we turned and faced everyone and I bowed to right and left, George stood with hat off, the band played 'God save the King', then we got into the postilion carriage escorted by the bodyguard and the whole crowd cheered and cheered. Lord Kitchener had never moved – he raised his white helmet and stood like a sphinx and our procession moved away and we left Simla and its troubles behind us forever.[6]

The most prescient final thoughts on departure appear in E.M. Forster's *A Passage to India*. Forster lived in Northern India in 1921–2, working as secretary to the Maharaja of Dewas Senior. He found the state 'an untidy ant-hill' which was 'slackly administered' and quickly reached the conclusion that until a strong degree of self-government was granted to the Indians, there was little hope of proper relations between the two races. In his novel, Aziz, the young Muslim doctor who is wrongfully accused of molesting Miss Quested, tells his friend Fielding, a school principal, that there is no point in seeking his forgiveness for the way things developed.

> 'Clear out, clear out, I say. Why are we put to so much suffering? We used to blame you, now we blame ourselves, we grow wiser. Until England is in difficulties we keep silent, but in the next European war – aha, aha! Then is our time.' He paused, and the scenery, though it smiled, fell like a gravestone on any human hope. They cantered past a temple to Hanuman – God so loved the world that He took monkey's flesh upon Him – and past a Saivite temple, which invited to lust, but under the semblance of eternity, its obscenities bearing no relation to those of our flesh and blood. They splashed through butterflies and frogs; great trees with leaves like plates rose among the brushwood. The divisions of daily life were returning, the shrine had almost shut.
> 'Who do you want instead of the English? The Japanese?' jeered Fielding, drawing rein.
> 'No, the Afghans. My own ancestors.'
> 'Oh, your Hindu friends will like that, won't they?'
> 'It will be arranged – a conference of Oriental statesmen.'

'It will indeed be arranged.'

'Old story of "We will rob every man and rape every woman from Peshawar to Calcutta," I suppose, which you get some nobody to repeat and then quote every week in the *Pioneer* in order to frighten us into retaining you! We know!' Still he couldn't quite fit in Afghans at Mau, and, finding he was in a corner, made his horse rear again, until he remembered that he had, or ought to have, a motherland. Then he shouted: 'India shall be a nation! No foreigners of any sort! Hindu and Moslem and Sikh and all shall be one! Hurrah! Hurrah for India! Hurrah! Hurrah!'

India a nation! What an apotheosis! Last comer to the drab nineteenth-century sisterhood! Waddling in at this hour of the world to take her seat! She, whose only peer was the Holy Roman Empire, she shall rank with Guatemala and Belgium perhaps! Fielding mocked again. And Aziz in an awful rage danced this way and that, not knowing what to do, and cried: 'Down with the English, anyhow. That's certain. Clear out, you fellows, double quick, I say. We may hate one another, but we will hate you most. If I don't make you go, Ahmed will, Karim will, if it's fifty five-hundred years we shall get rid of you; yes, we shall drive every blasted Englishman into the sea, and then' – he rode against him furiously – 'and then,' he concluded, half kissing him, 'you and I shall be friends.'

'Why can't we be friends now?' said the other, holding him affectionately. 'It's what I want. It's what you want.'

But the horses didn't want it – they swerved apart; the earth didn't want it, sending up rocks through which riders must pass single file; the temples, the tank, the jail, the palace, the birds, the carrion, the Guest House, that came into view as they issued from the gap and saw Mau beneath: they didn't want it, they said in their hundred voices: 'No, not yet,' and the sky said: 'No, not here.'[7]

Forster was considered at the time to have exaggerated the poisonous effects of colonialism on relations between Indians and the British, but with hindsight it is extraordinary how perceptive he was. Dennis Castle's satirical novel, *Run Out the*

Raj, provides an amusing portrait of the eventual departure of
the British on the eve of Independence. The novel is set in a
fictitious hill station where the local wing-commander calls a
meeting to discuss details of the regiment's withdrawal.

Amid the applause and laughter he drew himself up and
bellowed, 'BOY!'

As the rest of the committee were recovering from this
entirely unexpected shout, Akkar Singh, senior bearer at
the Queen's Club, opened the door.

'Bara pegs, eck dum, Akkar Singh,' ordered the wing-
commander, 'the sub-cheese to go on the R.A.F. chitty.'

'Large whiskies for everyone, sahib? All on account.
Atchcha.'

The Sikh bearer backed out, his bloodshot eyes nar-
rowed in his bearded, high-boned face. The ancient
monastic door hung loosely on 18th-century iron hinges.
And, as always, when any committee sat, Akkar Singh
removed a small cork, its head rounded smooth and tarred
to match the remaining iron bolts of the upper hinge band,
and applied his ear to the hole. Worn smooth by generations of Indian ears which, from within, would only
appear as a knot in the oak, this listening post revealed the
scandals of British club members reported for drunken-
ness, bouncing cheques or adultery. For nearly a hundred years the British had firmly believed Indians to be
psychic. What the bazaar knew today, GHQ would know
tomorrow. Bearers would tell their office-masters of
their postings and promotions long before the top-secret
notification arrived from Delhi for decoding.

While an embarrassment, this constant leakage of
information was also regarded with some inverted pride
by the exiled British. India was a land of mystery and
magic wavelengths and they adored writing 'home' about
it. But, in reality, the key to this riddle could be found
in wide-meshed shutters, ill-fitting windows and porous
doors – plus the incredible carrying power of the British
whisper. Add, too, a bona fide reliance upon service wives
not repeating, over tea, their husbands hush-hush postings
to more superior stations and the extraordinary British

belief that an Indian clerk could type out top-secret orders without understanding them, and all India's mystique and uncanny djinnism could be accounted for.

Akkar Singh had already known for three days that the R.A.F. were leaving Tophar for his cousin was a clerk in Air H.Q. Delhi. Now all R.A.F. servants in Tophar had been warned to make ready with tears, blackmail and theft for the departure of their masters. They would never see them again, so officers who foolishly left their packing to their bearers while they drank themselves insensible at the Queen's Club farewell party or crept through the shrubbery for a final fling in a lady's bed would, on opening their baggage in Delhi two days later, find very few personal belongings left. Many a Harrods shirt would end its days flapping round the skinny knees of an 'untouchable' latrine sweeper, cricket boots would become a new fashion among Tophar goatherds and an Adastrian (RAF) blazer would lose its glory on the shoulders of a money-lender, huddled by his hookah outside his bazaar go-down.[8]

There is still an unnecessary deference shown to British visitors to India but at least relationships on an equal footing are now perfectly possible, which was not the case when one race ruled and the other was subjugated.

Earthly reality for tens of millions of Indians is destined to be miserable for generations to come. No person who takes in all the various facts about political unrest and population growth can doubt that the future is bleak. Philip Mason, the ICS officer who first went to India in the 1920s, emphasized this cruel reality in his autobiography.

India hits you full in the face with misery. There is misery everywhere; starved, mangy dogs, gaunt lame ponies; beggars that sicken the beholder. In the back streets of the towns, people are huddled together in hideous squalor; there are flies everywhere, wasted limbs, festering sores. Unless you take the way of St Francis of Assissi, you cannot live as a sane man with open eyes among such sights. You must close your eyes, harden your heart and do what you can. If you are in any sense a ruler, you must make your heart harder still, because any just system of rule must make laws and treat all men according to categories. A just judge cannot play father to the prodigal son. Hard cases make bad law, they say, and if that is so, good law makes hard hearts. Just as Indians felt that all their problems would be solved by independence, so I felt obscurely that to leave India, and to stop being an official, would release me from a burden of which I had taught myself not to think. But it is not a burden of which one can ever be quite rid; it is part of being human.[9]

The sense of quaint unreality which pervades many Indians' thoughts about their country can be ascribed to a fear of confronting the painful reality that exists in each and every state of the country. In the early 1960s V.S. Naipaul believed that this blinkered approach was merely an easy way to avoid harsh everyday existence.

It is well that Indians are unable to look at their country directly, for the distress they would see would drive them mad. And it is well that they have no sense of history, for how then would they be able to continue to squat amid their ruins, and which Indian would be able to read the history of his country for the last thousand years without anger and pain? It is better to retreat into fantasy and fatalism, to trust to the stars in which the fortunes of all are written – there are lecturers in astrology in some universities – and to regard the progress of the rest of the world with the tired tolerance of one who has been through it all before. The aeroplane was known to ancient India, and the telephone, and the atom bomb: there is evidence in the Indian epics. Surgery was highly developed in ancient India; here, in an important national newspaper, is the text of a lecture proving it. Indian shipbuilding was the wonder of the world. And democracy flourished in ancient India. Every village was a republic, self-sufficient, ordered, controlling its own affairs; the village council could hang an offending villager or chop off his hand. This is what must be recreated, this idyllic ancient India; and when *panchayati raj*, a type of village self-rule, is introduced in 1962 there will be so much talk of the glories of ancient India, so much talk by enthusiastic politicians of

hands anciently chopped off, that in some villages of the
Madhya Pradesh state hands will be chopped off and people
will be hanged by village councils.

Eighteenth-century India was squalid. It invited conquest. But not in Indian eyes: before the British came, as
every Indian will tell you, India was rich, on the brink of
an industrial breakthrough; and K.M. Munshi says that
every village had a school. Indian interpretations of their
history are almost as painful as the history itself; and it is
especially painful to see the earlier squalor being repeated
today, as it has been in the creation of Pakistan and the
reawakening within India of disputes about language,
religion, caste and region. India, it seems, will never cease
to require the arbitration of a conqueror. A people with
a sense of history might have ordered matters differently.
But this is precisely the saddening element in Indian
history: this absence of growth and development. It is a
history whose only lesson is that life goes on. There is only
a series of beginnings, no final creation.[10]

Since then, Naipaul has been back to the Subcontinent several
times, and after his most recent visit in 1989, says that 'In 27
years I had succeeded in making a kind of return journey, shedding my Indian nerves, abolishing the darkness that separated
me from my ancestral past.' He has also changed his earlier
opinion about the absence of growth and development in Indian
history.

What I hadn't understood in 1962, or had taken too much
for granted, was the extent to which the country had been
remade; and even the extent to which India had been
restored to itself, after its own equivalent of the Dark
Ages – after the Muslim invasions and the detailed,
repeated vandalising of the North, the shifting empires,
the wars, the 18th-century anarchy. The twentieth-
century restoration of India to itself had taken time; it
could even seem like a kind of luck . . . People everywhere
have ideas now of who they are and what they owe
themselves. The process quickened with the economic
development that came after independence; what was hidden in 1962, or not easy to see, what perhaps was only

in a state of becoming, has become clearer. The liberation
of spirit that has come to India could not come as release
alone. In India, with its layer below layer of distress and
cruelty, it had to come as disturbance. It had to come as
rage and revolt. India was now a country of a million
mutinies. A million mutinies, supported by twenty kinds
of group excess, sectarian excess, religious excess, regional
excess: the beginnings of self-awareness, it would seem,
the beginnings of an intellectual life, already negated by
old anarchy and disorder. But there was in India now what
didn't exist 200 years before: a central will, a central
intellect, a national idea. The Indian Union was greater
than the sum of its parts; and many of these movements
of excess strengthened an Indian state, defining it as the
source of law and civility and reasonableness . . .

Excess was now felt to be excess in India. What the
mutinies were also helping to define was the strength of
the general intellectual life, and the wholeness and
humanism of the values to which all Indians now felt they
could appeal. And – strange irony – the mutinies were
not to be wished away. They were part of the beginning
of a new way for many millions, part of India's growth,
part of its restoration.[11]

While one may quibble with Naipaul on the details, his
remains the most stimulating and thoughtful voice on the fate
of India.

The effect of India on the newcomer can cause considerable
confusion to the uninitiated. Ivan Illich, the radical educa-
tionalist, visited India in the early 1970s and found much to confirm his prejudices against highly centralized Western society.
He was a guest of Romesh and Raj Thapar, two prominent
liberal publishers, who introduced him to various like-minded
souls in New Delhi.

He suddenly felt he was in a place that was familiar – and
so far removed from what he had expected. 'Even your
peasants are not uneducated. They may not know how
to read and write but their minds are able to roam over
a philosophical plane, which is quite unusual.' I tried to
bring him down to earth. 'Don't be carried away by what

we say – there is a yawning gap between our words and action of any kind.' But he was unbelieving and went back to his adopted home in Mexico armed with books on Hindi and Sanskrit, determined to learn the language before his next visit, determined to somehow get through to the real India, to find that elusive chord of communication.

I feared for him and his impending disillusionment but could not stifle his enthusiasm in any way.

Illich set off on his quest for the 'real India' and was out of touch with the Thapars for several months.

. . . one morning as I entered the office I saw a gaunt, sad man sitting with my secretary, looking like a burnt out case, familiar and yet unrecognisable. I passed him by but something about the look in his eyes brought me back. 'Ivan,' I almost cried. . . . 'What's happened? Something terribly traumatic has happened. I can tell from your face.' And then reluctantly he came out with his story, his brush with the 'real' India.

Starting from the more civilised south, he had worked his way to Banaras, that city which claims to hold the soul of this country. There he looked around, talked to people and decided to stay with a priest who offered him hospitality. On the floor, in a little verandah, open to the sky. The first result was diarrhoea which sapped all his strength; the second was that all his possessions were stolen from him amidst the chanting and the ritual of that holy of holies. Abandoned and friendless, he lay there not having the physical strength or the money to take himself off, to flee from the real face of India, cruel and uncaring. How he finally managed to get to Delhi, I never found out. It was a trauma of gigantic proportion, more emotional than physical. 'I never knew how feeble I really was until I got some hot water this morning to shave. I just loved it,' he said. But he looked frail, that burning fire in his eyes had been extinguished by our heartlessness, and we both felt he needed immediate medical attention. We suggested he take the first flight out of India and he did, thank the Lord. I had a little note from him after that

saying, 'Raj, you were right. I went into a coma for
a week after I reached Zurich.' This episode made me
feel more than ever that if one survives India one can
survive the worst hell. Perhaps it is the theory of transmigration that keeps us going, that waiting for another
birth.[12]

The American journalist Elizabeth Bumiller was based in
New Delhi in the mid-1980s and wrote a book describing the
fate of women in India, in which she concluded with her own
impressions before her departure.

India, the country that once made me feel as if I were free-
falling in space, was home. Delhi, once so foreign and
overpowering, had evolved into a lovely, vaguely dull
suburb to which I was always happy to return after my
other adventures. . . . I never have had patience with
people who romanticized India, but as I write these last
pages in Tokyo, in a modern, Westernized house, with
all the latest conveniences but none of the charm of our
old place on Prithvi Raj Road, I am afraid I am perilously
close to sinking into sentiment. When I look at our pictures of India now, of meals on the mud floor of Bhabhiji's
house, or of peacocks on the ramparts of Rajasthan, or of
our garden of dahlias, it does not seem possible to me that
I lived there. India seems part of another time, as if it were
a dream I had before awaking one morning. And yet, this
nostalgia has overcome me only since I left. While living
in India, the day-to-day irritants – power shortages,
water shortages, erratic phones, heat, dust, months of
stomach troubles – always balanced out the romance . . .
I was too bewildered to love India in the beginning,
although I felt that I somehow should. Nor did I love it
at the end, when I realized that it is neither possible nor
right to 'love' a country where there still exists such
widespread poverty and injustice. What I can say,
selfishly, is that I loved my life in India. The country
brought a depth and a richness to my experience that I had
never known before and changed many of my assumptions
that I had brought with me.[13]

It is fitting that the most moving comment on departure should be by Jawaharlal Nehru in his last will and testament, which he composed in 1954. He always had a hearty contempt for religious mumbo-jumbo from any quarter and wished the major part of his cremated ashes to be scattered over the countryside: but for a small portion, he had a different journey in store, which they finally underwent after his death in 1964.

The Ganga, especially, is the river of India, beloved of her people, round which are intertwined her racial memories, her hopes and fears, her songs of triumph, her victories and her defeats. She has been a symbol of India's age-long culture and civilisation, ever-changing, ever-flowing, and yet ever the same Ganga. She reminds me of the snow-covered peaks and the deep valleys of the Himalayas, which I have loved so much, and of the rich and vast plains below, where my life and work have been cast. Smiling and dancing in the morning sunlight, and dark and gloomy and full of mystery as the evening shadows fall, a narrow, slow and graceful stream in winter and a vast, roaring thing during the monsoon, broad-bosomed almost as the sea, and with something of the sea's power to destroy, the Ganga has been to me a symbol and a memory of the past of India, running into the present, and flowing on to the great ocean of the future. And though I have discarded much of past tradition and custom, and am anxious that India should rid herself of all shackles that bind and constrain her and divide her people, and suppress vast numbers of them, and prevent the free development of the body and the spirit; though I seek all this, yet I do not wish to cut myself off from the past completely. I am proud of that great inheritance that has been, and is, ours, and I am conscious that I too, like all of us, am a link in that unbroken chain which goes back to the dawn of history in the immemorial past of India. That chain I would not break, for I treasure it and seek inspiration from it. And as a witness of this desire of mine and as my last homage to India's cultural inheritance, I am making this request that a handful of my ashes be thrown into the Ganga at Allahabad to be carried to the great ocean that washes India's shore.[14]

NOTES

All books were published in London unless otherwise stated.

1. ARRIVAL

1. Victor Jacquemont, *Letters from India*, 1834, Vol. 1, p. 87.
2. Mark Twain, *More Tramps Abroad*, 1897, p. 238.
3. Nearchus, quoted in Arrian, *Indica*, XVI, trans. J.W. McCrindle, in *Ancient India as Described by Megasthenes and Arrian*, 1877.
4. Strabo, *The Geography of Strabo*, trans. H.L. Jones, Cambridge, Mass., 1944.
5. *The Travels of Fa-hsien (399–414 AD), or Record of the Buddhistic Kingdoms*, trans. H.A. Giles, 1923, pp. 20–1.
6. Hiuen Tsiang, [Hsien Tsang], *On Yuan Chwang's Travels in India*, trans. Thomas Watters, 1904–5, pp. 147–8.
7. Alberuni, *Alberuni's India*, trans. E.C. Sachau, 1910, pp. 22–3.
8. *Babur-Nama*, trans. A.S. Beveridge, 1922, p. 518.
9. *The First Englishmen in India*, ed. J. Courtenay Locke, 1930, pp. 19–20.
10. *Early Travels in India, 1583–1619*, ed. William Foster, Oxford, 1921, p. 14.
11. *A Collection of Voyages and Travels (The Journal of Sir Thomas Roe)*, ed. Awnsham Churchill, 1704, Vol. 1, p. 772.
12. Edward Terry, *Purchas his Pilgrimes*, 1625, Vol. 2, p. 1464.
13. *Memoirs of William Hickey*, ed. Alfred Spencer, 1913, Vol. 1, p. 163.
14. *The Life and Times of Mrs Sherwood*, ed. F.J. Harvey Darton, 1910, p. 242.
15. Reginald Heber, *Narrative of a Journey through the Upper Provinces of India*, 1828, Vol. 1, pp. 2–4.
16. William Howard Russell, *My Diary in India*, 1860, Vol. 1, p. 86.
17. Manuscript of the Indian Journal of Edward Lear (22 November 1873) in the Houghton Library, Harvard University.
18. P.N. Furbank, *E.M. Forster: A Life*, Oxford, 1979, Vol. 1, p. 225.
19. Robert Byron, *An Essay on India*, 1931, p. 19.
20. Francis Yeats-Brown, *Bengal Lancer*, 1930, pp. 8–9.
21. Robert Lutyens, letter to his mother, private collection.
22. *Collected Letters of Evelyn Waugh*, ed. Mark Amory, 1980, p. 389.
23. Arthur Koestler, *The Lotus and the Robot*, 1960, p. 1.
24. Alan Ross, *Blindfold Games*, 1986, p. 39.
25. Sashti Brata, *India the Perpetual Paradox*, New York, 1985, pp. 15–16.

26. Hugo Williams, *All the Time in the World*, 1966, p. 107.
27. Patrick Marnham, *The Road to Katmandu*, 1971, pp. 139–40.
28. Anita Desai, *Baumgartner's Bombay*, 1988, p. 13.

2. CLIMATE

1. Edward Thompson, *An Indian Day*, 1927, p. 73.
2. *Rig Veda*, trans. W.D. O'Flaherty, 1981, p. 173.
3. Subandhu, *Vasavadatta, A Book of India*, ed. B.N. Pandey, 1965, p. 138.
4. *The Travels of Marco Polo*, trans. Ronald Latham, 1958, p. 267.
5. *Babur-Nama*, trans. A.S. Beveridge, 1922, p. 518.
6. François Bernier, *Travels in the Mogul Empire*, 1934, pp. 240–1.
7. Peter Mundy, *The Travels of Peter Mundy*, 1914, Vol. 2, p. 40.
8. *Memoirs of William Hickey*, ed. Alfred Spencer, 1923, Vol. 3, p. 343.
9. Jawaharlal Nehru, *The Discovery of India*, 1946, p. 16.
10. Victor Jacquemont, *Letters from India*, 1834, Vol. 1, p. 91.
11. Virginia Surtees, *Charlotte Canning*, 1975, pp. 205–6.
12. F.A. Steel and G. Gardiner, *The Complete Indian Housekeeper and Cook*, 1921, p. 205.
13. Frank Richards, *Old-Soldier Sahib*, 1936, p. 240.
14. Alan Ross, *Blindfold Games*, 1986, p. 41.
15. Patrick Marnham, *The Road to Katmandu*, 1971, pp. 136–7.
16. Edward Terry, *A Voyage to East India*, second edition 1777, pp. 43–95.
17. John Hobart Caunter, *The Oriental Annual*, 1834, pp. 6–10.
18. E.M. Forster, *The Hill of Devi*, 1953, p. 55.
19. Alexander Frater, *Chasing the Monsoon*, 1990, p. 259.
20. Victor Jacquemont, *Letters from India*, 1834, Vol. 1, p. 227.
21. Emily Eden, *Up the Country*, 1930, p. 293.
22. Sir Henry Cunningham, *Chronicles of Dustypore*, 1875, p. 234.
23. *The Letters of Edwin Lutyens to His Wife*, ed. Claire Percy and Jane Ridley, 1985, p. 245.
24. Richard Burton, *Goa and the Blue Mountains*, 1851, p. 353.
25. E.F. Knight, *Where Three Empires Meet*, 1892, pp. 26–7.
26. Jawaharlal Nehru, *The Discovery of India*, 1946, pp. 8–9.

3. MUTINY AND PARTITION

1. William Howard Russell, *Mutiny Diary*, 1858, Vol. 1, p. 299.
2. George Curzon, *Leaves from a Viceroy's Notebook*, 1926, p. 32.
3. 'The Outbreak of the Indian Mutiny', *Journal of the Society of Army Historical Research*, 1955, p. 33.
4. Field Marshal Lord Roberts, *Forty Years in India*, 1897, Vol. 1, pp. 123–4.
5. J.G.Farrell, *The Siege of Krishnapur*, 1973, pp. 296–7.

6. William Howard Russell, *My Diary in India*, 1860, Vol. 1, p. 329.
7. Queen Victoria to Lady Canning, Windsor Castle, 22 October 1857.
8. Sita Ram Pande, *From Sepoy to Subedar*, 1873, final chapter.
9. Michael Edwardes, *The Battle of Plassey*, 1963, p. 148.
10. Francis Buchanan, *A Journey from Madras through Mysore, Canara, and Malabar*, 1807, p. 65.
11. Bishop Reginald Heber, *Narrative of a Journey through the Upper Provinces of India*, 1828, Vol. 1, p. 626.
12. Edward Thompson, *An Indian Day*, 1927, pp. 12–14.
13. George Orwell, *Burmese Days*, London, 1935, pp. 122–3.
14. Ibid. p. 275.
15. Brigadier-General R.E.H. Dyer, GOC Amritsar, in his official report explaining the shooting, p. 96.
16. Jawaharlal Nehru, *Autobiography*, 1936, p. 43.
17. Sir Penderel Moon, *Divide and Quit*, 1961, p. 267.
18. *The Contemporary Conservative, Selected Writings of Dhiren Bhagat*, ed. Salman Kurshid, New Delhi, 1990, pp. 180–1; originally published in *The Spectator*, 8 August 1987.
19. Ibid., pp. 180–2.
20. Khushwant Singh, *Train to Pakistan*, New Delhi, 1988, p. 9.
21. Sir Penderel Moon, *Divide and Quit*, 1961, p. 269.

4. THE RULERS

1. *The Ramayana*, trans. R.T.H. Griffith, Benares, 1915, Vol. 2, p. 57.
2. *Ancient India as Described by Megasthenes and Arrian*, trans. J.W. McCrindle, 1877, p. 27.
3. 'Asoka Rock Edict 6', trans. D.C. Sircar, in B.N. Pandey, *A Book of India*, 1965, p. 26.
4. *The Laws of Manu*, 1886, trans. G. Buhler, Oxford, *Sacred Books of the East*, Vol. 25 (vii, 3–5), p. 8.
5. Ibn Battuta, *Travels in Asia and Africa*, 1929, p. 184.
6. Sir H.M. Elliot and Professor John Dowson, *The History of India as Told by its Own Historians*, 1871, Vol. 3, pp. 430–6.
7. *Early Travels in India, 1583–1619*, ed. W. Foster, 1921, p. 17.
8. *Memoirs of Jahangir*, trans. Alexander Rogers, 1909–14, pp. 307–9.
9. *Early Travels in India, 1583–1619*, ed. W. Foster, pp. 106–12.
10. Warren Hastings, 1921, in his introduction to Wilkins' translation of the *Bhagwat-Gita*, 1785.
11. Ram Mohan Roy, *Exposition of the Practical Operation of Judicial and Revenue Systems of India*, 1831, p. 18.
12. Abbé J.A.Dubois, *Description of its Character, Manners, and Customs of the People of India, and of their Institutions, Religious and Civil*, Oxford, 1906, xxiii.
13. Victor Jacquemont, *Letters from India*, 1834, Vol. 1, p. 277.

14. Lord William Cavendish-Bentinck in his foreword to the Abbé Dubois' book, *Hindu Manners, Customs and Ceremonies*, 1906.
15. Lady Canning in a letter to her mother, in Virginia Surtees, *Charlotte Canning*, 1975, p. 218.
16. David Dilkes, *Curzon in India*, 1969, p. 64.
17. Jawaharlal Nehru, *An Autobiography*, 1936, p. 417.
18. V.S. Naipaul, *An Area of Darkness*, 1964, p. 56.
19. Jan Morris, *Destinations*, 1980, p. 57.
20. R.K. Narayan, *A Writer's Nightmare*, Delhi, 1988, p. 223.
21. Philip Mason, *A Shaft of Sunlight*, 1978, p. 97.
22. G.K. Das, *E.M. Forster's India*, 1977, pp. 71–2.
23. Verrier Elwin, *The Tribal World of Verrier Elwin*, Oxford, 1964, p. 66.
24. Mohammed Ali Jinnah, *Some Recent Speeches and Writings of Mr Jinnah*, Lahore, 1946–7, pp. 174–80.
25. S. Gopal, *Jawaharlal Nehru*, Oxford, 1975, Vol. 1, p. 255.
26. Lord Wavell, *Viceroy's Journal*, Oxford, 1973, 1 July 1946.
27. S. Gopal, *Jawaharlal Nehru*, Oxford, Vol. 1, p. 363.
28. Extract from 'Partition' in *Collected Poems of W.H. Auden*, ed. Edward Mendelson, 1991, p. 803.
29. James Cameron, *An Indian Summer*, 1974, p. 102.

5. RELIGION

1. James Cameron, *An Indian Summer*, 1974, p. 42.
2. *The Rig Veda* Benares, Second edition 1896–7, 2 vols, X, Hymn 129.
3. A.L. Basham, *The Wonder that was India*, 1954, pp. 240–1.
4. *The Upanishads*, trans. Juan Mascaro, 1965, pp. 49–50.
5. *The Bhagavad Gita*, trans. Juan Mascaro, 1962, p. 8.
6. A.L. Basham, *The Wonder that was India*, 1954, 'Address to Sigala', p. 181.
7. Twelfth Rock Edict in *Sources of Indian Tradition*, ed. Ainslie T. Embree, 1988, Vol. 1, p. 147.
8. *On Yuan Chwang's [Hsuen Tsang] Travels in India*, ed. Thomas Watters, 1904, pp. 180–1.
9. Alberuni, *Alberuni's India*, trans. E.C. Sachau, 1910, pp. 19–22.
10. Khushwant Singh, *A History of the Sikhs*, Oxford, 1983, Vol. 1, p. 29.
11. Ibid., pp. 31–2.
12. William Sleeman, *Rambles and Recollections of an Indian Official*, 1844, p. 480.
13. Victor Jacquemont, *Letters from India*, 1834, Vol. 2, p. 306.
14. Richard Burton, *Goa and the Blue Mountains*, 1851.
15. Abbé J.A. Dubois, *Description of the Character, Manners and Customs of the People of India*, Oxford, 1906, p. 26.
16. Mulk Raj Anand, *Untouchable*, 1935, p. 128.
17. *Journals and Letters of the Rev. Henry Martyn*, ed. Rev. S. Wilberforce, 1839, pp. 371–2.

18. Ibid., Vol. 2, p. 139.
19. Mary Martha Sherwood, *The Life and Times of Mrs. Sherwood*, ed. F.J. Harvey Darton, 1910, p. 374.
20. John Beames, *Memoirs of a Bengal Civilian*, 1961, p. 196.
21. Abbé, J.A. Dubois, *Description of the Characters, Manners and Customs of the People of India*, Oxford, 1906, p. 29.
22. M.K. Gandhi, *Young India, 1919–1922*, New York, 1923, pp. 472–7.
23. Nirad C. Chaudhuri, *The Autobiography of an Unknown Indian*, 1951, p. 123.
24. Shiva Naipaul, *Beyond the Dragon's Mouth*, 1984, p. 277.
25. V.S. Naipaul, *An Area of Darkness*, 1964, p. 70.
26. Arthur Koestler, *The Lotus and the Robot*, 1960, p. 113.
27. Ibid., p. 153.
28. Abbé J.A. Dubois, *Description of the Character, Manners and Customs of the People of India*, Oxford, 1906, pp. 128–9.
29. Paul Theroux, *The Great Railway Bazaar*, 1975, p. 129.
30. Hugh Milne, *Bhagwan, The God that Failed*, 1986, p. 93.
31. Robert Byron, *An Essay on India*, 1931, p. 59.
32. Nirad C. Chaudhuri, *The Autobiography of an Unknown Indian*, 1951, p. 209.

6. Travel and Transport

1. Rudyard Kipling, *Kim*, 1901, p. 190.
2. Jawaharlal Nehru, *The Discovery of India*, 1946, p. 51.
3. Eric Newby, *Slowly Down the Ganges*, 1966, p. 246.
4. Geoffrey Moorhouse, *Calcutta*, 1971, p. 138.
5. Ibn Battuta, *Travels in Asia and Africa*, 1929, p. 183.
6. *General History of the Mogol Empire, Memoirs of M. Manouchi*, trans. F.F. Catrou, 1708 pp. 85–87.
7. *Early Travels in India, 1583–1619*, ed. William Foster, Oxford, 1921, p. 244.
8. Jean-Baptiste Tavernier, *Travels in India*, trans. V. Ball, 1889, Vol. 1, pp. 38–9.
9. Victor Jacquemont, *Letters from India*, 1834, Vol. 1, p. 154.
10. Richard Burton, *Goa and the Blue Mountains*, 1851, p. 250.
11. Rudyard Kipling, 'The Overland Mail' in *Foot-service to the Hills*, 1943, p. 33.
12. Geoffrey Clarke, *The Post Office of India and its Story*, 1921, pp. 5–6.
13. James Cameron, *An Indian Summer*, 1974, p. 17.
14. Trevor Fishlock, *India File*, 1982, p. 3.
15. G.W. Steevens, *In India*, 1899, p. 251.
16. Bibhutibhusan Banerji, *Pather Panchali*, 1929, trans. T.W. Clark and Tarapada Mukherji, 1968, pp. 135–6.
17. E.W. Robinson-Horley, *Last Post*, 1985, p. 38.

18. Jon and Rumer Godden, *Two Under the Indian Sun*, 1966, pp. 148–9.
19. Denis Kincaid, *Cactus Land*, 1934, pp. 55–6.
20. Alexander Frater, *Beyond the Blue Horizon*, 1986, pp. 209–13.
21. V.S. Naipaul, *India: A Million Mutinies Now*, 1990, pp. 136–7.

7. THE GREAT CITIES

1. Francis Yeats-Brown, *Bengal Lancer*, 1930, p. 122.
2. *Early Travels in India, 1583–1619*, ed. William Foster, Oxford, 1921, pp. 20–1.
3. Reginald Heber, *Narrative of a Journey through the Upper Provinces of India*, 1828, Vol. 1, p. 282.
4. *Edward Lear's Indian Journal*, ed. Ray Murphy, 1953, p. 45.
5. Raghubir Singh, *Banaras, Sacred City of India*, 1987, pp. 16–17.
6. *The Traveller's Dictionary of Quotation*, ed. Peter Yapp, 1983, p. 463.
7. John Fryer, *A New Account of East India and Persia*, ed. William Crooke, 1909, Vol. 1, pp. 171–3.
8. Gillian Tindall, *City of Gold*, 1982, p. 64.
9. Louis Bromfield, *Night in Bombay*, 1940, p. 57.
10. Shiva Naipaul, *Beyond the Dragon's Mouth*, 1984, p. 254.
11. Ibid., p. 262.
12. Shoba De, *Socialite Evenings*, New Delhi, 1989, p. 120.
13. Eliza Fay, *Original Letters from India*, 1925, pp. 161–3.
14. Maria Graham, *Journal of a Residence in India*, 1812, pp. 123–4 and 130–1.
15. Rudyard Kipling, *City of Dreadful Night*, 1888, pp. 3–5.
16. *Memoirs of William Hickey*, ed. Alfred Spencer, 1913, Vol. 3, p. 211.
17. William MacIntosh, *Travels in Europe, Asia and Africa*, 1782.
18. Geoffrey Moorhouse, *Calcutta*, 1971, pp. 93–4.
19. Leopold von Orlich, *Travels in India*, 1845, Vol. 2, pp. 29–30.
20. *Storia do Mogor; or, Moghul India*, trans. William Irvine, 1907, Vol. 1, pp. 183–5.
21. *Three Mughal Poets*, trans. Ralph Russell and Kurshid ul Islam, 1968, pp. 67–8.
22. Victor Jacquemont, *Letters from India*, 1834, Vol. 1, p. 189.
23. Robert Byron, *Letters Home*, ed. Lucy Butler, 1991, p. 151.
24. Tom Pocock, *Alan Moorehead*, 1989, p. 122.
25. Khushwant Singh, *Delhi*, New Delhi, 1989, p. 1.
26. Jan Morris, *Destinations*, 1980, p. 32.

8. VILLAGE INDIA

1. E.M. Forster, *A Passage to India*, 1924, pp. 116–17.
2. James Forbes, *Oriental Memoirs*, 1813–15, Vol. 2. pp. 416–17.

3. Reginald Heber, *Narrative of a Journey through the Upper Provinces of India*, 1828, Vol. 1, pp. 13–14.
4. Sir William Sleeman, *Rambles and Recollections of an Indian Official*, 1844, p. 394.
5. Ibid., p. 322.
6. Rabindranath Tagore, *Selected Short Stories*, trans. William Radice, 1991, pp. 22–3 (Letter No. 23, 23 June 1891).
7. Nirad C. Chaudhuri, *The Autobiography of an Unknown Indian*, 1951, p. 5.
8. Ibid., pp. 46–7.
9. Bibhutibhusan Banerji, *Pather Panchali*, trans. T.W. Clark and Tarapada Muhkerji, 1968, pp. 282–3.
10. Robert Byron, *An Essay on India*, 1931, pp. 51–2.
11. Denis Kincaid, *Durbar*, 1933, pp. 174–5.
12. F.L. Brayne, *Socrates in an Indian Village*, Delhi, 1929, pp. 33–4.
13. Verrier Elwin, *The Tribal World of Verrier Elwin*, Oxford, 1964, pp. 61–2.
14. M.K. Gandhi, *Collected Works*, New Delhi, 1958–78, Vol. 85, pp. 32–3 and Vol. 75, p. 216.
15. Premchand, *The Gift of a Cow*, trans. Gordon C. Roadarmel 1968, p. 166 (published in Hindi under the title *Godaan* in 1936).
16. Prafulla Mohanti, *My Village, My Life*, 1973, p. 14.
17. R.K. Narayan, *Under the Banyan Tree*, 1985, p. 14.
18. V.S. Naipaul, *An Area of Darkness*, 1964, pp. 252–4.
19. Robin Moore, *Paul Scott's Raj*, 1991, pp. 53–4 (Lecture to Writer's Summer School, 1967, *Muse*, pp. 51–69).
20. Sarah Lloyd, *An Indian Attachment*, 1984, p. 45.
21. Ibid., pp. 45–7.
22. Upamanyu Chatterjee, *English, August*, 1988, pp. 255–6.
23. Philip Mason, *A Thread of Silk*, 1984, p. 99.

9. MAHARAJAS

1. Lord Curzon, Address delivered in Jaipur, 1902.
2. James Tod, *Annals and Antiquities of Rajasthan*, 1829, Vol. 1, p. 530.
3. Emily Eden, *Up the Country*, Oxford, 1930, pp. 207–18.
4. Victor Jacquemont, *Letters from India*, 1834, Vol. 1, p. 395.
5. Sir William Sleeman, *Journey through the Kingdom of Oude*, 1858, Vol. 1, p. 81.
6. Edward Lear, 'The Akond of Swat', *Nonsense Songs and Stories*, 1894, pp. 84–6.
7. A.E.W. Mason, *The Broken Road*, 1907, p. 32.
8. Private Frank Richards, *Old-Soldier Sahib*, 1936, p. 188.
9. Lloyd I. Rudolph, 'The Self as Other', in Mariola Offredi (ed.), *Proceedings of the Eleventh European Conference on South Asia*, Delhi, Manohar and Columbia.
10. Louis Bromfield, *The Rains Came*, 1937, pp. 21–3.

11. J.R. Ackerley, *Hindoo Holiday*, 1932, p. 18.
12. Ibid., p. 28.
13. Charles Chenevix Trench, *Viceroy's Agent*, 1987, p. 17.
14. Philip Mason, *A Shaft of Sunlight*, 1978, p. 207.
15. Charles Chenevix Trench, *Viceroy's Agent*, 1987, pp. 129–30.
16. Ibid., pp. 143–4.
17. Lord Wavell, *Viceroy's Journal*, Oxford, 1973, p. 333, 12 August 1946.
18. Philip Ziegler, *Mountbatten*, 1985, p. 409.
19. Charles Chenevix Trench, *Viceroy's Agent*, 1987, pp. 346–7.

10. DEPARTURE

1. Ruth Prawer Jhabvala, *How I Became a Holy Mother and other Stories*, 1981, p. 9.
2. *Memoirs of William Hickey*, ed. Alfred Spencer, 1913, Vol. 4, p. 382.
3. Ibid., Vol. 4, p. 405.
4. Miss Emma Roberts, *Oriental Scenes, Sketches and Tales*, 1832.
5. Victor Jacquemont, *Letters from India*, 1834, Vol. 2, p. 355.
6. *Lady Curzon's India*, ed. John Bradley, 1985, pp. 161–2.
7. E.M. Forster, *A Passage to India*, 1924, p. 280.
8. Dennis Castle, *Run Out the Raj*, Folkestone, 1975, p. 6.
9. Philip Mason, *A Shaft of Sunlight*, 1978, p. 215.
10. V.S. Naipaul, *An Area of Darkness*, 1964, p. 201.
11. V.S. Naipaul, *India: A Million Mutinies Now*, 1990, pp. 516–18.
12. Raj Thapar, *All These Years: A Memoir*, New Delhi, 1991, pp. 361–3.
13. Elizabeth Bumiller, *May You Be the Mother of a Hundred Sons*, 1990, p. 282.
14. Jawaharlal Nehru, *An Anthology*, ed. Sarvepalli Gopal, Delhi, 1980, pp. 647–8.

ACKNOWLEDGEMENTS

Acknowledgement is due to the following for kindly giving permission to reproduce copyright material:

Aitken & Stone Ltd: Shiva Naipaul, *Beyond the Dragon's Mouth*; V.S. Naipaul, *An Area of Darkness* (André Deutsch and Penguin Books) and *India: A Million Mutinies Now* (William Heinemann).

Sashti Brata: Sashti Brata, *India the Perpetual Paradox* (William Morrow, New York).

Jonathan Cape Ltd: Charles Chenevix Trench, *Viceroy's Agent*.

Chatto & Windus Ltd (one of the publishers in the Random Century Group Ltd): J.R. Ackerley, *Hindoo Holiday*; Nirad C. Chaudhuri, *The Autobiography of an Unknown Indian*; Sir Penderel Moon, *Divide and Quit* and *Strangers in India*.

Columbia University Press: Ainslie T. Embree, *Sources of Indian Tradition*.

Davis-Poynter Ltd: Prafulla Mohanti, *My Village, My Life*.

Ravi Dayal Publishers (New Delhi): Khushwant Singh, *Train to Pakistan*.

André Deutsch Ltd: Philip Mason, *A Shaft of Sunlight*.

Eland Books: John Beames, *Memoirs of a Bengal Civilian*; Sarah Lloyd, *An Indian Attachment*.

Faber and Faber Ltd: W.H. Auden, 'Partition', in *Collected Poems of W.H. Auden* (ed. Edward Mendelson); Upamanyu Chatterjee, *English, August, An Indian Story*; Frank Richards, *Old-Soldier Sahib*.

Hamish Hamilton Ltd: Alan Moorehead, *A Year of Battle*; Paul Theroux, *The Great Railway Bazaar*.

Harper Collins Ltd: B.N. Pandey, *A Book of India*; Alan Ross, *Blindfold Games*; Philip Ziegler, *Mountbatten*.

William Heinemann Ltd: Anita Desai, *Baumgartner's Bombay*, by permission of Rogers, Coleridge & White Ltd, Literary Agents; R.K. Narayan, *Under the Banyan Tree*; Paul Scott, *My Appointment with the Muse*.

David Higham Associates: Francis Yeats-Brown, *Bengal Lancer*.

Hutchinson & Co. Ltd: Arthur Koestler, *The Lotus and the Robot*.

Government of India, Publications Division: the writings of M.K. Gandhi.

King's College, Cambridge, and the Society of Authors as representatives of the E.M. Forster Estate: *A Passage to India* and *The Hill of Devi*.

The Lutyens family: Robert Lutyens, unpublished diary.

Macmillan London Ltd: James Cameron *An Indian Summer*; Jon and Rumer Godden, *Two Under the Indian Sun*.

Patrick Marnham: Patrick Marnham, *The Road to Katmandu* (Macmillan).

John Murray Ltd: Robert Byron, *Letters Home* (ed. Lucy Butler); Trevor Fishlock, *India File*; Ruth Prawer Jhabvala, *How I Became a Holy Mother*; Ray Murphy (ed.), *Edward Lear's Indian Journal*; Virginia Surtees, *Charlotte Canning*.

Nehru Memorial Museum and Library (New Delhi): the writings of Jawaharlal Nehru.

Eric Newby: Eric Newby, *Slowly Down the Ganges* (Hodder and Stoughton).

Oxford University Press: Claire Percy and Jane Ridley (eds.), *The Letters of Edwin Lutyens to His Wife*; Lord Wavell, *Viceroy's Journal*.

Oxford University Press (New Delhi): K. Das, *India: A Traveller's Anthology*; Verrier Elwin, *The Tribal World of Verrier Elwin*; S. Gopal, *Jawaharlal Nehru*; Khushwant Singh, *A History of the Sikhs*.

Oxford University Press (New York): Jan Morris, *Destinations*.

Penguin Books Ltd: Mulk Raj Anand, *Untouchable*; Alexander Frater, *Chasing the Monsoon* and *Beyond the Blue Horizon*; Juan Mascaro (trans.), *The Upanishads* and *The Bhagavad Gita*; W.D. O'Flaherty (trans.), *Rig Veda*; Rabindranath Tagore, *Selected Short Stories* (trans. William Radice).

Penguin Books India Pvt. Ltd: Shoba De, *Socialite Evenings*; R.K. Narayan, *A Writer's Nightmare*; Khushwant Singh, *Delhi*.

Random House, Inc. (New York): Elizabeth Bumiller, *May You Be the Mother of a Hundred Sons*.

Professors Lloyd I. and Susan Rudolph: 'Amar Singh's Story: a diary of becoming Indian under the Raj, 1898–1905' (forthcoming).

Alan Ross Ltd: Hugo Williams, *All the Time in the World*.

Routledge Kegan and Paul Ltd: Peter Yapp (ed.), *The Traveller's Dictionary of Quotations*.

Royal Archivist at Windsor Castle: one letter from Queen Victoria; one letter from the Duke of Windsor.

Michael Russell (Publishing) Ltd: Philip Mason, *A Thread of Silk*.

Martin Secker & Warburg Ltd and the Estate of the late Sonia Brownell Orwell: George Orwell, *Burmese Days*.

Seminar Publications (New Delhi): Raj Thapar, *All the Years*.

Sidgwick & Jackson Ltd: A.L. Basham, *The Wonder that was India*.

Raghubir Singh: Raghubir Singh, *Banaras, Sacred City of India* (Thames and Hudson Ltd).

The Spectator: Dhiren Bhagat, *The Spectator*, 8 August 1987 (reprinted in *The Contemporary Conservative, Selected Writings of Dhiren Bhagat*, ed. Salman Kurshid, Viking, New Delhi, 1990, pp. 180–1).

The Estate of Edward John Thompson: Edward Thompson, *An Indian Day* (Alfred A. Knopf).

Times Newspapers Ltd: *The Times Special Report on the Punjab*, 1947.

Unwin Hyman Ltd: Bibhutibhusan Banerji, *Pather Panchali* (trans. T.W. Clark and Tarapada Mukherji); Premchand, *The Gift of a Cow* (trans. Gordon C. Roadarmel).

Auberon Waugh: Letter from Evelyn Waugh in Mark Amory (ed.), *Collected Letters of Evelyn Waugh* (The Estate of Laura Waugh).

Weidenfeld and Nicolson Ltd: J.G. Farrell, *The Siege of Krishnapur*; Geoffrey Moorhouse, *Calcutta*.

INDEX

NOTE: page numbers in **bold** indicate quotations and extracts from writings